BEDROCK

FOR

A CHURCH ON THE MOVE

By

MERWYN S. JOHNSON

Previous Publications:

Locke On Freedom: An Incisive Study of the Thought of John Locke, Austin, 1978.

Resource Materials for the Study of Christian Theology and Ministry, Charlotte, 2016.

Case Studies in the Life and Theology of Dietrich Bonhoeffer, Fourth Edition, Charlotte, 2016.

"Calvin's Treatment of the Third Use of the Law and its Problems," in *Calviniana* (16th Century Journal, 1988).

"The Three-Legged Stool: Pietism and Post-modern Theology," in *Theology Between East and West* (Wipf and Stock, 2002).

"Gospel and Law in the Theology of Karl Barth," in *The Westminster Handbook to Karl Barth* (Westminster John Knox, 2013).

"The Idiom of Scripture, Leviticus 18:5, and Theology—at a Time of Paradigm Shift," *Bulletin of Biblical Theology* (August 2017).

BEDROCK

FOR

A CHURCH ON THE MOVE

By

MERWYN S. JOHNSON

ICSM, Charlotte NC
2019

Bedrock for a Church on the Move.
Copyright © 2019 by Merwyn S. Johnson.
All rights reserved.
Published by In Christ Supporting Ministries,
7615 Colony Road, Suite 210, Charlotte, NC 28226.
Phone: 704-554-2490. Facsimile: 704-442-8214.
Contact for permissions:
info@inchristsupportingministries.org

Printed in the United States of America. No part of this book, including text and diagrams, may be used or reproduced in any manner whatsoever without written permission except in the case of brief quotations embodied in critical articles and reviews. For information or requests, address the Publisher.

Cover design by Kwackin' LLC,
with further assistance from Mark Fortenberry Photography

Library of Congress Cataloging-in-Publication Data
Johnson, Merwyn S. (1938-)
    Bedrock for a Church on the Move — 1st edition.
ISBN 978-1-7335142-0-0

1. Christianity—21st century.

2. New Reformation/paradigm shift/post-modernism.

3. Reformed theology.

BEDROCK
FOR A CHURCH ON THE MOVE

Contents

List of Sidebars	vii
Thank You	viii
Permissions	ix
Abbreviations for Versions of the Bible	x
Preface	xi
1. God's Covenant Community	1
2. In Christ	11
3. The Vision: Law and Gospel	19
4. The Triune God	29
5. The Word of God	45
6. Grace and Predestination	59
7. Union with Christ: What Does It Mean to be Saved?	69
8. Is Jesus Only the Means of Our Salvation?	83
9. The Total Work of Christ for Our Redemption	89
10. Christ and the Golden Rule	101

Contents

11.	The Marks of the True Church	121
12.	Is Authentic Christian Community Even Possible?	137
13.	What Does It Mean to be a Confessional Church?	145
14.	Are We Participants in or Instruments of God's Mission?	163
15.	Church and World	177
16.	The Universality of the Gospel	189
17.	Historical Christian Paradigms and the Current Paradigm Shift	205
18.	Afterword: Bedrock for a Church on the Move	219
	About the Author	243

List of Sidebars

P.1	On Theological Paradigms in General	xiii
1.1	Command and Do	3
1.2	Variations of the Covenant as Stated in the Bible	5
1.3	Covenant Space with God	9
3.1	The Law after Christ, a Spectrum	24
4.1	Names for God in the Old Testament	30
4.2	The Trinity: Father to Son	32
4.3	The Trinity: What the Spirit Does	37
5.1	God's Word	47
5.2	The Word and the Words	49
5.3	The Word and the Spirit	50
5.4	The Word *then* and the Word *now*	52
6.1	Time and Eternity	67
7.1	Calvin on Justification and Sanctification	77
9.1	Jesus and the Main Views of Atonement	95
9.2	God as the Human Jesus Christ	99
10.1	Interactions of the Golden Rule at Three Levels	103
10.2	Forms of The Golden Rule in the Bible	111
10.3	The Golden Rule over Time	120
11.1	Church as the Body of Christ Extended (Early)	124
11.2	Church as Participation in Christ's On-going Life (Reformation)	127
11.3	Church as Mission and its Rhythms (Mod-Piet)	129
11.4	Emphases in the Marks of the True Church	130
13.1	Major Written Confessions of Faith	146
15.1	Barth on Church and World	185
15.2	Bonhoeffer on Church and World.	186
17.1	Historical Paradigms of Christian Theology	207
18.1	Post-World War II Liberals and Conservatives	223
18.2	2010 Revision to the *PC(USA) Book of Order*	236
18.3	Overview: Presbyterian Dispute over Gays and Lesbians in the Church, 1978-2011	240

Thank You

To Jack Haberer, then-editor of *The Presbyterian Outlook*, for your openness to my ideas, detailed editorial advice, and patience over time.
To my long-running discussion partners,
- beginning with
    Beverly Neale Johnson (wife);
    Carolyn Johnson Crawford (sister);
    Sarah Johnson Kromer (daughter); and
    Neale T. Johnson (son);
- Kim Robertson Matthews, Danette Osborne-Smart, and Sarah Kromer for reading through this manuscript with a fine-tooth comb and providing invaluable feedback;
- The whole ICSM team, a sounding board for ideas and approaches and willing helpers no matter what the job;
- To mentors and others who stood with me at critical points along the way:
    Balmer Kelly, Jan Milic Lochman, Jane and Bedford Moore, John Leith, Wellford Hobbie, Prescott Williams, Randall T. Ruble, Julius Garbett, Anestine Crawford, Glenn Graham Curles, Jean Poe; and
- The many church people, students, colleagues, fellow ministers, and brothers and sisters in Christ with whom I have been privileged to interact over the years.

All these people have been the crucible for my emerging ideas, forcing me to refine questions and hold insights in the fire of life, life under God, indeed in the blazing truth of God's forgiving love. Our best ideas and insights come from life shared with others. That is certainly the case for me. So, I must give my greatest thanks to the One in whose providence my path crossed with all these others and in whose glory is the joy of human life.

Permissions

The Presbyterian Outlook has given me written permission to modify and publish the essays previously printed in the pages of the *Outlook* as articles in the series, "The Roots of Our Discontent," from March 2006 to January 2011. I have edited all these essays, sometimes substantially, and added several others, notably:
- "God's Covenant Community" (1);
- "Union with Christ: What does it mean to be saved?" (7);
- "Christ and The Golden Rule" (10, Part 1);
- "Historical Christian Paradigms and the Current Paradigm Shift" (17); and
- "Afterword: Bedrock for a Church on the Move" (18).

With gratitude I acknowledge the following publishers who have granted permission to use quotations from their publications within the framework of their "fair use" policies:

From Westminster John Knox Press, for:
- Karl Barth, *The Humanity of God*, translated by John Newton Thomas. Atlanta: John Knox Press, 1960.
- John Calvin, *Institutes of the Christian Religion*, edited by John T. McNeill, translated by Ford Lewis Battles. Philadelphia: Westminster Press, 1960.
- John Leith, editor, *Creeds of the Churches*, Third Edition. Atlanta: John Knox Press, 1982.

From Augsburg Fortress Press, for:
- Dietrich Bonhoeffer, *Dietrich Bonhoeffer Works,* Volumes 1-17, General Editor Wayne Whitson Floyd, Jr. Minneapolis: Augsburg Fortress, 1996-2014.

Abbreviations
For Versions of the Bible Used

RSV   Revised Standard Version
New York: Oxford University Press, 1977.

NRSV New Revised Standard Version
San Francisco: HarperCollins, 2006.

NIV   New International Version
New Jersey: International Bible Society, 1984.

KJV   King James Version
Philadelphia: Universal Book and Bible House, n.d.

ESV   English Standard Version
Wheaton: Crossway Bibles, 2001.

Biblical quotations are usually ascribed to one of the versions listed. The author's direct translations from the Hebrew or Greek text of the Bible are indicated by [AT]. Quotations from the Bible are set apart by italics, not by quotation marks. Abbreviations for individual books of the Bible are those used by the RSV, NRSV, NIV, and ESV.

Following historic precedents, the book refers to the two main divisions of the Christian Bible as the Old and New Testaments. The whole Bible bears witness to Jesus Christ and the testament, or covenant, in his name. The Old Testament points forward anticipating Christ; the New Testament points back to Christ as the fulfillment of the Old Testament. Both are indispensable to the Christian religion.

PREFACE

This book addresses the current turmoil in American Christianity and culture. The Church[1] is at a crossroads, often trapped by its own message. For Christians, only Jesus Christ can provide bedrock for such a time as this.

American Christianity has boxed itself in at two crucial points. (1) The message of salvation, including the afterlife, typically focuses on Jesus dwelling in our hearts to make us good, make society good, and through us make others good. This message raises tough questions from within. If we do not feel Jesus in our hearts, is God still there? Are we still saved? Is it finally up to us to make ourselves good? Where, then, does God fit in? (2) Many American Christians set up a distinction between the Church as the place where God dwells and the World as a secular place without God. Does our World now confidently embrace secularism? If so, how do Christians—and the Church—fit into such a World? On both fronts, the Church now faces a crisis of authenticity, relevance, and community.

The true Christian bedrock, Jesus Christ, offers new directions for moving forward. When the message shifts from claiming that *Christ is in us* to affirming that *we are in Christ*, the emphasis changes from embodying God in ourselves to participating in what God is doing all around us. The mantra, *where the Church is, there is Christ,* gives way to *where Christ is, there is the Church.* God's gracious presence brings out joy in every moment, and in Christ we experience a vigorous fellowship with God and others in all of life.

---

[1] Church with a capital "C" indicates the broader Christian movement, while church with a lower-case "c" indicates individual congregations or denominations (unless cited by name).

This book draws on the Bible and Christian theology to reflect on Jesus Christ as bedrock for a Church on the move. Many essays in this book began as a series entitled "The Roots of Our Discontent," published in *The Presbyterian Outlook*, between March 2006 to January 2011, when the Presbyterian Church (USA) was struggling with the question of ordaining gays and lesbians. I realized then as now that the underlying concerns go well beyond that particular issue. We are in fact going through a sea change—a paradigm shift—in American religion and culture.

As used here, a theological paradigm is the shared world view of Christians during a given time frame, usually in blocks of several hundred years (see Sidebar P.1). Paradigms rarely shift from one to another. Later paradigms do not disprove previous paradigms. At a certain point in time, however, the earlier paradigm just does not work well or make sense for life as Christians face it. God is the same, creation is the same, the Bible is the same, certainly the bedrock in Christ is the same, as is truth in Christ's name. In God's time, however, things move on, and, in faithfulness to God, Christian self-understanding and practice change as well. We are, I believe, in the middle of such a paradigm shift today.[2]

The prevailing Christian paradigm, Modernism-Pietism runs from 1650 to 2000, with carryover into the present. This paradigm has been one of the most successful eras in the history of the Christian religion. The era, however, as indicated above, has trapped itself in its own language and habits. The questions raised from within have reached a tipping point where this approach to being Christian no longer works well and at some points cannot be sustained. That signals the need to move to a new paradigm.

---

[2] See Sidebar P.1 concerning the basis of paradigm language. See Essay 17 and Sidebar 17.1 for the main historic paradigms of Christianity.

> *Sidebar P.1. On Theological Paradigms in General.*
>
> Church historians have long marked periods in Church history. Theological paradigms cover a constellation of beliefs and practices that operate for a period, usually centuries, and then shift to another constellation, driven by internal pressures and unresolved questions.[3]
>
> Four over-arching paradigms stand out after the first century. While scholars disagree over the specific dates of these periods, they agree on the four paradigms, namely,
> i. The Early Church, 33-600.
> ii. The Middle Ages, 600-1350.
> iii. The Protestant Reformation, 1350-1650. The time frame includes the Renaissance and Catholic Reformation.
> iv. Modernism-Pietism, 1650-2000, Modernity coupled with Pietism, including the Enlightenment and Post-modernism.
>
> See Jaroslav Pelikan, *The Christian Tradition: A History of Development of Doctrine*, 5 vols. (Chicago: U.Chicago Press, 1971-89).
> Hubert Cunliffe-Jones, ed, *A History of Christian Doctrine*, (Philadelphia: Fortress Press, 1978).
> David J. Bosch, *Transforming Mission: Paradigm Shifts in Theology of Mission* (Maryknoll, NY: Orbis Books, 1991).
> Phyllis Tickle, *The Great Emergence: How Christianity is Changing and Why* (Grand Rapids: Baker Book House, 2008).
> Bosch and Tickle assert that we are now in the middle of a paradigm shift.

---

[3] The important book by Thomas S. Kuhn shows how paradigms work in scientific research as science changes and grows over time from one paradigm to another: *The Structure of Scientific Revolutions*, (University of Chicago Press, 1st edition, 1962; 2nd edition, 1970; 3rd edition, 1996).

Dealing with theological paradigms, these essays are deliberately theological. At its best:
- Theology deals with practical insights into daily life.
- Theology provides insights more than conclusions, befitting authentic pilgrims on a journey together. Accordingly, theology is fluid, conversational, constantly in motion, yet true to God and ourselves.[4]
- Christian theology concerns insights into life with God, centered in the person of Jesus Christ, who is the reality of God with us (*Emmanuel*), and whose on-going, active life defines our lives. Such theology is the study of God, not religion.
- Theology at its best deals with truth and justice for all humanity, not sectarian beliefs. God's forgiving love sees all things as they really are and raises up the lowly and the undeserving to communion—salvation—with God.
- Theology sets up insights for which awe before God—faith—is the beginning and the reference point for all human knowledge, wisdom, and worldviews. Christian theology thus cannot be bound to religion in general, and may in fact shape the foundations of the culture in which it resides.[5]

---

[4] Scripture is essential to this journey and grounds every step of the way. The knowledge of God and of ourselves recalls the opening line in Calvin's *Institutes* (1.1.1): "Nearly all the wisdom we possess, that is to say, true and sound wisdom, consists of two parts: the knowledge of God and of ourselves."

[5] See Proverbs 1:7, Job 28:28, John 8:31-32, 1 Cor 1:21-25, and the remarkable chapter 8 of Proverbs. Reason and knowledge cannot start themselves. They require a starting point or a place to stand other than themselves. Simple faith—awe before God, or, as the Old Testament puts it, *the fear of the Lord*—provides that essential starting point. At the same time, the starting point cannot sit still, but works itself out, with rigorous understanding and full participation in the reality of earthly life, ... and, I dare add, with rigorous understanding and full

- Considered in paradigms, theology is dynamic and alive, bringing out the overarching issues sharply and clearly as well as the moving, interactive parts. Such theology offers practical insights for individuals, churches, and leaders.

My aim in this book is to clarify the paradigm from which we are emerging and look for a frutiful direction going forward. Each essay is self-standing and does not have to be read in a particular order. The last essay, "Afterword: Bedrock for a Church on the Move," highlights where the crises of focus, relevance, authenticity, and community stand out today. It could serve as the introduction to the whole book. I put this essay last, however, so that the current urgency of our situation would not detract from the self-standing insights of the other essays. You can jump to the assessment of the current situation or move directly into the insights where I believe Christians today will find bedrock for a church on the move, centered in Jesus Christ.

Merwyn S. Johnson,
Charlotte, North Carolina
February 2019

---

participation in the activity of God at every moment of our lives. This approach follows Augustine ("I believe in order to understand."), Anselm ("faith seeking understanding"), and the Protestant reformers (for whom the faith that unites us with Christ is the ground of all human freedom and endeavor).

ESSAY 1

GOD'S COVENANT COMMUNITY

With a simple refrain that echoes throughout the Bible, *I will be your God, and you will be my people,* God establishes a covenant community with humanity for all time.[1] The covenant community provides a space where even sinful humans can abide with God and with one another. Within that space we awaken to God's active presence in all aspects and events of our day-to-day lives, like flowers to the sun. The covenant has two sides, God's and ours. From God's side God is totally self-giving. We see this clearly in God's on-going providence and creative activity. We see it also and most notably in Jesus Christ, who is God incarnate, crucified, and risen as one of us.

The human side, however, has never lived up to its expectations. We humans fall short no matter how hard we try. Turned in on ourselves, our self-concern gets in the way. We do not do everything badly. We just never do anything with pure goodness. Our best efforts are ambiguous, and we cannot tell the difference between what is really good and what is not. Because on the human side we have never lived up to covenant expectations, God couches the human side of the covenant in mercy, that is, on God's side. For the Bible God's self-giving begins at the point of creating us and continues *while we were yet sinners* (Rom 5:8).

To make God's covenant community plain, this essay takes two steps. The first step moves away from the widespread, modern Christian view of covenant as a tit-for-tat contract, which misses the foundational community

---

[1] See Ex 6:7, Lev 26:12, 1 Peter 2:8-10.

to which the Bible is pointing. The second step explores covenant as the place where we commune with God, a true community with God, with one another, and with all humanity.

1. The Covenant is more than a contract.

For many modern American Christians the Gospel operates like a contract in which God offers and we accept, God acts and we respond, and/or we do something for God and God does something for us. God offers us salvation in the form of love, blessing, peace of mind, well-being. From within the contract perspective: as long as we accept the contract and do our part, we will receive some benefit or reward. If not, we risk God's wrath, curse, and condemnation, including the punishments of hell.

What God gets from such a contract is not so clear. Humans, however, are caught in an endless round of calculations to keep the contract going and get what we need from God. This perspective turns
- the Bible into a book of rules to keep,
- the Church into an institution that tells people what to believe and do, and
- religion into a set of requirements for obtaining salvation, goodness, or blessing.

In this system God's assigned role is to uphold the divine offer and deliver the goods earned.

Sidebar 1.1 diagrams how the contract works. From above, God commands humans to do good deeds as their duty to God. From below, humans are to do as God commands. If they obey the commands, they obtain the blessings. If they do not obey the commands, they miss the rewards and get the punishments. The terms of the contract do not change if we substitute faith for good works. Requiring faith from the heart, certain beliefs, or even just good intentions, still sets up a contract that depends on what we do. Whether faith or good works, we still wind up pursuing the modern American mantra, "If it's to be, it's up to me."

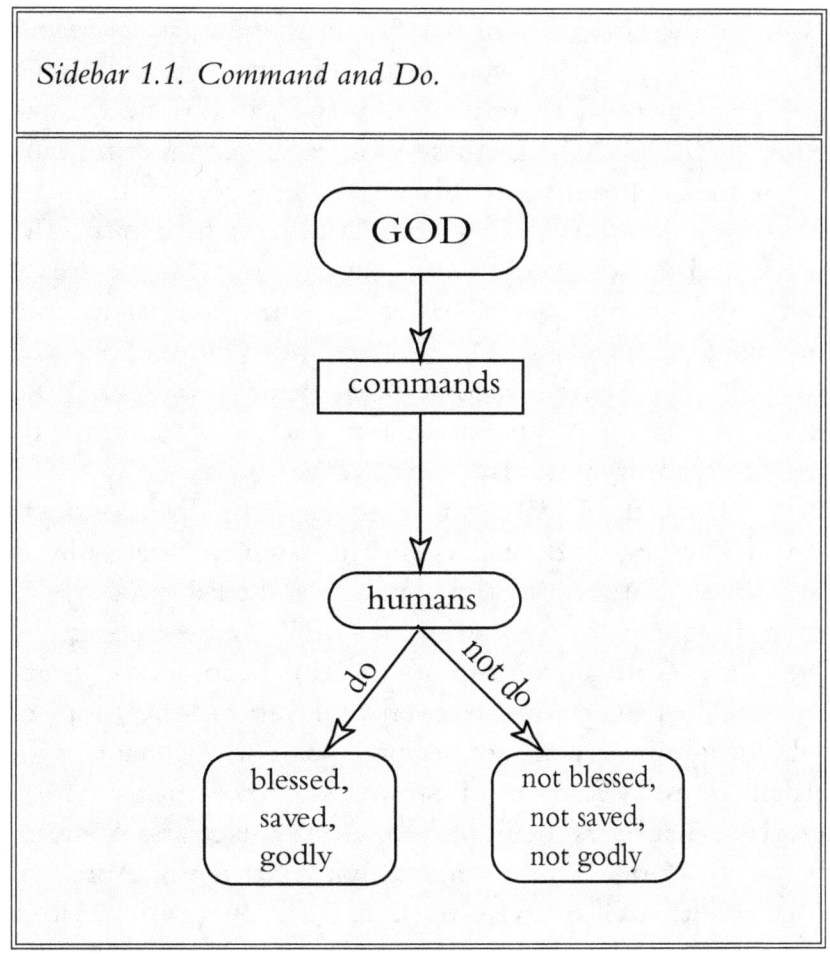

Sidebar 1.1. Command and Do.

Once delivered, God's role within this contract is secondary, even irrelevant, except as an enforcer. If it is up to us to obey the commands, make ourselves good, and get the benefits on our own, what further need do we have of God? We wind up focusing on the commands and not on the God who commands them.

Many Christians regard the Old Testament covenant as a contract and the New Testament as a release from it. "Testament," of course is the Latin word for covenant. Reinforcing this view of the Old Testament, some recent scholars see parallels between God's covenant with Israel and Ancient Near Eastern suzerainty treaties (Late Bronze Age, ca. 1200 BC).[2] In these treaties the conquering emperor makes promises to his vassal kings. He will confer blessings upon them if they honor and serve him in specific ways, and curses upon them if they do not. Such a treaty remains a contract even between the unequal partnership of suzerain and vassal. On this reading, God parallels the suzerain, the Hebrew people parallel the vassals, the Old Testament covenants parallel the treaties, and a command-and-do reading of the Biblical covenant holds.

But is the Old Testament covenant finally a contract? A quick review of Biblical covenant statements (see Sidebar 1.2) shows that, even with the parallels, the Bible follows its own, unique path. Neither in the Old Testament nor in the New does God's covenant with creation become a contract.

The Bible states the covenant in various ways, none of which requires a contract perspective. The covenants with Adam (i) and Wisdom (vi) show God covenanting with a creation that bears the impress of God's image and wisdom, yet is not God. The covenants with Noah (ii), Abraham (iii), and Jesus Christ (viii-xi) show God covenanting with a

---

[2] See George E. Mendenhall and Gary A. Herion, "Covenant," in *Anchor Bible Dictionary*, ed David Noel Freedman (New York: Doubleday, 1992), vol 1, 1179-1202, for a good summary of the non-Biblical sources. The conclusion, 1201, risks lumping the Biblical covenant together with a contract along with the early suzerainty treaties.

Sidebar 1.2. Variations of the Covenant as Stated in the Bible.

i. OT Covenant with Adam	Genesis 2:15-17
ii. OT Covenant with Noah	Genesis 9:8-17
iii. OT Covenant with Abraham	Genesis 15:17-20, 17:1-8
iv. OT Covenant with Moses	Exodus 19:1-6, commands spelled out in Ex 20:1-17/Deut 5:1-21
v. OT Covenant with David's Kingly Line	2 Samuel 7:14; Isaiah 55:1-5
vi. OT Covenant with Wisdom	Proverbs 8:1-36; Job 28:12-28
vii. OT Covenant within	Jeremiah 31:31-34
viii. NT Covenant as Kingdom of God	Mark 1:14f/Gospels; and parables of Matthew 13
ix. NT Covenant, in Christ's blood (crucifixion and resurrection)	Matthew 26:26-29 and parallels; Hebrews 9:15; 1 Cor 11:23-25
x. NT Covenant with Word made Flesh	John throughout: notably, 1:1-18; 8:31-32; 15:1-17
xi. NT Covenant in Christ	Paul throughout: notably, Rom 8:28-39; Phil 2:5-13; 2 Cor 5:14-19; Eph 1:3-14, 2:4-10

created humanity who is not-righteous and who cannot make themselves righteous before God. In all eleven covenant statements, God's covenant promises occur repeatedly

in the *absence* of the appropriate, even requisite, human responses. As parts of God's gracious self-giving, *the outcomes are simple gifts of*
- life (i, iii, vi),
- no world-ending flood (ii),
- descendants, land, and, blessings (iii),
- perpetual kingdom (v, viii),
- righteousness from within (iii, vii, ix-xi), and
- deliverance/salvation and eternal life with God (iv, viii-xi).

The gift-giving of the Biblical covenants does not remove the human side! God still expects a complete self-giving from the human side, corresponding to God's total self-giving. With constant shortfalls, however, the human side is incapable of keeping its part. In that respect the life, death, and resurrection of Jesus Christ encompasses *both* the divine side of the covenant *and* the human side. The Old Testament thus finds the distinctively Biblical sense of covenant culminating in the New Testament.

2. The Covenant as a place where ...

The contrast between covenant and contract becomes sharper when we discover that the God who gives the commands also keeps them. Because God is keeping the commands, they redefine every moment in terms of God's presence and activity.[3] Like God's wisdom inherent in creation, the commands form a running interface be-

---

[3] For John Calvin the primary use of the law ("third use of the law") is to show us the nature of God's will. The "command of God" does the same for Karl Barth, pointing to the reality of God at the moment. For Mendenhall also, *op. cit.*, 1200b: "the ultimate character of one's religious obligations proceeds from the character of God." The Heidelberg (1563) and Westminster (1648) catechisms of the Reformation interpret the Ten Commandments this way, one-by-one.

tween God and us. The *commands* say as much about *God* as they say about the *humans* to whom they are directed. For example,
- When God commands *thou shalt not kill,*
    what does it say about God? ...
        that God values human life and fosters it everywhere.
- When God commands *thou shalt not steal,*
    what does it say about God? ...
        that God provides for us and preserves our well-being even down to the least among us.
- When God commands *thou shalt not lie,*
    what does it say about God? ...
        that God is true and prizes truth.

When we find ourselves—to our great surprise and amazement—actually keeping these commands, we find ourselves in company with God, who as a vital part of the covenant community is keeping them at this very moment.

From the beginning, the Old Testament covenants aim to establish the place where God will be our God, where we will be God's people, and where we live together with God (see Sidebar 1.2). The Bible does not usually state the Ten Commandments (Ex 20:1-17, Deut 5:1-21) as imperatives at all, but most often in the future tense: *you shall not kill, you shall not lie, you shall not steal*. They point to a future reality where God and humans live in full communion together. The commandments establish that future as a reality in which we participate here and now.

Following the Old Testament lead, the New Testament also portrays Jesus Christ as a covenant, a place where we abide with God and God with us. The New Testament starts with Jesus Christ as his own, historical person. Even as a human being, he is the reality of God with us, *Emmanuel* (Matt 1:23):

As Jesus Christ is toward us, so is God.
    and
As Jesus Christ is toward God, so are we.

United with Christ by the Spirit, we participate in God's covenant in Christ, whether
- living in his kingdom (covenant viii),
- sharing in his life-blood (ix),
- abiding in his Word (x), or
- simply being in him and he in us (xi).

God's words of command create an on-going covenant space for us (see Sidebar 1.3). The ten words or commands of the Mosaic covenant are interconnected, like the rules of a game. While the rules of a game are usually "must" statements, taken together they describe the field of play where players interact with one another. We do not play the game to keep the rules. The rules focus our attention on the play, on the skill and fun of playing hard, and on the fellowship of playing even in competition with other players.

Moreover, precisely as the human Jesus Christ, God is a player keeping these commands. Jesus fulfills the commands (Matt 5:17) and, without abolishing them, replaces them with himself as the location of our life with God. The Old Testament covenant notion of keeping God's commands carries over directly to the New Testament notion of abiding in Jesus Christ. As Jesus says,

> *When [ean] you keep my commandments, you will abide in my love, just as I have kept my father's commandments and I am abiding in his love.*[AT]   (John 15:10)

The Greek word *ean* here can mean either "if" or "when." "If" makes the sentence conditional, a contract. "When" makes it a statement of fact, circumscribing the place where we fellowship with God and others. Taken all together, the sentence reads as a fact statement, which removes the sense of a command-and-do contract. The commands point instead to the place where God is present and active as God's own person, concretely as the incarnate, crucified, risen Christ. There God abides with us and we with God, finding joy in fellowshipping together (John 15:11).

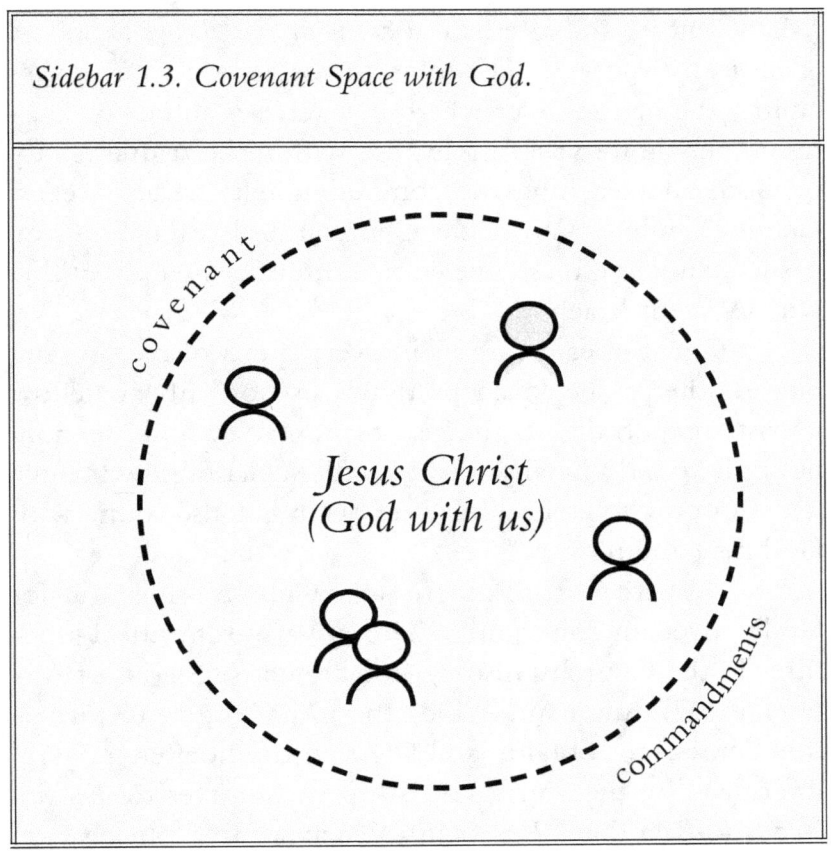

Sidebar 1.3. Covenant Space with God.

So, when Jesus says, *This is my commandment, that you love one another as I have loved you* (John 15:12 RSV), he is pointing to the complete, mutual self-giving of God's covenant people. Not that we can out-of-ourselves keep that commandment, sinners that we are. But Jesus did, and, united with him by the power of the Spirit, we participate in his having done so and we immerse ourselves more and more in what he is doing here and now.

So, when Jesus utters the Great Commission, he couches it in his own covenantal activity—before: *All power [or authority] in heaven and on earth has been given to me*[AT] (Matt 28:18)—and after: *Lo, I am with you always to the end of the age*[AT] (Matt 28: 20b). Jesus, that is, goes before us, discipling the nations over which he exercises authority, baptizing people into sharing his life within the triune reality of God, and teaching the commandments he also keeps. Centered in Jesus Christ, the Church thus lives, moves, and has its being as God's covenant community in a direct line with Ancient Israel.

Christ goes before us in every arena of life. Loving one another as he loved us draws us not only to fellow Christians but also to the rest of humanity and creation, not only to individuals but also to the societies in which we live, not only to eternal life after death but also to life with God here and now.

"Where Christ is, there is the Church" rings true for God's covenant community. This cry arose at critical junctures in the Church's history, notably with Ignatius of Antioch (†107), Augustine (†430), the 16th Century Reformation confessions of faith, and Dietrich Bonhoeffer (†1945).[4] Energized by the Spirit, Christ opens our eyes to *the least among us* (Matthew 25:40, 45). When we find ourselves in this covenant space, to our great surprise and amazement we also find ourselves in the presence and reality of God, with whom to live is life itself.

---

[4] The mantra also shows up in the current Presbyterian Church (U.S.A.) *Book of Order* (F-1.02).

ESSAY 2

IN CHRIST

This essay focuses on two different ways to articulate the Gospel, one using the phrase, *Christ in me/us* and the other using the phrase *me/us in Christ*. Both phrases belong to the Bible, especially Paul and John, but Western Christianity over the last 350 years has stressed *Christ in me/us* almost to the exclusion of the other phrase. With this emphasis Christianity grew in huge numbers during the 18th-19th centuries.

The over-balance, however, has probably run its course. We are now experiencing its down side. Recapturing the sense of *me/us in Christ* may be a way out of our current impasse, opening up fresh insights into the gospel and new energy for the Christian Church today. After

(1) looking more closely at the two phrases,

this essay considers how the phrases understand

(2) the presence of God,

(3) authentic Christian community, and

(4) the challenges both phrases have to face.

1. Christ in Us vis à vis Us in Christ.

The phrase *Christ in us* concentrates on the interior self of the Christian believer and looks for an embodiment of Christ in us. The traditional liberal perspective draws from Luke 17:21 to say *the kingdom of God is within you* (KJV, NIV). The Greek words can also mean *among you* (RSV, NRSV), but classical liberals prefer the other reading. Once within the heart, they say, the kingdom will manifest itself in the ideals of love, peace, and justice, which in turn will flow out for the benefit of all.

The traditional conservative perspective appeals to the experience of conversion. Being convicted of our sins and persuaded that Christ died for us, we are to pray, *Come dwell in my heart, Lord Jesus* (from Ephesians 3:17). With Jesus living in our hearts, they say, we sinners experience an actual change in our lives, namely, a new-found love for God and other people, a commitment to moral living, and a joyful hope for eternal life.

Some real differences separate these two sides, as we know from listening to the liberal-conservative debates over the last century. More striking, however, is what they share together—a concentration on the interior self, looking for the embodiment of Christ or the kingdom of God within the believer. Even with variations such as *the Spirit dwelling in us,* or *God in us working through us,* the phrase *Christ in me/us* fits both liberals and conservatives.

What do we actually talk about when we use these phrases? When we speak of *Christ in us,* we transpose Christ into language about *ourselves:* what has happened to *us,* what *we* like about it, what makes *us* happy or relieved, or what the benefit is to *our* tribe or to *our* cause.

By contrast, when we speak of *us in Christ,* we transpose ourselves into language about *Christ.* The focus is upon *Christ,* who *Christ* is (*Emmanuel, God with us, Savior, Lord*), what *Christ* is doing here and now, and how the gospel in *Christ's* name goes forward. What appears to be only a slight difference in language hides some large theological consequences.

2. The Presence of God.

Concerning the presence of God, *Christ in us* locates God *within us,* dwelling in *our hearts* by *our faith,* perhaps going where *we* go. When *our faith* is weak, however, is God less present with us? Is God more present when *our faith* is strong? Doubt is a real threat here, because it may signal the absence of God. In the face of devastating terrorist attacks, tsunamis, hurricanes, fire storms, and disease epidemics, the question becomes even more urgent, Where was God? Was God perhaps absent from us at such moments, even if *we* and God-in-us were there?

By contrast, the phrase *us in Christ* locates us wherever *Christ*—or God—is. "God is everywhere" is probably too broad a statement to be meaningful. Better is to say, "God is always somewhere," concretely, that is, *in Christ*. If we are *in God* (or *in Christ, in the Spirit*) and God is always somewhere, then we are always where God is. We will always be in God's presence, no matter how bad things get, even when we do not believe in God. Being *in Christ,* we seek to identify concretely the God in whose presence we always find ourselves—precisely the way the Bible talks about God.

3. *Christian Community.*

These two phrases project very different notions of community. Following an embodiment model, *Christ in us* says the Christian community is where the believer is, that is, as an association of largely like-minded individuals. The Church is thus set apart from the World. God (Christ, the Spirit) dwells in believers one-by-one and among them collectively, but God does not dwell the same way in the World where no believers are. With high levels of faith, love, spiritual experience, devotional and moral purity to attract and hold believers, such communities can and often do sustain themselves effectively apart from the World.

By contrast, the phrase *us in Christ* says: *Where Christ is, there is the Christian community.*[1] The Church, that is, is not

---
[1] See Jürgen Moltmann's discussion in *The Church in the Power of the*

defined by the people who join it, but by Jesus Christ, who, energized by the Spirit, draws people together and sustains them as a community. For this reason, the majority of Reformation confessions talk about three marks of the true Church. A true Church exists, they say, wherever the Word is purely preached, the Sacraments are rightly administered, and church discipline or discipleship is exercised. These marks point to Jesus Christ, who, empowered by the Spirit, gathers people together around the Gospel and governs their lives: one-by-one, as a community (mutually), and at those places where Christians engage the world at large.[2]

4. Challenges.

Both approaches to community produce challenges to be overcome—or endured. *Christ in us* invites us to ask, How much is Christ really *in us*? How much more is the Spirit *in some of us*, and how much less in others? And for the devout the question is urgent, How much is enough? Quantifying Christ *in us* moves very quickly to comparisons and finger pointing among Christians, both individuals and denominations.

No one can deny the authenticity of faith, hope, and love whenever we find them in such communities. These are, after all, the evidences of *God in us*. Maintaining the evidences of God's presence, however, takes an enormous, sustained human effort and energy. Even a partial breakdown of the evidences becomes a crisis of faith, as if God is absent from the Church. The quantifying and the comparisons are also inherently divisive and destructive of authentic Christian

---

Spirit (San Francisco: Harper and Row, 1977), 122ff.

[2] These considerations shape the Reformation forms of church order, notably Lutheran and Presbyterian. See the PC(USA) *2011/13 Book of Order* F-1.0201–1.0205, previously G-1.0100a–d.

community. I believe we are experiencing these several dynamics in congregational church life, denominations, and at every level of the Church at the present time.

By contrast, the phrase *us in Christ* joins us with Christ, binds us together with everyone else who is in Christ, and focuses our attention on what God is doing all around us.[3] If there is any faith or hope or love—no matter how much or how little—that is an authentic Christian community in Christ's name. *In Christ's name* means Christ actually mediates our relationships with one another more than we mediate Christ to one another.[4] And, with a diversity of gifts given to a diversity of people in Christ, we live not for ourselves or for our own claims of right and privilege, but for the sake of Jesus Christ. As the head of the Church, Jesus Christ creates this community and governs it himself, energized by the Spirit. The body of Christ thus remains centered in Christ and not in its members..

The challenges of *us in Christ* are to keep alive the vision of Christ at the center of life and to avoid becoming merely self-serving. Though we can strive vigorously for a vision of Christ through effective preaching and worship, teaching, mutual love, intercessory prayer, and active discipleship, we cannot guarantee the authenticity or power of the vision. Like the activities themselves the authenticity and power still have to come as gifts from God the Holy Spirit, who frees us from having to do these activities as a self-motivated, demand requirement.

The other challenge of *us in Christ* is that we will spend our energies on ourselves and not look for the face

---

[3] See Colossians 1:15-17.
[4] See Dietrich Bonhoeffer, *Discipleship: Dietrich Bonhoeffer Works, Vol. 4* (Minneapolis: Augsburg Fortress, 2001), 92-99; and *Life Together* in *Dietrich Bonhoeffer Works, Vol. 5: Life Together and Prayerbook of the Bible* (Minneapolis: Augsburg Fortress, 1996), 43-44.

of Christ all around us. According to Scripture and the Reformed tradition, Christ is at the center of the world, which was both created and redeemed through God the Son, Jesus Christ (John 1:3, 3:16). So, the way we deal with other people, the world around us, and the issues of our common life is the way we deal with Christ (Matthew 25:40, 45). Wherever we see people beset by evil, burdened by need, torn by conflict or war, or broken in body and spirit, we are looking into the face of Christ. To participate in the on-going, active life of Christ is a high calling and a tall order, which takes constant discernment, caring, courage, and risk-taking for the sake of Christ. The Church exists, that is, in following—not containing—Christ and in spending itself for the sake of Christ and the Gospel (Mark 8:34-38).

This essay appears to set the two phrases, *Christ in us* and *us in Christ*, at odds with each other. The Bible actually sets them side-by-side (John 15:1-17, Romans 8 and Paul *passim*). For the Bible, the larger term is *us in Christ*. That is, Christ is not in us unless and until we are first in Christ. The branches engrafted into the vine precede the life-giving sap flowing through the branches (John 15:1-8). The abiding in Christ comes before Christ's abiding in us (John 15:9-10, 16). Similarly, the wisdom of the universe in Christ (Ephesians 1) precedes the love of God dwelling in our hearts by faith (Ephesians 3:16-19).[5]

Above all, *us in Christ* keeps us from reducing *Christ in us* to a container notion of either the individual believer or the Christian community. The emphasis on *Christ in us* has dominated the epoch of Pietism from 1650 to the present, to the point of ignoring the other phrase. Has the time

---

[5] Note the accent on the faith and love OF Christ in Ephesians 3:12 and 17b-19a, Galatians 2:16, 20, and elsewhere, as in KJV and footnotes to the RSV, ESV, NRSV, and NIV.

come to correct that imbalance? This move is at the heart of Dietrich Bonhoeffer's theological breakthrough in the mid-20th century, grounded in Karl Barth at the front end and extended by Jürgen Moltmann at the back end. Maybe balancing the two phrases can move the Christian Church to a fresh perception of the Gospel and help embattled church people engage the paradigm shift now underway.

ESSAY 3

THE VISION: LAW AND GOSPEL

Law-and-Gospel takes us to one of those surprising, mountain top vistas where, once there, everything looks different, sparkling with fresh insights into beauty and excellence and energized with grace and freedom. The vista before us, centered in an active fellowship with Christ, is life with God as a joyful participation in God's goodness without possessing or dispensing it as our own. Having tasted it, we cannot get enough of it. We pursue it not because we must, but because we really want to.

How do we get there? Do we have to do something in order to obtain God's love for us, for humanity, for salvation? By itself the Law seems to say yes, that we must strike a bargain with God—be or do something worthy enough for God to love, justify, approve, or save us. Does that then throw us into an unavoidable trap of works righteousness? By itself the Gospel seems to say no, that life with God is pure blessing—God's mercy triumphs over all and requires nothing from us. Does that then throw us into an unending sea of permissiveness? Which one of these two approaches to Law and Gospel is right? Or does one cancel out the other? Can they be combined—Law-and-Gospel—with a different outcome altogether?

This essay aims to recapture the freedom and joy at the root of Law-and-Gospel, asking:
(1) How does American Christianity distort the issue?
(2) How does Law-and-Gospel arise for the Bible and the Protestant Reformers?
(3) What happens to the Law after Christ? and
(4) What will sustain the gift character of the Gospel?

1. How does American Christianity distort Law-and-Gospel?

Law-and-Gospel was central to the Protestant Reform of the Christian Church, 1517-1650. The issue shaped everything Reformation leaders like Martin Luther and John Calvin had to say, as well as the Lutheran and Reformed confessions of the day.[1] By 1650, however, other voices came to the forefront and set in motion the dynamics with which we are wrestling today. In the movement known as Pietism,[2] Christians emphasized the indwelling of God in the believer and our internal experience of God. That led to a different parsing of Law-and-Gospel which has prevailed ever since.

On the one hand, American Christians often hear the Gospel as a new law telling us what we have to do in order to be saved. The good news about Jesus Christ is an offer, we are told, and all we have to do is . . . [you can fill in the blank:] receive it, repent and believe, make a decision for Christ, have enough faith, believe certain things, do certain things, obey, make a proper response, love others from the heart, love all people inclusively, prove authentic faith by our good deeds, pursue peace with justice, *etc.* From this perspective, the Gospel turns into a transaction in which *we* have to do our part or lose the benefits of the contract.

On the other hand, American Christians today often hear that the Gospel of God's love in Jesus Christ supersedes and does away with the law altogether. With the love

---

[1] For Lutherans see the Lutheran *Book of Concord*, trans and ed Theodore G. Tappert (Philadelphia: Fortress Press, 1959), from 1577. For Presbyterians and Reformed see the confessional documents of the current Presbyterian Church (USA), Reformed Church in America, and Christian Reformed Church, for whom the most important documents come from the Reformation era.

[2] See Roger Olson and Christian Collins Winn, *Reclaiming Pietism* (Grand Rapids: Wm. B. Eerdmans, 2015).

of Christ in our hearts, we are told, we are enabled to do all that is expected of us and nothing further is required of us. Indeed, if Christ or the Spirit is truly embodied in us, can we do any wrong?

For the first perspective, the Gospel becomes a blatant calculation of rewards and punishments, an appeal to raw self-interest, and a rigorous demand that looks like a new Law. For the second perspective, the Gospel becomes mere permissiveness, justifying the sin as well as the sinner and setting up an avenue to self-righteousness. Either way, the Biblical message of the Gospel is lost and the resulting formation of human life becomes seriously distorted. When the Gospel is distorted, so is the Law. The Christian conversation on all sides today is at risk of falling into these pitfalls, and missing altogether the Biblical issue of Law-and-Gospel.

2. How does Law-and-Gospel arise in the Bible and Reformers?

The issue of Law-and-Gospel for Paul and the Protestant reformers plays out quite differently from modern American Christianity. For Paul, the Law encompasses moral demands which come from the Ten Commandments, from Scripture as in *the law and the prophets,* and from the law of nature as created by God. The Law demands perfection in keeping it, so it shows us specific places—sins—where we go wrong (Romans 3:20). The Law shows us the inescapable breadth and depth of human sin, especially but not only in moral matters.

The bigger problem emerges, however, when, having repented of our sins and wanting to do better, we try harder to do what the Law requires of us. Now as admitted sinners we try to produce out of our tainted selves the worthiness that the Law requires, and a goodness we no longer have. So we focus more and more upon the Law, what we have to do to keep it, and what benefits we can get when we do. In the process, we pay less and less attention to the Lawgiver.

We effectively put the Law in the place of God—which is idolatry—and we turn the simple sin(s) of violating the Law into a condition of sinfulness from which there is no human avenue of escape. The harder we try to keep the Law, the more we distance ourselves from God.[3] If we quit trying, we prove ourselves to be the sinners we were at the start. We are trapped in a vicious circle of our own making. Because the Law both triggers and increases our sin, Paul calls the Law *the power of sin* (1 Cor 15:56), and he cries out for release from *this body of death* (Rom 7:24, 1 Cor 15:57). Idolatry is the underlying problem of the Law for sinners, not legal demands forced upon unwilling human subjects and enforced legalistically.

For Paul and the New Testament, the Gospel pertains to what Jesus Christ does to free us from this deep, profound bondage to sinfulness. The Reformers and the Reformation confessions present the Gospel in the same way. Jesus Christ, that is, fulfills all the requirements of the Law (Matt 5:17f; Gal 3:13). He was born according to the Law. He lived by the Law. He taught the Law. He died under the curse of the Law upon sinners. And he rose again from the dead, with a humanity that manifests what God intended through the Law from the beginning.

Fulfilling the Law at every point, Jesus Christ replaces it with himself (John 15:10, Romans 10:4) and refocuses our attention upon God. Though the Law is God-given and tells us much about God, the Law is *not* God and never will be. Jesus Christ can re-direct our attention toward God . . .

---

[3] The key passages are Romans 3:20 coupled with 5:20, and chapter 7, plus Galatians 2:15-3:14. The KJV has the most reliable English translation of these passages. See also the alternative readings in the footnotes of RSV, NRSV, and NIV.

because he *is* God as a human being. And when united with Christ by faith, we refocus upon God and no longer have to make ourselves righteous or worthy under the Law. The Gospel centers us on Jesus Christ and his accomplishments.

3. What happens to the Law after Christ?

The question remains: What happens to the Law after Christ? What role does the Law play for us after we become united with Christ?

Four answers to this question surfaced during the Protestant Reformation (see Sidebar 3.1, next page). Two of them sound like the false alternatives presented earlier. At one end of the spectrum (the "antinomians"), the Law after Christ has been superseded; now only the Gospel applies. Trying to sweep away the Law along with the Old Testament, the antinomians turn the Gospel into a new law which we have to keep, or they set up requirements in other terms (*e.g.*, relationships of love or goodness).

At the other end of the spectrum ("Papists" at the time), the Law was re-established as faith working through love, good works as the demonstration of true faith, or keeping the Law as something the Gospel enables Christians to do from within. The Law remains thereby the final measure of the Gospel.

Midway in the spectrum (Luther and the "Lutherans") the Law functions to set up the Gospel: the Law accuses in order for the Gospel to save the condemned sinner. Preaching the Law highlights particular human sins; preaching the Gospel serves as God's antidote to those sins. Luther's rediscovery of the Law and its dynamics made the issue of Law-and-Gospel central to the whole Reformation. His approach does not re-erect the Law after Christ (Gal 2:18) but gives up a constructive role for Law going forward.

> *Sidebar 3.1. The Law after Christ, a Spectrum.*
>
> - Papacy/Roman Catholic
>   Law and Gospel side-by-side, equally demanding.
>   Gospel (faith) enables Law (works).
>
> - Lutheran
>   Law reveals human sins and sinfulness,
>   Christ (Gospel) fulfills and replaces Law.
>   After Christ, Law-and-Gospel are repeated, to
>   stir faith in Christ and good works as fruits.
>
> - Reformed/Presbyerian
>   Law reveals human sins and sinfulness,
>   Christ (Gospel) fulfills and replaces Law.
>   In Christ, Law is refocused on the Lawgiver and
>   where humans live in daily fellowship with God.
>
> - Antinomian/Anabaptist
>   Law is abolished, superseded by Christ (Gospel).

Also in the middle of the spectrum is the Reformed option based on John Calvin's "third use of the law," which "finds its place among believers in whose hearts the Spirit of God already lives and reigns."[4] Luther articulates two uses of the Law,[5] but not three. Those most close to Luther talk

---

[4] John Calvin, *Institutes of the Christian Religion*, Bk 2, Ch 7, Para 12, 360.
[5] These are (i) to restrain human sin (by threats of punishments) and (ii) to reveal the depths of human sins and sinfulness as idolatry. A "third use" first appears in Philip Melancthon's 1535 *Commentary on Galatians*

about a third use of the Law, but only as part of a back-and-forth repeat of Law-and-Gospel, as described above. Calvin builds on Luther's key insights and develops a clear option within them. According to Calvin, Jesus Christ transforms the Law itself when he fulfills it and substitutes himself for it. Christ refocuses our attention on the Law-giver, to whom God's commands have always pointed. Now in Christ, the commands help redefine every moment in terms of the presence and activity of God. They tell us:

- what God is like (what kind of God wants us to act this way?),
- what God is doing at any given moment (God keeps the commandments, too), and
- where we who love God will want to be, in fellowship with God (sharing life together with God and with one another).

Calvin brings out the loving, merciful, and gracious intent in each of the Ten Commandments, because that is how the Gospel presents God.[6] For people who love God, to do anything contrary to God's manifest activity is simply unthinkable. Like parents and children in a loving family, everyone wants to fellowship with God in whatever God is doing at the moment, whether deeds of justice, peace, or simple goodness. Or, like the rules of a game that detail the interactions, relationships, and field of play, the force of the commandments after Christ is descriptive, not prescriptive. The result is neither legalistic nor permissive, but nevertheless promotes profound ethical reflection and vigor.

---

and emerges in the much later *Formula of Concord*, Art. VI, in the Lutheran *Book of Concord, op cit.*, 479f.

[6] See the treatment of the Ten Commandments in Calvin's *Institutes*, Book 2, Chapter 8; *The Heidelberg Catechism* (1563); and *The Westminster Larger and Shorter* catechisms (1647). See also Luther's Small and Large Catechisms, in the Lutheran *Book of Concord, op. cit.*, 342–344, 465–411.

4. What will sustain the gift character of the Gospel?

One more pitfall remains. We could assume that all we need to do is understand the issue of Law-and-Gospel, believe it, and apply it to the life of the Church like any other doctrine. That would make the doctrine depend upon what we do with it. The Gospel would turn into another Law, something we have to do—a new contract, transaction, or calculation, with its own set of demand requirements (see Sidebar 1.1, Command-and-Do diagram).

The Gospel, however, including the "third use of the law," contains an underlying gift character. For Calvin, the Reformation confessions, and Paul (1 Cor 12:3) alike, the faith that unites us with Christ is the Holy Spirit at work (John 3:8). So, when we find ourselves in fact doing such things as believing the Gospel, sharing it with others, loving one another, and seeking peace with justice—often to our great surprise and amazement—we also find ourselves in the active presence of the living God, with whom to live is life itself.

In other words, the Gospel is more than an offer. Our human response, including the whole Christian life, is part of the gift. Paul sums it up rather well in Ephesians 2:8-10:

For by grace you have been saved through faith, and this gift [is] from God, not from us; not from works, that no one might boast. For we are his workmanship, created in Christ Jesus for good works, which God prepared beforehand that in them we walk.[AT]

Notice that the gift extends to our good works, which God creates and prepares as occasions for participating in God's activity at the moment.[7] So, the Law shares the gift character of the Gospel, similarly rooted in God's mercy and

---

[7] Also the *"if"* of Romans 10: 9 and John 15:10 is probably better translated *"when in fact...."* John 3:17ff provides a similar explanation of John 3:16.

forgiving love. As gifts, the Law and the Gospel are not finally at odds with each other, but overlap and inform each other utterly.

All this:
- comes from God alone,
- as the work of Christ alone (God as a human being, who accomplishes all that is required of us),
- through faith alone (the work of the Holy Spirit uniting us with Jesus Christ and his righteousness),
- by grace alone (wherein both the work of Christ and our believing-and-doing are gifts pure and simple).

From this mountain top vista flows a vigorous life with God every moment of every day, and it is ours to enjoy with freedom!

ESSAY 4

THE TRIUNE GOD

Trinitarian language for God arose when the early Christians faced a crisis concerning who Jesus Christ is in relation to God. Is Jesus God acting as a human being, or is he merely an instrument through which God was sending some kind of message, perhaps making an offer of salvation? When they perceived that the Gospel itself was at stake in this question, they redefined the moment in terms of Trinitarian language for God (and Jesus) and rallied the whole Church around it. The Christian Church faces such a defining moment today. Perhaps the time has come to reaffirm the Trinity as the "summary of the Gospel of Jesus Christ."[1]

This essay covers
(1) the origins of the Trinity in the Old Testament,
(2) Trinitarian affirmations about Jesus Christ,
(3) Trinitarian affirmations about the Spirit, and
(4) Trinitarian affirmations about Oneness among the three "persons."

1. Origins in the Old Testament.

The origin of Trinitarian language starts with the Bible's concern for *the name of God* and the reality that stands behind that name (see Sidebar 4.1 on Old Testament names for God). When God confronts Moses about the risky venture of rescuing the people of God from slavery in Egypt, Moses knows the people will ask him for the name of the One who sends him: *When they ask me, "What is his name?"*

---

[1] *Report of the Task Force on Peace Unity and Purity of the Church* (PUP Report), as adopted by the 2006 PC(USA) General Assembly at Birmingham AL, p. 3, citing Karl Barth.

Sidebar 4.1. Names for God in the Old Testament.

"In the OT, far from being a mere label or an external description, a name expresses the profound reality of the being who carries it. ... To speak or act 'in someone's name' is to participate in the reality expressed by that name."★

Two names for God stand out in the OT:
- *Yawheh* (ca. 6,800 times in the OT), based on the verb "to be": *God [Elohim] said to Moses, "I am [yiwha] who I am [yiwha]." Say this to the people of Israel: "I am [yiwha] has sent me to you."* (Ex 3:14, RSV/NRSV). The word was considered too holy to utter, so it was transposed into a substitute, *my Lord [Adonai],* for speaking. The Greek translation is *Lord [kurios],* in both OT and NT.
- *Elohim* (ca. 2,500 times in the OT), based on the generic word for God, *El,* rendered in the plural (*Elohim,* gods), but used as a name in the singular, pre-empting all other gods. Hence the Shema (Deut 6:4): *Hear, Israel, the Lord [Yahweh] our God [Elohim], the Lord [Yahweh] [is] One..* The plural form of the word is not found in other Semitic languages of the day.
- These two names are often combined and given an historical reference, as above and in *The Lord [Yahweh] the God [Elohim] of your fathers, the God [E.] of Abraham, the God [E.] of Isaac, and the God [E.] of Jacob sends you; this is my name forever* (Ex 3:15, 3:16, RSV).

★ H. Michaud, "Name," *A Companion to the Bible,* ed J-J von Allman (New York: Oxford University Press, 1958), 278a-279b. See also "Names of God in the NT and OT," *Harper's Bible Dictionary* (San Francisco: Harper and Row, 1985), 684a-687a.

what shall I say to them? (Ex 3::13) God gives him two names: *I AM WHO I AM* (3: 14) and *The Lord, the God of your fathers, the God of Abraham, the God of Isaac, and the God of Jacob* (3:15). Likewise when Jesus utters the Great Commission to his disciples, he introduces Trinitarian language as a name: *going, we are to baptize people into the name of the Father and of the Son and of the Holy Spirit*[AT] (Matt 28:19).

Jesus' own name is important in this regard. At his birth, he is named Jesus, which means *he will save,* to which is added the prophetic tags *Emmanuel (which means, God with us)* (Matt 1:23) and *Son of the Most High* (Luke1:32) in the line of Davidic kings. God has bestowed on Jesus this name, *that in his name every knee would bow ... and every tongue confess that Jesus Christ is Lord*[AT] (Phil 2:9-11). John sees his whole purpose in writing to be *that you may believe that Jesus is the Christ, the Son of God, and that believing you may have life in his name* (John 20:31, RSV).

Even more specifically, the father-son language of the Trinity comes from God's covenant with David, in which God promises that *I [God] will be to him [David's heir] a father, and he shall be to me a son*[AT] (2 Sam 7:14, 1 Chron 28:6). Jesus applied this covenant to himself and understood himself to be a king and messiah in the line of David (see Matt 1; 22:41-46; Luke 1:31-33). So, Jesus prays to God as Son to Father (Matt 11:25-27, John 17:1-26) and speaks openly about God as his Father (John 5:17-18, 6:37-46, 10:25-30, 14:6-11).

By definition there can be no son without a parent, and no father without a child. Natural parents and their children resemble one another sometimes laughably in walk, talk, mannerisms, and appearance. That is because, having the same DNA, they belong to each other as members of the same family, bone-of-bone and flesh-of-flesh. The family

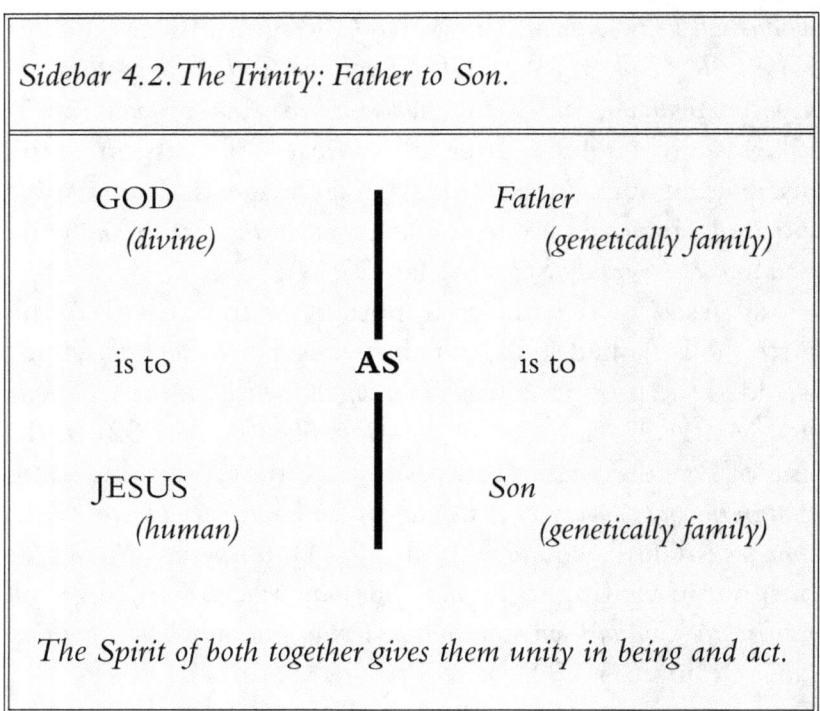

connection in trinitarian language is the same even if we substitute daughter for son or mother for father.

So, when Jesus prays to God as Son to Father (Matt 11:25-26, John 17), he makes the stunning connection: Jesus the human is to God the divine as a son is to his father (see Sidebar 4.2). They are family, "of the same substance or being."[2] As parent and child they care for and uplift one another (John 14:13, 17:1) the way families do at their best.

Jesus also applies the messianic passage from Isaiah to himself, *The Spirit of the Lord God is upon me*[AT] (Luke 4:18, 21, quoting Isa 61:1). *God is Spirit*, says Jesus, and we are to worship the Father in spirit and truth (John 4:23-24). New Testament statements about the Spirit are explicitly linked to

---

[2] This is the *homousios* of the *Nicene (325) and Constantinopolitan (381) Creeds*. See creeds and discussion in Leith, *Creeds of the Churches*, 28-33.

both the Father and the Son. The Spirit, that is, comes from both the Father and the Son (John 15:26-27) and unites them as members of the same family in being and act. The Spirit also makes God powerful among humans: *where the Spirit of the Lord is, there is freedom* (2 Cor 3:17-18).

As a name, Trinitarian language for God is not a concept or an explanation of God. Father-Son-Spirit provide us a concrete language to call upon God by name in life and in worship. When God's name is uttered, the reality of God stands before us, both *God with us* (*Emmanuel*) and God beyond us (*my thoughts are not your thoughts, neither are your ways my ways, says the Lord*, Isa 55:8 RSV). In both instances we share in the presence and activity of the living God.

As such the Trinity is not an attempt to divide God into pieces and parts or define God in rational terms. The Trinity is not a composite of Biblical proof-texts or pictorial images of one kind or another, whether metaphors, similes, or allegories.[3] Trinitarian language in the Bible is not even exclusively male-gender. Father and son are male in both Biblical languages, but spirit is feminine in Hebrew (Isa 11:2) and neuter in Greek (John 14:26).

2. Affirmations about Jesus Christ (Sidebar 4.2).

Following from the familial connection of Father to Son, the first and primary affirmation of the Trinity is the incarnation of God as a human being, or, in other words, the divinity of the human Jesus Christ. Whether stated as *Jesus is the Son of God* or *Jesus is Lord*, this affirmation permeated the entire New Testament centuries before the Council of Nicaea in 325 CE or the Church ever used the word "Trinity."

---

[3] The Hebrew of 2 Sam 7:14 and 1 Chron 28:6 draws the connection of father-to-son as an analogy, as in Sidebar 4.2, not as a simile or a metaphor.

The early Christians were quite aware of the questions raised by the incarnation of God as the human Jesus. They debated openly and honestly whether God could become a human being and still remain truly God, or the human could become God and remain truly human, or whether God could suffer and die as humans do. These questions, however, arose historically and logically only *after* the primary affirmation that Jesus is God as a human being.

Notice the phrasing here is not "God *in* a human being," where Jesus' humanity could convey a "container notion" of the incarnation,[4] or an instrument to be used and then discarded. *In Christ God was reconciling the world to himself* (2 Cor 5:19 RSV/NRSV) is a statement of *where* God is reconciling, not the means or instrumentality of God's reconciling activity. *In Christ* marks off the covenant space where God abides as God among humans and where God acts—as the human Jesus—to save a sinful humanity.

The poignancy of the Gospel stands out when we see the extent to which God as the human Jesus embraces our humanity. For John Calvin the depth of the incarnation arises from the question, How near does God have to come to us in order to save us?[5] Reflecting the Biblical accents, early Christian creeds like the *Apostles* and *Nicene* narrate the birth, sufferings, and death of Jesus, to show the extent to which God stoops to our human condition, enfolds us in God's mercy, rescues us from our bondage to sin, and initiates a new humanity. Paul goes so far as to say, God *made him to be sin who knew no sin, so that in him we might become the righteousness of God* (2 Cor 5:21, RSV/NRSV). The humanity of the Son is as important as the divinity of the Son for

---

[4] T.F. Torrance makes this point in his writings. See, for example, *Space, Time, and Incarnation* (Oxford University Press, 1969) and *Incarnation: The Person and Life of Christ* (InterVarsity Press, 2008).

[5] Calvin, *Institutes*, Book 2, Chapter 12, paragraph 1, pages 464-5.

our salvation. As the Son of God, Jesus Christ includes both humanity and divinity.

At bottom, this discussion of the incarnation is about authenticity. When dealing with Jesus Christ, are we really dealing with God or something less than God?

- When we say Jesus loves us, do we mean that Jesus is only a surrogate through whom God acted? Or, to the contrary, do we mean that *God* is really and truly the One loving us *as the human Jesus*?
- When we say Jesus suffered and died for our sins, do we mean that Jesus is like a scapegoat that God used—sacrificed—to attain reconciliation with humanity? Or, do we mean that *God* is the One forgiving us *as the human Jesus*?
- When we say Jesus died on the cross and rose again from the dead, do we mean that Jesus is a mere example, a sage, perhaps a metaphor, of God's pledge to humanity, by which God demonstrates love and shows us how to love back? Or, do we mean that *God as the human Jesus* is acting to conquer sin, evil, and death once and for all, and in the process recreate a new humanity?

In other words, is Jesus the real thing, *i.e.*, really God? Or, is Jesus merely an instrument, something less than God, in and through which God communicates indirectly God's love, purposes, and moral instruction to a wayward humanity?

The priest Arius triggered the Council of Nicaea in 325 CE when he offered an instrumental solution to the Christians of his day. For him the Son was a creature, Jesus Christ, who as such could not be fully God, though God could work through him to create the world and make known God's will for creation. The Son, says Arius, is more than human but less than fully divine, while the real God remains at a distance, unknowable and inaccessible to humans.

Living in an advanced, technological, largely utilitarian society, we are strongly attracted to an instrumental view of Jesus. But if Jesus Christ the Savior is primarily a means to an end—our salvation—is he not more or less replaceable with other instruments that can do the same thing? In the question of instrumentality, the early Christians saw the Gospel itself at risk. They answered with a profound grasp of what the Bible says on the matter, both Old and New Testaments, that Jesus Christ is nothing less than God as a human being, acting for the salvation of humanity.

Furthermore, the Trinity rules out a one-dimensional, top-down, self-sufficient idea of power. As "father" is bound to "son" and *vice versa*, the Father's almighty power as "maker of heaven and earth"[6] is bound to the Son's intentional vulnerability as Savior and servant Lord. God's activity of creation is tied to God's activity of redemption; and the lowly Jesus Christ on the cross is the touchstone of God's power over all creation.[7] For Christians, then, the measure of all legitimate power—whether political, economic, military, psychological, or institutional—is how well it serves the weak, the poor, the oppressed, the needy, and the least among us, with whom God the Son (Jesus Christ) explicitly identifies (Matt 25:40, 45).

The Trinitarian distinction between Father and Son leads to a differentiated idea of real power. As Jesus says to his disciples, *Whoever would be great among you must be your servant* (Matt 20:26-28). And Paul adds: *Sufficient for you is my [God's] grace, for my power is made perfect in weakness*[AT] (2 Cor 12:9).

3. Affirmations about the Spirit (Sidebar 4.3).

The importance of the Spirit cannot be overstated. The discussion, however, is elusive As Jesus points out, the

---

[6] *Apostles Creed* (ca. 180), *Nicene Creed* (325), *Constantinopolitan Creed* (381).
[7] See Col 1:15-20; 1 Cor 1:18-31.

Spirit is like the wind,[8] which

> *blows where it wills, and you hear the sound of it, but you do not know whence it comes or whither it goes; so it is with every one who is born of the Spirit.* (John 3:8 RSV)

Sidebar 4.3. The Trinity: What the Spirit Does.

The Spirit:
- *unites Father and Son*—Matt 28:19; Mark 1:10-11; John 10:30, 14:25, 25:26; Rev 4:21-22.
- *gives life*—Gen 1:2 (-31); Job 33:4; Psalm 104:30; Psalm 139:7, 13; Ez 37: 5, 14; Romans 8:6, 11; Hebs 9:14.
- *unites us with Jesus Christ*—John 3:8, 16; Ro 8: 1-4, 11; I Corinthians 12:3; 2 Cor 3:17-18; Eph 2:13-14, 3:14-19; I John 4:2-3.
- *works to bring about*—
  our knowledge of God (John 14:25-26; I Cor 2:1-16);
  our confession that "Jesus Christ is Lord" (I Cor 12:3);
  our cry "Abba, Father!" (Ro 8:15; Gal 4:6);
  our awareness of God's love and hope (Ro 5:5; Ro 8:16-17, 23-25; Gal 5:5);
  our abiding in God and God in us (I John 4:13-16).
- *gives gifts*—
  faith, hope, and love (I Cor 12:4-7, 13:13);
  the fruit of love, joy, peace, patience, kindness, goodness, faith, gentleness, self-control (Gal 5:22);
- *provides*—*the unity and energy for Christians in community with one another* (Eph 2:18-22, 4:1-6; 2 Cor 3:17-18); plus *individual strengths for the sake of the whole* (I Cor 12:4-11; Eph 4:11-16).

---

[8] In Hebrew and Greek, the word for wind is the same for word or spirit.

So, the Spirit only shows up in its effects on other things (see Sidebar 4.3). The Spirit is the unity and power of Father-and-Son taken together, but the Spirit lies hidden within the language of the other two persons of the Trinity. The Spirit provides the unity and energy for Christians in community, but the Spirit lies hidden in the concrete language of the Christian community. Uniting us with Christ, the Spirit gives us the confession *Jesus is Lord* and the cry *Abba, Father!* but the Spirit lies hidden in the concrete specificity of these phrases as they are spoken. Likewise, in Christ the Spirit gives us faith, hope, love, good works, truth, and other fruits, but the Spirit lies hidden in these concrete realities.

The question of authenticity arises here, too, as it does in relation to the human Jesus Christ (see Sidebar 4.2). Are our faith, our hope, and our love merely the natural responses of our own hearts and minds, sense of transcendence, or feelings of affection for others? Or, on the contrary, does our experience of these things really and truly reflect God's concrete manifestations within and among us? In other words, is the faith, hope, love, joy, and peace we experience actually God the Spirit at work? That is the claim of the New Testament Christians. Where the authenticity of the Son has to do with whether Jesus Christ is really God as a human being, the authenticity of the Spirit has to do with whether our experience really touches God acting within and among us here and now, joining us with the faith, hope, and love of Jesus Christ.

The Bible never confuses God's Spirit with human spirits. That was already clear in the Old Testament. The prophets spoke when God's Spirit was upon them, as Isaiah says of himself: *The Spirit of the Lord God is upon me, because the Lord has anointed me to bring good tidings to the afflicted* (Isa 61:1). Similarly, of the servant precursor of Jesus Christ, Isaiah says, *Behold my servant, whom I uphold, my chosen, in whom my soul delights; I have put my Spirit upon him, he will bring forth justice to the nations* (Isa 42:1).[9] Because of the Spirit upon them, the prophets called their prophecies *the word of the Lord* (*e.g.*, Ez 37:15).

Nonetheless, the prophets distinguish between God's Spirit and their human spirits, as in the case of Ezekiel: *The Spirit lifted me up and took me away, and I went in bitterness in the heat of my spirit, the hand of the Lord being strong upon me* (Ez 4:14 RSV). Paul maintains that distinction even when he speaks of the Spirit dwelling in us. The Spirit that dwells within us (Rom 8:11) bears witness with our spirits that we are children of God (Ro 8:16), but does not thereby replace our spirits.

The truth is that the Gospel of Jesus Christ, together with the faith, hope, and love that accompany it, flies in the face of life as we know it. Raw, human experience is filled with evil and injustice, sickness and death, senseless destruction and loss, human stupidity and foolishness all around us and within. It is counterintuitive for Christians to regard God's wisdom as truth, to believe that the crucified Jesus is Lord (God), to love our enemies and forgive those who sin against us, or to rejoice in the midst of sorrow and have peace amidst turmoil. For those who demand evidence or earthly wisdom (1 Cor 1:22), nothing can smooth out the chaos or dog-eat-dog feel of human existence.

For this reason, Paul explains why he came among people with a message of *nothing ... except Jesus Christ and him crucified, ... in weakness and in much fear and trembling* (1 Cor 2-4 RSV). He did so *in demonstration of the Spirit and of*

---

[9] See also Isa 11:1-3 (RSV): *There shall come forth a shoot from the stump of Jesse, and a branch shall grow out of his roots. And the Spirit of the Lord shall rest upon him, the spirit of wisdom and understanding, the spirit of counsel and might, the spirit of knowledge and the fear of the Lord.*

power, that your faith might not rest in the wisdom of men but in the power of God (1 Cor 4-5). The Spirit given to our spirits allows us *to understand the gifts bestowed on us by God* (1 Cor 2:12), especially those attached to Jesus Christ. In Christ by the power of God's own Spirit, we live with faith, hope, and love against all odds.

Where Paul speaks of a mutual indwelling of God's Spirit and our spirits, John talks about a mutual abiding of us in God and God in us. *Every spirit which confesses that Jesus Christ has come in the flesh is of God* (I John 4:2 RSV). That confession is how we recognize or *know the Spirit of God* (*ibid.*). Thus do *we know that we abide in him and he in us, because he has given us of his own Spirit* (I John 4:13). In sum,

> *Whoever confesses that Jesus is the Son of God, God abides in him, and he in God. So we know and believe the love God has for us. God is love, and he who abides in love abides in God, and God abides in him.* (I John 4:15-16)

The discussion of mutual abiding coincides utterly with the same language concerning Jesus as the Son of God in the Gospel of John (15:1-11). Here, too, distinct from but proceeding from both the Father and the Son, the Spirit of truth which dwells with and in us (John 14:17) will teach us all these things (14:25).

Neither the mutual abiding in John nor the mutual indwelling in Paul replaces our spirits with God's Spirit, makes our spirits divine, or domesticates one to the other. This is a critical point, lest we lapse into the instrumentalist trap once again. The mutual abiding-and-indwelling establishes a human fellowship with God and one another that for us is both freedom from sin and joy in the present moment. We now live and move and have our being in God (Acts 17:28)—united with Jesus Christ, filled with the Holy Spirit, and rejoicing in the God of all creation.

Grace is another way the New Testament presents the operations of the Spirit, as in Ephesians 2:4-10:

> *But God, being rich in mercy, through the great love with which he loved us, and we being dead as to sins, [God] made us alive together with Christ (by grace you have been saved), indeed [God] raised up and seated [us] in the heavenly places in Christ Jesus, that in the coming ages he might show the immeasurable riches of his grace in kindness toward us in Christ Jesus. For by grace you have been saved through faith; and this not of yourselves, [it is] the gift of God; not from works, lest anyone might boast. For we are [God's] workmanship, created in Christ Jesus for good works, which God prepared beforehand, that in them we walk.*^{AT}

4. Affirmations about the Oneness (Perichoresis).

The working of Father, Son, and Spirit together also signals a primary affirmation of the Trinity (*perichoresis*). Whenever one is at work, the other two are at work as well. Calvin puts it this way:

> To the Father is attributed the beginning of activity, and the fountain and wellspring of all things; to the Son, wisdom, counsel, and the ordered disposition of all things; but to the Spirit is assigned the power and efficacy of that activity.[10]

Similarly, Karl Barth interprets each of God's primary activities—creation, reconciliation, and redemption—in terms of the Trinitarian persons at work. The concrete take-off point for each is the Son. The source of each is the Father. The effective power of God at work with each activity and with all taken together is the Spirit.[11] Though Father,

---

[10] *Institutes*, Book 1, Chapter 13, paragraph 18, pages 142-3.
[11] The Trinity governs Karl Barth's entire theology, as he spells it out at the end of *Church Dogmatics*, Volume 1, Part 2, (EdinburghT & T Clark,

Son, and Spirit each contribute something distinct, they act inseparably as One at every point *(perichoresis)*.

God's oneness is more than a concept, say, of monotheism, because, again, God is a name more than a concept. As the Shema says, *Hear, Israel, the Lord our God, the Lord [is] One*^{AT} (Deut 6:4). We are easily overwhelmed by the sheer details, fleeting changes, and disconnections of day-to-day human life. In the midst of constant fragmentation, the Shema addresses us by name (Israel) and declares that our manifold experiences in nature and history have a unity that gathers everything together with meaning and directs it with focused intentionality. God is the One who does this. The Shema continues into verse 4: *and you shall love the Lord your God with all your heart, and with all your soul, and with all your might.*^{AT} Loving God, we participate in God's singular reality.

So, with the Trinitarian name of God: Jesus says plainly, *I and the Father are one* (John 10:30). "One" here does not mean "same," collapsing all distinctions between them. Neither is Jesus Christ the Son merely an instrument or manifestation of God. The two are so bound to each other as son to father—child to parent—that where one of them is, there is the other also. God deals with us as the human Jesus, so we cannot deal with God and not deal with Jesus Christ.

Within the Trinity itself, Father, Son, and Spirit come together as three, yet the three are so bound to one another in their unity—the *perichoresis*—that they retain their differences. The interplay of their differences makes the whole—the Oneness—more than the sum of its parts, as a body is more than the sum of its members or a human life is more than the sum of its moments on earth. To call upon one trinitarian person is to invoke all three, and God's Oneness remains a mystery.

1956), § 24, pp. 870-884.

Modernity, like early Christians, has a strong temptation to collapse the Oneness of God into sameness. Some in the Early Church historicized the persons of the Trinity across time, tying each person of the Trinity to a different period in history in which God appears:
- as Father from the time of creation to Christ (coincides with the Old Testament);
- as Son for the time of Jesus' life, death, and resurrection (coincides with the New Testament gospels); and
- as Spirit from the time of the Church at its beginning to the end time (coincides with the New Testament Acts-Letters-Revelation).

Such an approach reduces the variations of the three persons to a sameness over time and minimizes the humanity of Jesus Christ. The early Christians called this "modalism" and rejected it.

In modern times modalism has been combined with the notion of progressive revelation,[12] which values the latest manifestations of God above the earlier ones. Biblically and historically that emphasizes the period of the Spirit, the period of the Church, and the last book of the Bible, Revelation. These accents come at the expense of the rest of the Bible and the other parts of the Gospel, and invite speculation about the future, whether there may be a fourth, as-yet-undisclosed "mode" of God's manifestation or history.

Modalism takes another modern form when trying to avoid male-gender specific language for God in baptisms

---

[12] "Progressive revelation" is a theme discussed in the 20th Century by both conservative and liberal Biblical scholars. C.I. Scofield along with a host of popular preachers and writers added speculation about seven stages in history in his widely-used *Scofield Reference Bible*, first published by Oxford University Press in 1909, with successive revisions as recently as 1967. He combines fundamentalism with various premillennial and dispensational speculations.

and benedictions. In this approach the role of Creator replaces Father, the role of Redeemer replaces Son, the role of Sustainer or Sanctifier replaces Spirit, and an overall instrumental reckoning of the Trinity takes center stage. As we have seen, Father-Son-and-Spirit are bound together internally (cannot have one without the other) in a way that is not the case with Creator-Redeemer-Sustainer. Furthermore, at its heart Trinitarian language for God does not depend on gender-specific language. The essential point of the Trinity remains the incarnation of God as a real human being, which, along with the gifts of the Spirit, place us authentically in the presence of the living God.

The Trinity truly goes to the heart of the Gospel, centered in Jesus Christ, that is, grounded in the reality of *God with us*. The Triune God gathers people together, shapes them, and sustains them as an authentic Christian community, *where two or three are gathered together in my name* (Matt 18:20). To utter the Trinitarian name—Father-Son-and-Spirit—is to commune with the gracious presence, power, and activity of the living God.

ESSAY 5

THE WORD OF GOD

All the essays in this book cite the Bible regularly as source for the substance of each essay. The time has come to discuss the Bible directly, especially how different people can reach different meanings from the same text. The competing interpretations are enough to shake our confidence in the Bible as "our only rule of faith and obedience."[1] As a people of the Book, the Church cannot leave this topic to the skepticism swirling around us.

This essay considers why and how the Bible functions powerfully among us. The aim is to reaffirm a basic, Reformed view[2] of the Bible and point a way beyond the road blocks that beset the Christian Church today in the middle of an epochal paradigm shift. The essay covers:

(1) the Bible as the Word of God to us today, and the circles of
(2) the Word and the words,
(3) the Word and the Spirit,
(4) the Word then and the Word now, and
(5) takeaways from the discussion.

1. The Bible as the Word of God to Us Today

The Bible is the Word of God because it comes from God. *One does not live by bread alone, but by every word that comes from the mouth of God* (Deut 8:3, Mark 4:4 NRSV). The Bible—Scripture—conveys in writing the miracle of God's

---

[1] *Westminster Larger Catechism*, q. 3, PC(USA) *Book of Confessions*, 7.113.
[2] "Reformed" comes from the Protestant Reformation. The term initially referred to Martin Luther (†1546) and was later applied more specifically to John Calvin (†1564) and the Swiss reformers.

speech to humankind, interpreting all created life in the light of God's on-going, gracious activity. It tells us who God is, what God's saving mercy is to a sinful humanity, and what God wants for our lives going forward. The Bible, however, does not stand alone as the Word of God and cannot be understood apart from at least three other facets: the Word made flesh, the Word proclaimed, and the Word as God's act.

The Bible itself points directly to Jesus Christ, *the Word made flesh* (John 1:14), the Word who is God (John 1:1). The Old Testament looks forward to Christ, while the New Testament looks back upon him.[3] Both bear witness to Jesus Christ as the supreme Word of God. Without this connection with Jesus Christ, the Bible would be just another book, perhaps a book of wise teachings or an interesting window on ancient history. The Bible draws its importance as the Word of God from the Christ who is *God with us* (*Emmanuel*, Matt 1:23)—to whom the Bible points in writing.

The Bible also functions as God's Word in worship. There the Bible is read and interpreted for life today at the center of a community of people gathered around Jesus Christ. We call this facet the Word of God proclaimed and engage it as preaching and the sacraments, both in local congregations and in governing bodies.[4] The Word of God proclaimed is grounded utterly in Scripture, and like the Bible draws its importance as the Word of God—its truth—from its ties to Jesus Christ, the Word incarnate. Exercised in worship, the Bible brings our daily life into the light of Christ's presence and activity. Scripture also functions as God's Word when we study the Bible in our homes, in groups, or alone.

As the Word of God written, the Bible stands between the Word Incarnate and the Word proclaimed. The Scrip-

---

[3] The connection to Christ explains why Christians refer to their Scriptures as the Old Testement and the New Testament.

[4] Governing bodies like sessions, diaconates, or consistories; or, more broadly, presbyteries, synods, national assemblies, or annual conferences.

tures of the Old and New Testaments in writing are indispensable to the Christian message and community. So, the Bi-

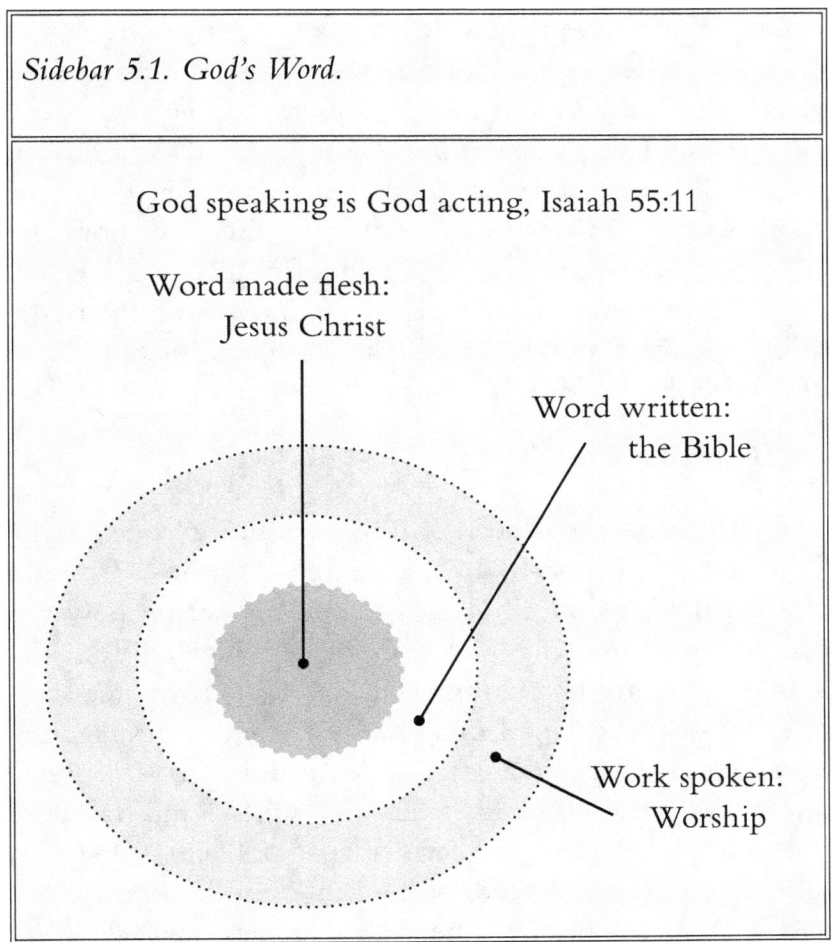

Sidebar 5.1. *God's Word.*

God speaking is God acting, Isaiah 55:11

Word made flesh:
Jesus Christ

Word written:
the Bible

Work spoken:
Worship

ble deserves the high authority given to it, enough to be called the Word of God straight away. Yet the Bible cannot stand apart from the truth of its own message, namely Jesus Christ as the Word incarnate. Neither can it stand apart from the place where it is exercised as proclamation in the context of worship. So, the Word of God includes all three—the Word incarnate, the Word written, and the Word proclaimed.

These three facets belong inseparably together (see Sidebar 5.1), and not one of them diminishes the other two.

The umbrella for all three is how the Word of God points to what God is saying and doing. According to the Bible, when God speaks God acts, and when God acts God speaks. God said, *let there be light; and there was light* (Gen 1:3; see also John 1:1-5; Psalm 33:9). The Word of God spoken always accomplishes what God intends (Isa 55:10-11). As God's speech and activity at every point discussed above, the Word of God defines human life in terms of God's life.

Three circles further clarify the inner workings of the Bible: the Word and the words, the Word and the Spirit, and the Word *then* and the Word *now*.

2. The Word and the Words.

Modern discussions of Biblical authority often highlight the words one-by-one, assuming that the words and the Word are identical. The Word and the words, however, are not the same. The Word cannot be separated from the individual words that comprise it. The Bible is written with specific words to be taken seriously as they stand: Hebrew words in the Old Testament, Greek words in the New Testament, and our own words when we translate and transpose the Bible's words into modern languages. There is no Word of God without the words of the Bible, one-by-one.

At the same time, the Word emerges only when the words are put together into a larger whole with a coherent meaning. By themselves individual words do not carry equal weight: one "if," "and," and "but" does not mean the same as every other "if," "and," and "but." Words in a jumble without some coherence make no sense for life. The authority of these words, like their meaning, hinges on how they work together to shape the Word of God.

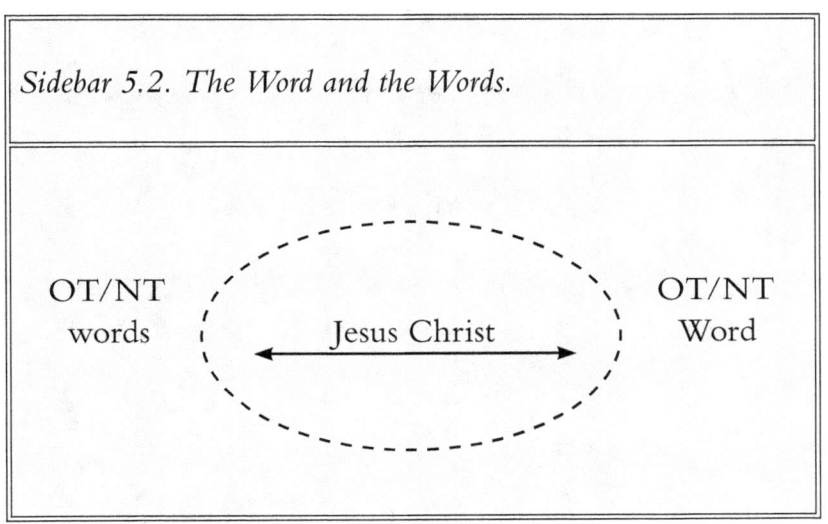

Sidebar 5.2. The Word and the Words.

Furthermore, *something*, namely, Word with a capital "W," has to draw all the words together, focus their meaning, and present them in their wholeness. Such wholeness is more than the sum of its parts, as a human life is more than the sum of its body parts or moments in time. The Word, too, is going to be more than the sum of the words.

The Bible itself names the Word which pulls together the sense of its words. Jesus Christ is the Word that *is God* (John 1:1), the Word *through whom all things were made* (John 1:2-3), the Word that *became flesh and dwelt among us full of grace and truth* (John 1:14). The words of the Old Testament all point forward to Jesus Christ. The words of the New Testament all point back to Jesus Christ. Jesus Christ elevates all these writings to a true, authentic revelation, namely, the Word of the living God.

The Word and the words form a circle (see Sidebar 5.2). We cannot say which one comes first. The Word cannot be reduced to the words or the words to the Word. Yet we cannot have one without the other.

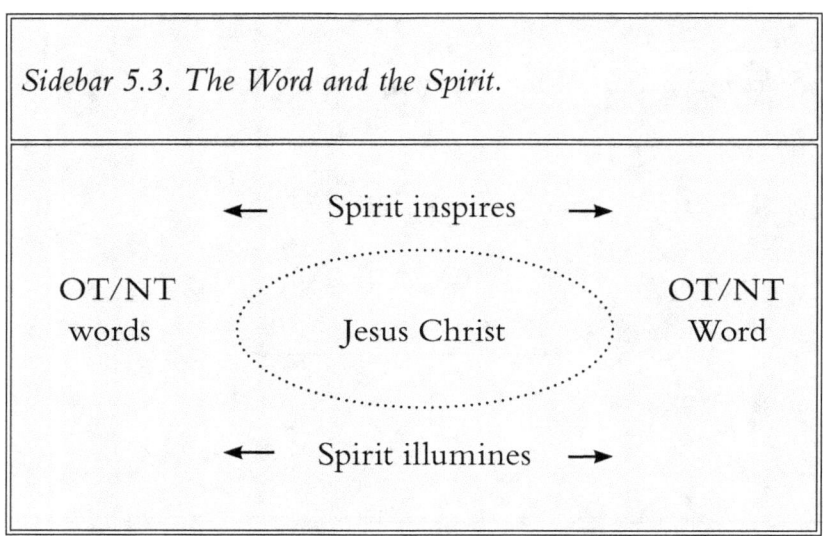

Sidebar 5.3. The Word and the Spirit.

3. *The Word and the Spirit.*

According to the Bible and Reformed confessions, both the Word of God and the words of the Book require the Spirit of God to make them powerful. *No one can say 'Jesus is Lord' except by the Holy Spirit,* says Paul (1 Cor 12:3, NRSV), and again: *The letter kills, but the Spirit gives life* (2 Cor 3:5, NRSV). According to the *Westminster Confession of Faith* (1646):

> notwithstanding [the perfections of Scripture], our full persuasion and assurance of the infallible truth and divine authority thereof, is from the inward work of the Holy Spirit, bearing witness by and with the Word in our hearts.[5]

The Spirit was essential to producing the Bible at its points of origin, then sustaining it over time. The Bible indeed comes *from God* by the inspiration of the Spirit. Likewise the illumination of the Spirit is essential for the Bible to point *to God*

---

[5] Chapter I, Paragraph V, quoted from John Leith, *Creeds of the Churches,* Third Edition, *op cit.,* 195.

today and make the Bible powerful in our lives. The Spirit, that is, urges us to read or hear the words of Scripture, helps us understand the individual words drawn together as the Word of God, and leads us to take both the Word and the words to heart, making them effective for life. The Bible functions for revelation today because God illumines the book with the same Spirit that inspired it.[6]

Word and Spirit thus form a circle (Sidebar 5.3). We cannot tell which one comes first, the Word or the Spirit. Yet we cannot have one without the other. The Word of God which is Jesus Christ and the Spirit of God work together to make the words of the Bible powerful for human life.

4. The Word Then and the Word Now.

Interpreting the Bible often bogs down in rules or techniques. At one end are the techniques of Bible study, *i.e.*, research into historical context, word meanings, and the clear sense of the text. At the other end are rules for "applying" the text to life today or drawing doctrinal conclusions.

What happens between these two poles deserves closer attention. The lower side of the diagram (see Sidebar 5.4), from *now to then,* moves from the ever-present concern for life today into the Biblical text written for people in another time and place. To let the text speak with its own voice, we study closely what they said to and among themselves for the issues of their lives—exegesis—before we turn to their message to us in very different times and settings.

To complete the circle, however, we have to return to where we began, lest we get stuck in the past. The upper side of the diagram, from *then to now,* moves from immersion in the life and times of these ancient people back to our own. Every true interpreter of Scripture takes this step, asking how

---
[6] *Westminster Confession*, Chapter 1, Paragraph VI, *ibid.*, 195-196.

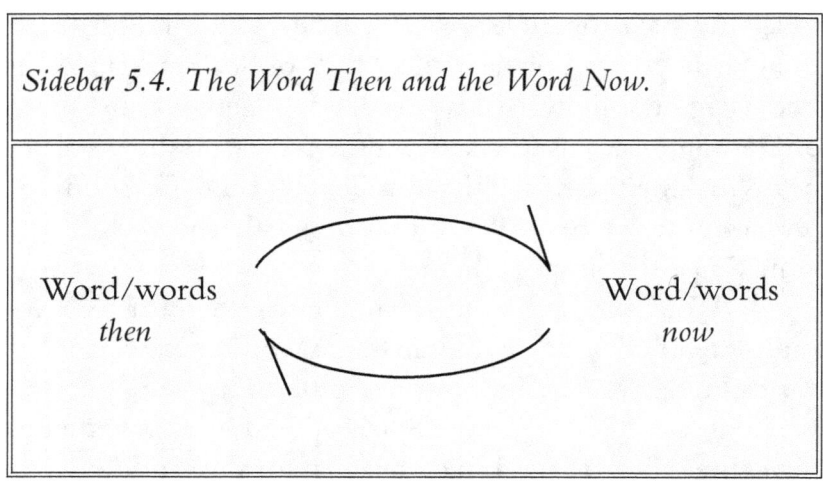

Sidebar 5.4. The Word Then and the Word Now.

a particular text brings light and direction to our footsteps today, the Word of God for today. Besides completing the circle, the search for meaning today shapes what we expect to find when we first approach the Book (from *now* to *then*).

For all interpreters, the simple task of Biblical interpretation today is to bridge the historical gap between then and now, them and us, their issues and ours. Here is yet another circle, running *from the Word now*—the Book in our hands–*to the Word then*—the Book at its points of origin–*and back again*. Once again, the circle cannot be reduced to one part alone, which part comes first is not obvious, and we cannot have one part without the others. Amazingly, faithful Christians have found ways to navigate this circle for the modern era and proclaim the Gospel today with all the power it had at its beginning. Four strategies for navigating the circle stand out. The following illustrates the strategies using Luke 15:1-7, the parable of the lost sheep.

a. Timeless Truth.

The first strategy transposes the text of Scripture into a timeless truth that is the same today and every day. Two distinct approaches have emerged using this strategy. One approach sees Jesus speaking to the mixed crowd of sinners, Pharisees, and disciples (1-2). In the parable, the good shepherd is God, who risks everything to search for the one lost sheep *until he finds it*, as in verse 4. *For God*, that is, *every individual has an infinite value*, which at its best is the human experience of God for everyone everywhere all the time.[7]

For the other approach, Jesus is addressing the sinners before him (1-2). The parable shows how the human condition as lost sheep or sinners always stands in need of salvation. Jesus Christ is the good shepherd who comes to find and save us from our lostness, at great cost to himself. *Through Christ God offers every lost sinner salvation if only we repent*, as in verse 7. Both the sin and the salvation apply to us today as much as to sinners then.[8]

This strategy uses the enduring truths of the Gospel to bridge the historical gap between the text and us. The parts of the text that do not pertain to these truths just drop away. The similarity of these two approaches—timeless truth—is as striking as their dissimilarity—the human experience of God *vs.* the drama of salvation. These approaches often align as liberal *vs.* conservative, but the labels do not always fit, as the footnote representatives show. The other three strategies are less easily identifiable in partisan terms. By reconsidering what it means to be Biblical, these four strategies may force us to rethink what we call liberal and conservative.

b. Timebound Truth.

A second strategy immerses modern people in the timebound, revelatory experience or relationships manifest

---

[7] *E.g.*, Adolph Harnack, Harry Emerson Fosdick, Paul Tillich, Haddon Robinson, and Eugene Peterson.

[8] *E.g.*, J. Greshan Machen, George W. Truett, Carl F.H. Henry, and Millard Erickson.

in Luke 15:1-7. This strategy, too, allows two approaches. For one approach Jesus is speaking to the sinners as the lost sheep, for whom the shepherd risks all else to search until he finds it. Like the shepherd, God extends the same boundless mercy to unworthy sinners. *Identifying with the sheep and reliving its experience, we, too, can share God's boundless, ineffable mercy to sinners*, as in verse 4c. The experience transforms us for joyful, vigorous living today.[9]

For the other approach within this strategy, Jesus is likewise speaking to the sinner, perhaps also to the Pharasees who are grumbling (1-2). This approach highlights the relational identity of the sheep: first lost, then found, and now belonging to God along with the rest of the flock. Placing ourselves within these relationships, traced down through the ages, *we too belong to God, and our identity is thus defined and shaped along with the rest of the flock*, as in verse 6c. The ninety-nine righteous would do well to take notice.[10]

These two approaches maximize the literary-historical tools for studying every detail of the text, to bridge the time gap. They highlight what is important to the truth of the Gospel and winnow out the rest.

c. Common Point of Reference.

A third strategy, also with two approaches, recognizes that the people, situations, and issues of the text *then* may be very different from those *now*, so it looks for a common point of reference or horizon shared by both timeframes. For one approach, in which God is the common point of reference (*the same yesterday, today, and tomorrow,* Hebrews

---

[9] *E.g.*, C.H. Dodd, Samuel Terrien, Phyllis Trible, Will Wilimon, and Walter Wink.

[10] *E.g.*, Ernst Troeltsch, H. Richard Niebuhr, Sallie McFague, Lewis Smedes, Marcus Borg, and Diana Butler Bass.

13:8), Jesus is addressing the grumbling of the Pharisees and scribes in Luke 15:1-7. The passage, that is, shows a *God who, like the shepherd, rejoices in seeking and finding lost sheep*, as in verse 5. For all sheep, however, participating in God's joy is the gift of living in God's presence every moment of every day, especially when recovering sinners who were lost.[11]

The other approach under this strategy sees Jesus justifying to the Pharisees why he is eating with sinners (1-2). Here, humanity-under-God is the common point of reference. Jesus' aim is to help us recover our true humanity in daily living. So, like the shepherd working with a lost sheep: *having been lost and found, the sheep repents and returns to the place of authentic humanity-under-God*, as in verse 7. The contrast with the 99 sheep (the righteous persons who need no repentance), namely, the Pharisees and scribes, is stark. We face such alternatives daily.[12]

Like all the strategies, the common point of reference in both variations bridges the time gap between *then* and *now*, and concentrates the message that comes through.

d. Typology.

A fourth strategy looks for patterns or types that are similar *then* and *now*. If we can find similar life circumstances *then* and *now*, the message *now* can correspond with the message *then*. One approach takes a more situational-historical angle, the other a more verbal-literary angle. For historical typology, Jesus is addressing the situation of sinful people lost in Jesus' day—the sheep in Luke 15:1-7. *As Jesus reached out to the lost sheep in his day (search until he finds them), so Jesus reaches out to sinners (us) today*, as in verses 4 and 1-2. That is good

---

[11] *E.g.*, Karl Barth, Paul Scherer, James Cone, Stanley Hauerwas, and Frederick Buechner.
[12] *E.g.*, Rudolf Bultmann, Schubert Ogden, and Davie Napier.

news for sinners and sets the appropriate role for religious leaders.[13]

Literary typology, looks for the word patterns with which Jesus made his impact on sinners and Pharisees at the time—patterns that, when faithfully repeated, presumably will have the same impact today. The response to Jesus and his parable is striking. *Sinners once lost and now found, today as of old, will hear God's Word of grace and joy in Jesus' words: "repentance" is a celebration*, as in verse 7. The Pharisees, on the other hand, will grumble self-righteously like the 99 sheep who hear "repentance" as a command for uniformity.[14]

The typologies are notable for jumping back-and-forth between *then* and *now* to bridge the historical gap. They, too, focus on what is important in the text and let the rest go.

All eight approaches strive to faithfully interpret the Bible as the Word of God for our time. Each is effective in the hands of its respective interpreters. One does not deny the others, even when the outcomes for a given passage are different. Furthermore, these approaches do not offer a cafeteria of options from which we can pick or choose one according to the passage or the situation; nor can they all simply be combined into one. Switching from one to another is difficult because each approach involves its own theological convictions. A shift from one to another is like a conversion experience: when it happens, there is no turning back.

Interpreting Scripture today entails tracing the whole circle between the Word *then* and the Word *now*. One part entails the other, and which comes first is not always obvious. Traversing the circle, each of us is most likely using one of these eight bridges to interpret Scripture. That makes identifying our respective bridges crucial to our own clear grasp of the Gospel, to our own working theology, and to honest conversation with one another on issues that divide us. During a time of paradigm shift, informed theological discussion is crucial for the Christian Church going forward.

---

[13] *E.g.*, Gerhard Von Rad, Billy Graham, Edmund Steimle, Barbara Brown Taylor, James Forbes, and Jürgen Moltmann.

[14] *E.g.*, Fred Craddock, Thomas G. Long, David Buttrick, and Anthony Thiselton.

5. Takeaways from this Discussion of the Word of God.

This discussion of the Bible leaves us with several takeaways.

First, *predictions of the demise of the Bible and its authority are premature.* The authority of the Bible derives from its subject matter or object, namely, God, and how it functions in God's hands, namely, at the point of proclamation in worship within the community God gathers around Jesus Christ. The authority of the Bible will stand as long as God makes it so, as the Gospel of Jesus Christ.

Second, *efforts to ground the authority of Scripture in something other than God invariably go awry.* From early on, the Modernist-Pietist era sought to establish the truth value of Scripture from *outside* the Bible. That was the project of the 18th Century Enlightenment. Obvious candidates for outside criteria are timeless reason; the timebound facts of history or of science; and human experience, the feelings we have in relationships with God and life. These extra-Biblical foundations lie behind the misleading question, "do you take the Bible literally (*i.e.*, as historical or scientific fact) or figuratively (*i.e.*, imaginatively, detached from reality)?" In truth, "taking the Bible figuratively" is bound utterly to what the text says literally, as literature, and "taking the Bible literally" should mean taking the figurative parts figuratively. Literal *vs.* figurative readings are false alternatives, the same ones that led the Early Church to get stuck in allegorical interpretations. By and large, modern Biblical interpreters have come to terms with these outside criteria, and they have found ways to bridge the time gap between *now and then, then and now* faithfully.

Third, to say it plainly, *the only criterion for the truth value of the Bible is God.* The *Westminster Confession* puts it succinctly:

> The authority of the holy Scripture, for which it ought to be believed and obeyed, dependeth not upon the testimony of any man or church, but wholly upon God (who is truth itself), the Author thereof; and therefore it is to be received, because it is the Word of God.[15]

---

[15] *Westminster Confession*, Chapter I, para IV, in Leith, *Creeds of the Churches*, 195.

In other words, the Bible is self-authenticating, which makes the circles of Word and words, Word and Spirit, Word then and Word now, vital to the conversation. These circles offer no outside vantage point or handles with which to break into the circles or break them up. The circles belong within the realm of God's activity, where they operate with transparency, rigor, and honesty. Only those living within that space will take them as authority. But in that realm the Bible functions indeed as the Word of God.

Fourth, *the very things that challenge us most about the Bible also make it authoritative for us.* The Bible obviously talks about other people, in other times and places, using other languages, facing other issues of life. For modern people, the differences are daunting, to say the least. The Word in writing nonetheless gives us access to these ancient people in all their humanity. The very distances force us to look outside our own times, places, and comfort zones for perspective about our daily walk with God. Clearly, that calls for paying close attention to both ends of this time frame, life *then* and life *now*. At one end, we will diligently seek the meanings of the Bible *then*, and, at the other end, we will engage one another in walking with God *now* in the light of Scripture. To help us along the way, we will want ministers who can read the Bible in Hebrew and Greek as well as immerse themselves in the current issues of life.

By God's own activity among us, *the Bible is the Word of God for us today.* That conviction holds no matter what challenges or changes we face today. As a community committed to Jesus Christ and life together in him, we dare not diminish the Bible or its importance for Christians on the move. The Bible—the Word of God focused upon Christ, exercised in worship, and energized by the Spirit—remains *a lamp to our feet and a light to our pathway* (Psalm 119:105) where *the light shines in the darkness, and the darkness has not overcome it*[AT] (John 1:5). With God behind it, that light shines into the future as it does in the present and has in the past.[16]

---

[16] For further discussion of this subject, see Merwyn S. Johnson, *The Voice of Scripture in the Church: Christians Interpreting the Bible Today*, publication pending.

ESSAY 6

GRACE AND PREDESTINATION

Sola gratia—grace alone—lies at the heart of the Gospel for all churches that trace their roots to the Protestant Reformation and earlier to Augustine (†430). Salvation, that is, comes from God alone in Christ alone through faith alone by grace alone. Grace preserves the gift character of each item in that list. Without grace, each of the other items risks becoming a mere means or method for human management or manipulation. When that happens, we quickly pick up the mantra, "if it's to be, it's up to me," and God takes a back seat. One way to move beyond the deep divisions within churches today may be to recover the profound, historic, Reformation accent on grace.

To get there, the following discussion considers:
(1) the dynamics of cheap and costly grace,
(2) where God's choosing and our choosing overlap, and
(3) how costly grace is connected with predestination.

1. The Dynamics of Cheap and Costly Grace.

Dietrich Bonhoeffer (1906-1945) highlights the issue of grace with his celebrated talk about cheap grace and costly grace. "Cheap grace," says Bonhoeffer, "is that grace we bestow on ourselves."[1] Cheap grace occurs on the one hand when we fixate on certain absolute principles or moral practices as the only way to be Christian. Clinging to such "laws," we focus more and more upon what we humans must do to be worthy, right, or good, but less and less upon

---
[1] Dietrich Bonhoeffer, *Discipleship: Dietrich Bonhoeffer Works*, Vol. 4, *op cit.*, 44. For the discussion of "cheap grace" vs. "costly grace," see 43-56.

God, from whom the principles and laws supposedly came. The result is a grace we bestow on ourselves.

On the other hand, cheap grace occurs when we dispense with the commandments altogether, declaring them too demanding or legalistic, hence contrary to the spirit of the Gospel and love. So, seeking to "do what is within us,"[2] we release ourselves permissively from the requirements of any Biblical laws that we perceive no longer pertain to us. The result is still cheap grace, a grace we bestow on ourselves. The Gospel itself can be cheap grace if it merely shows us how to satisfy our own religious, moral, or personal needs.

Costly grace, on the other hand, is costly because it joins us with Jesus Christ, who is *God with us* (*Emmanuel*), God as a human being (*the Word become flesh*). His death and resurrection are God's costly act for us and for our salvation. With his birth, life, teachings, death, and resurrection Jesus Christ fulfills every demand and requirement of the law for us and our humanity. Christ replaces the law with himself. Costly grace is to share in the costly life of Christ, united with Christ by faith, therein communing with God now and always. In Christ, we focus on the grace that comes from God instead of the grace we bestow on ourselves.

Two side points arise here. First, modern American Christianity tends to put grace and law at odds with each other. For many Americans, grace is the freedom of unrestrained human spontaneity, and law is the imposition of a closely regulated, legalistic system that restricts human freedom and spontaneity. These views of grace and law parallel the two sides of cheap grace noted above.

---

[2] The phrase, "do what is within us," sounds very modern but was highlighted by Martin Luther for its misuse in the Church of the late Middle Ages, in *The Heidelberg Disputation* (1518), thesis 16. See *Martin Luther's Basic Theological Writings*, ed Timothy F. Lull (Minneapolis: Augsburg Fortress, 1989), 41.

By contrast, for the Bible and the Protestant Reformers the problem of the law is not legalism but idolatry. Though God-given, the law and human freedom become idols when we embrace them apart from communing with God in everyday life. That is precisely what happens in cheap grace, where we put something in the place of God that is not God and ignore God in the process.

Second, while marking the gift character of God's working with us, grace does not mean we become passive or inactive. Quite the opposite, as we shall see. Sharing in Christ's death and resurrection does not leave us doing nothing or merely enabled to "do what is within us." True, in Christ we no longer have to make ourselves righteous. But living in the presence of God means paying close attention to God's majestic goodness all around us.

In Jesus Christ costly grace and God's commandments come together in amazing, down-to-earth ways. Christ fulfills the law, and in doing so restores its true purpose of pointing to the Lawgiver, God. That is, the commandments tell us something about the God from whom they came, about the God who keeps the commandments still, and about the Christ—*God with us*—who fulfilled them.

What kind of God wants us not to kill, covet, lie, commit adultery, or engage in some other sin? Such a God values life and truth, and rejoices at the well-being of others. What does the law tell us about God's purposes for humanity? Clearly, the God who keeps the commandments wants us to abide with God and one another in the same space, that is, in the arena marked off by the commandments. What do we learn about the God who, as the human Jesus, came among us to save us from our bondage to sin? God is the One whose own righteousness manifests itself in everlasting mercy. As a gift, the law points us positively to:

- who God is, majestic, gracious, loving, and righteous;
- where God is, always at hand, no matter how bad or difficult the situation;
- what God is doing at the moment, actively; and
- what we want to be doing, in active fellowship with God.

2. God's Choosing and Ours.

Grace matches God's choosing with our choosing in a way that preserves the gift character of salvation. Cheap grace robs us of salvation as a gift by focusing instead on what we humans have to do to secure it, such as a decision for Christ, a response of faith or good works, or a life lived well. The gift character of our salvation, namely, that salvation comes from God and not from ourselves, involves how God's choosing us overlaps and establishes our choosing God, without one choosing canceling out the other. That is what the Biblical concept of predestination accomplishes.

a. God's Choosing.

During the Protestant Reformation (1517-1650) the focus of predestination was upon the God who predestines. Later, during the Modernist-Pietist era (1650-2000), the focus shifted to the condition of the believer who is predestined. The main question for Pietism became, "Who is saved and who is not saved (am I?), and how do we get there?"

Pietism flourished against the backdrop of scientific interest in natural necessity and determinism, for which every cause has its effect, and every effect has its cause. By the latter half of the 19th Century and throughout the 20th Century, Pietism settled into the human freedom to choose as the cause and our salvation as the effect. Under Pietism God provides the *means* of salvation, Jesus Christ, but we humans still have to choose whether to accept the offer, be saved, and seek the kingdom, or be condemned by our refusal to do so.

In late Modernist-Pietism, free will has become the litmus test for Americans in both church and culture, along the whole spectrum from right to left. Some Christians adopt the language of response—God offers and we respond in a back-and-forth sequence—but the outcome still shifts the focus of grace from God's gift over to the human capacity to receive it. The accent on free will misses the Reformation insight into costly grace and makes salvation and good works a grace we bestow on ourselves.

To emphasize God's choosing, theologian Karl Barth (1886-1968) restates the doctrine of predestination-election with a bold and brilliant grasp of Scripture and the Reformation.[3] He prefers the term "election." For Barth, Jesus Christ—God as a human being—is both the electing God and the elected human, embracing our damnation and our salvation at the same time. No human individual is more damned than Jesus Christ, who died the death of a condemned sinner. In his dying all humans die (2 Cor 5:14). The salvation of humanity depends on it (2 Cor 5:21). But also, no human individual is more saved than Jesus Christ rising from the dead, and no one is saved except in rising with him (1 Cor 15:21-26, Rom 5:15-6:11).

The reality and the mystery of what God does as the human individual, Jesus Christ, establishes the costly grace of our salvation. Bound to Christ, grace is more than an offer. Grace is the gift of actively participating in his dying and rising. Our choosing is thus rooted in God's costly choosing, and costly grace never loses its gift character.

---

[3] Karl Barth, *Church Dogmatics,* Volume II, Part 2 (Edinburgh: T & T Clark, 1957), 3-506. See also Volume IV, Part 2 (Edinburgh: T & T Clark, 1958), Section 64, "The Exaltation of the Son of Man," 3-277.

b. Our Choosing.

Both Luther and the Reformed confessions of the 16th Century place an extraordinary emphasis on the human freedom that accompanies grace.[4] That freedom comes explicitly from our connection with God, not from separating our act of choosing from God's. As Jesus says, *When you abide in my word, you are truly my disciples, and you shall know the truth, and the truth will make you free*[AT] (John 8:31-32).

Free will, however, faces us with a freedom of disconnection. Free will is not a modern idea, but it has become a way for modern humanity to transcend a natural necessity that traps everything in a web of cause-and-effect—the modern day equivalent of fatalism. That is, for example, the perceived threat posed by Darwin's theory of evolution (1857), its spin-offs under the umbrella of "social Darwinism," or its cousin in Freudian psychology. The freedom to choose seems to offer a way to retain the human soul as a *supernatural dimension unique to humanity.

But to work, free will has to disconnect the human will from its surroundings. The "free" in "free will" creates a vacuum—a capacity, potential, or unfilled space—where humans can make impartial, value-neutral choices, unaffected by internal bias or outside influences. The "freedom" in "the freedom to choose" thus isolates us from the very considerations the will has to process in order to make choices.

In life, however, we never make choices in such a vacuum. The choices we face come at us relentlessly, moment by moment. We are weighed down by the people, problems, and situations that surround us. We are predisposed by our own prior choices, experiences, and inner feelings. Do we ever choose in a vacuum whether to breathe or eat, or what

---

[4] See Martin Luther's important exchange with Erasmus over predestination, in *The Bondage of the Will* (1525). See also the Reformation confessions in the PC(USA) *Book of Confessions (BC)*, 3.01-8.28.

clothes to wear? How to face the moment? Whom to befriend and attach ourselves? What to do with our lives? Or what we want to think or believe? The "freedom" in "freedom to choose" does not help us sift or process all the things that go into our choices. Such freedom is an abstraction from the actual choices we face and how we make them.

Freedom to choose also contains a hidden trap. If we ever sin or choose life apart from God, our wills are tainted. Our current choices are directly affected by our previous ones. Having sinned—once is all it takes—our wills operate by an inner default which is no longer impartial, completely open, or truly free in the free will sense. The choosing that corrupts itself cannot then uncorrupt itself without adding to its corruption. We do not lose our choosing, but we do lose the freedom of our choosing. With keen insight into the human condition, the Bible calls sin a bondage (Rom 8:15, 21) or slavery (John 8:34).

To recover the integrity of our choosing entails a freedom rooted in God's choosing. God acts to release us from the bondage of our wills to sin. To that end, the faith that unites us with Christ is a gift, the work of the Holy Spirit. In union with Christ, hence shaped and formed specifically by Jesus Christ, we become in God what we could never be if left to our own devices, just as we are. In Christ, moved by the Spirit of God and participating in the love of God (Phil 2:1), our wills function in the context of when and where *the Lord may be found* (Isa 55:6 RSV). *Living, moving, and having our being in the living God*[AT] (from Acts 17:28) energizes us—frees us—every moment of every day.

God makes choices, too, providentially both in the moments at hand and in the long term. God's choices overlap with our choices utterly. There is here no obliteration of human choosing. Neither is there any space between God's choosing and ours—no context that does not involve God and no freedom apart from God. God's very closeness establishes our choosing. Our choosing is more important, not less, because we do everything in conjunction with God's simultaneous act at the moment (Psalm 139:1-18, John 1:12-13 and 3:21).

3. Costly Grace and Predestination.

When God's choosing is joined with costly grace and our choosing is joined with God's in predestination, the result is often revolutionary activity.[5] By all accounts, that was the effect on Calvinism in the 16th and 17th centuries. The *Westminster Confession of Faith* (1646), for example, with predestination at its core, gave a theological justification for the rebellion of England's Parliament against her king.

Since God alone saves us, we are released from the burden of having to accomplish our own righteousness or salvation. We are free, that is, to get on with the more important task of living with God. What Calvin calls "the third use of the law" provides believers a clear, concrete sense of God at work among us and where we want to be.

So, we strive to keep the commandments with all our heart, mind, soul, and strength, because to live in communion with God is an end in itself. There is no higher joy in life. We are confident that what is begun with God's blessing, God will bring to completion at the right time (Phil 1:6). We cannot fail, no matter how difficult the task we face, how weak our efforts, how limited our resources, or how great the opposition against us. With God behind the endeavor we can throw ourselves into doing God's will—evangelism, social action, mission, whatever the task large or small—with total abandon.

---

[5] See Michael Walzer, *The Revolution of the Saints: A Study in the Origins of Radical Politics* (Cambridge: Harvard Univ. Press, 1965).

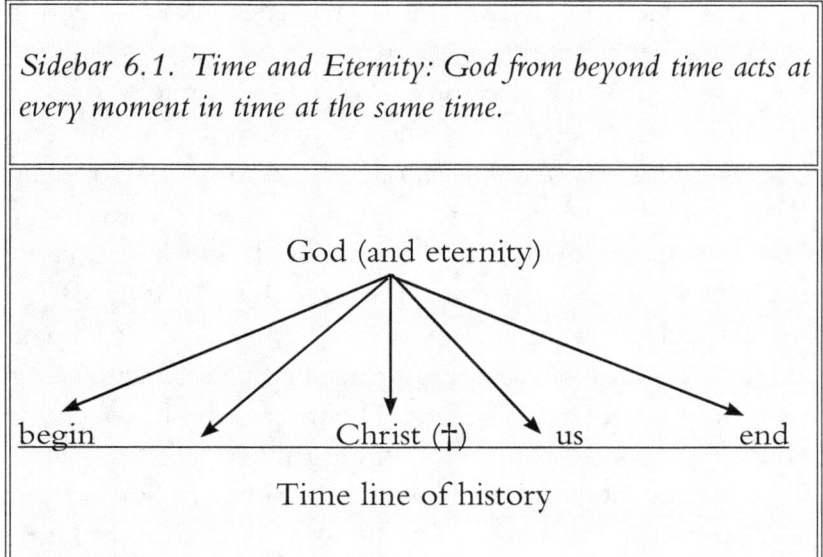

Sidebar 6.1. Time and Eternity: God from beyond time acts at every moment in time at the same time.

In the power of the Spirit, the Gospel frees us from our bondage to sin and from the cheap grace we bestow on ourselves. The same Gospel-and-Spirit frees us for life with God. This freedom comes from God's grace alone. As John says, *When the Son frees you, you will be free indeed*[AT] (8:36). *Where the Spirit of the Lord is, there is freedom,* says Paul (2 Cor 3:17 RSV). The Reformation confessions all concur on this.

How does predestination signal such grace and freedom? The "destination" in "pre-destination" refers to the time line of history from beginning to end (see Sidebar 6.1). The "pre-" in "pre-destination" locates God *outside* the time line of history, not merely before time. God, who creates both time and history, is not bound by time or the sequences of history as we creatures are. The "pre-" could as easily be "post-" or "mid-" or "two-thirds-destination." God from outside time acts at every moment of time … at the same time. And God engages all of time from within time, at the point of the timebound, human, historical Jesus.

In the Bible, covenant and predestination-election are close sister themes (see Sidebars 1.2 and 1.3). As we have seen, predestination-election conveys God's gracious favor[6] toward creation and God's chosen people, including Jesus Christ and *the believing-into-him-ones*[AT] (John 3.16). Covenant pertains to the arena where God abides with creation and God's people, and they abide with God. Speaking mainly of God's choosing, election embraces the choosing of the one elected. Speaking mainly of our choosing, the covenant activities we choose are always grounded in God's choosing. Each theme informs the other. The interaction between the two themes runs through the whole Bible.

In recent decades scientists and science fiction authors alike have been fascinated with the mystery of time and time travel. Across time, predestination highlights the vital particularities of our human lives one-by-one, moment-by-moment, because our every effort is *wrought in God* (John 3:21). That is the very opposite of obliterating our humanity in some kind of fatalism, luck, natural necessity, or pre-determinism.[7] *In God* our every action takes on a profound and important meaning at the moment.

Adolph Harnack, the great Lutheran historian of Christian theology, observes that whenever predestination— *"the confident belief in a God of grace"* [8]—shows up, it stirs a reformation, even a revolution. Maybe the time has come to recover its powerful meaning for the Church in our time.

---

[6] *Hesed*, in Hebrew, *charis* in Greek.

[7] "Fatalism" comes from the ancient Greek notion of "fate" and means that everything, including all our choices, is predetermined or bound by natural necessity. "Chance," or "luck," in which everything is totally random, also excludes human choosing.

[8] Italics as quoted, from Adolph Harnack, *What Is Christianity?* (New York: Harper Torchbooks, 1957. German original, 1900), 270, with discussion, 268-281. His main reference points are Augustine and Luther.

ESSAY 7

UNION WITH CHRIST: WHAT DOES IT MEAN TO BE SAVED?

Salvation stands at the heart of Christianity. Jesus is quite clear:

God so loved the world that he gave his only begotten Son, in order that every believing-into-him-one would not perish but have life eternal.[AT1] (John 3:16)

Jesus is also circumspect about this very salvation:

If anyone wants to follow after me, let him utterly deny himself, take up his cross, and follow me. For whoever may want to save his own life will lose it, but whoever shall lose his life for my sake and the Gospel's will save it.[AT2] (Mark 8:34b-35)

The Gospel, that is, cannot be a blatant appeal to human self-interest, rewards and punishments, or what we can get out of it. Salvation does not work that way. God does not work that way. The Gospel is above all about God's gift of living in communion with God—salvation—which comes down to union with Christ in his life, death, and resurrection.

To clarify the matter, this essay considers:

(1) the main Biblical images for union with Christ,
(2) how faith unites us with Christ,
(3) how salvation engages us in this life and beyond, and
(4) some obstacles we put in its way.

---

[1] The superscript [AT] indicates the author's translation. The Greek phrase *every believing-into-him-one* is based on a participle that states things as they are, *i.e.*, every person who in fact is already believing in Christ.

[2] Notice the contrast between *whoever may want* (conditional) and *whoever shall lose his life* (future). The future is a fact statement of things as they will be.

1. The Main Biblical Images for Union with Christ.

Union with Christ emerges from four strong images in the New Testament:
- As branches attached to the rootstock of a vine (John 15:1-11, 16-17; Rom 11:17-24);
- As adopted children brought into a natural family (John 1:12f and 3:3-8; 1 John 3:1-3; Rom 8:21-25, 29; Gal 3:35-4:7; Eph 1:5);
- As body members incorporated into the whole body (Rom 12:4-7; 1 Cor 12:12-30; Eph 1:23, 3:6, 4:4-16); and
- As family members drawn together in a functioning house or household (Eph 2:19-22; 2 Peter 4-10).

In all four images Jesus Christ is the one with whom we are united. He is the vine, the natural child, the body, and the house or household. John speaks of the union as a mutual abiding, of us in him and him in us.

Abide in me, and I in you. As the branch is not able to bear fruit by itself unless it abides in the vine, so you [cannot bear fruit] unless you abide in me.^{AT} (John 15:4)

Paul also speaks of *us in Christ* and *Christ in us*:

Anyone in Christ [is] a new creation; the old has passed away, behold, the new has come. ^{AT} (2 Cor 5:17)

I live, yet no longer I, but Christ is living in me. ^{AT} (Gal 2:20)

Both phrases, *us in Christ* and *Christ in us*, are vital. Both phrases make Christ intensely personal to us. But the life-giving, fruit-producing sap comes only from the rootstock of the vine, and the vine does not depend upon the branches in the same way the branches depend upon the vine. *Us in Christ* is the weightier phrase.

Likewise, union with Christ focuses first and foremost on *us in Christ*. The weight falls on Christ's perfect humanity not ours, on Christ's goodness not ours, and on

Christ's divinity not ours. Participating in the reality of Jesus Christ, we share in his attributes and accomplishments without having to duplicate them, and Christ defines our lives by his life.

Who, after all, is Jesus Christ that we might want to be united with him? He is the reality of God with us (*Emmanuel*, Matt 1:22). When Jesus says, *I am the vine; you are the branches* (John 15:5), he is recalling the Old Testament covenant, in which the commandments circumscribe the space where God will be our God and we will be God's people. God, who gave the commandments, also keeps them. As the human Jesus, God fulfills them. So, the commandments describe who God is, where God is, and what God is doing at the moment.[3] Jesus is referring to this covenant connection dirctly in John 15:10:[4]

> *When [ean] you keep my commandments, you will abide in my love, just as I have kept my father's commandments and I am abiding in his love.*[AT]

Jesus is describing what happens when, united or *abiding* with him, we find ourselves actively *abiding* with God. We keep the commandments not to gain favor with God nor to make ourselves actually good or worthy. Communing with God who is good, we participate in what God is also doing at the moment. We do not act to make a place for ourselves, but to enjoy the place God gives us *in Christ*.

> *I have said these things to you in order that my joy might be in you and that your joy might be full.*[AT] (John 15:11)

Luther, Calvin, and the Protestant Reformers of the 16th Century understand salvation to be union with Christ in this Biblical sense.

---

[3] This is the third and primary use of the law Calvin talks about in the *Institutes, op cit.*, Book 2, Chapter 7, Paragraph 12, pp. 360-1.

[4] The verse is better translated as a fact statement, with the Greek word *ean* translated as *when* instead of *if*.

2. How Faith Unites Us with Christ.

Union with Christ takes place by faith alone. The role of faith is to join us with Christ and the accomplishments of his life. Faith itself, the human act of believing, does not make us righteous, but unites us with the one who is righteous and clothes us in his righteousness, namely, Jesus Christ. The promise given to Abraham establishes this pattern already in the Old Testament, when God says to him:

> *I will make of you a great nation, and I will bless you, and make your name great, so that you will be a blessing. I will bless those who bless you, and the one who curses you I will curse; and in you all the families of the earth shall be blessed.*

(Gen 12:2-3, NRSV)

God's blessing here extends to others definitively through the person of Abraham. The *families of the earth*, that is, receive God's blessing when they are joined with God's blessing upon him. Abraham is Paul's poster child for how this works with Christ (Rom 4, Gal 3:6-9). We are blessed, or saved, solely by sharing in the faithfulness of Jesus Christ and the righteousness he accomplishes. As Paul says:

> *Now apart from the law the righteousness of God is manifest ... through the faith [or faithfulness] of Christ Jesus into all the believing-ones.*[AT 5] (Rom 3:21)

What is the difference between the activity of believing and doing good works? For Paul the works of the law, being *self*-generated, produce only *self*-righteousness. Faith as believing is still something we do, but it cannot generate itself. Believing cannot come from some inner capacity, good intention, special wisdom, or spiritual practice. Believing

---

[5] My translation follows the KJV closely and the NRSV/NIV footnote. See also Gal 2:15-21, where, referring to Christ, the Greek word *pisteos* can mean either faith or faithfulness. Modern translations uniformly change "the *faith/faithfulness of Jesus*" into "*our faith in Jesus*."

comes from beyond us, as a gift, unexpected and unconditional. *No one is able to say "Jesus [is] Lord" if not in the Spirit,*^{AT} says Paul (1 Cor12:3). Faith is a *fruit of the Spirit,* just like *love, joy, peace, patience, kindness, generosity, gentleness, and self-control* (Gal 5:22). With this in mind, Jesus says to Nicodemus,

> *The spirit blows where it wills, and you hear the sound of it, but you do not know whence it is coming or whither it is going; just so is every born-out-of-the-Spirit-one.*^{AT} (John 3:8)

The gift-character of our believing extends also to our so-called "good works." Paul says plainly:

> *For by grace you have been saved through faith;*
> *and this gift [is] from God, not out of ourselves;*
> *not from works, that no one might boast;*
> *for we are his [God's] workmanship, created in Christ Jesus for good works, which God created beforehand that in them we walk.*^{AT} (Eph 2:8-10)

As sinners, who among us can do a "good work" out of ourselves? Presuming that we can do so dooms our efforts before we begin. But when we find ourselves—to our great surprise and amazement—believing and walking *in union with Christ,* we find ourselves in communion with God, who is also walking in that place. We share thus in God's active life and in God's goodness all around us.

3. How Our Faith-Union with Christ Engages Us in Life.

The Protestant Reformers further elaborate faith in terms of *justification* and *sanctification.* The terms have become like theological jargon to us, unfamiliar and abstract. In truth, these terms are everyday realities of life.

Justification in everyday life deals with accountability. We are constantly making ourselves pleasing or accountable to someone. We justify ourselves first and foremost to ourselves. We also justify ourselves to others with whom we

share the web of life, such as:
- child to parents,
- husband to wife,
- student to teacher,
- soldier to commander,
- professional to colleagues,
- politician to voters, *etc.*
- friend to friend,
- wife to husband,
- businessperson to board,
- employee to boss,
- player to team,

Sanctification also comes from everyday life, having to do with being skilled or proficient at the things we love to do. In this sense, "being good" is not primarily a moral term, but signals things which we strive to "be good at" every day, such as:
- working at a job,
- gardening,
- building things with our hands,
- relating to family and friends,
- planning and organizing, *etc.*
- playing sports,
- cooking,

"Being good" at such things entails skill, effort, and practice:
- know how,
- energy and coordination,
- a taste for beauty,
- competence,
- personal integrity,
- a thirst for excellence, *etc.*

We spend most of our human energies justifying and sanctifying ourselves every day. When God enters the picture, we are face-to-face with our ultimate accountability or justification before the One from whom all life comes. In all our striving or sanctification we engage the One who creates the time of our lives and walks with us at every moment, whether we recognize it or not. With these realities in mind, our union with Christ affects daily living—our justifying and sanctifying—in three ways.

First, our union with Christ—salvation—is not only for a future life after death but also for the present. The Bible says as much about blessing now as it does about salvation to a future life (see Psalms 103-104). The present and the future life also belong together. In John's Gospel, *eternal life* refers to life in the presence of God here and now as well as forever (see John 3:16). To live fully awake to God's presence at any time is both blessing and salvation.

Second, our union with Christ—the grace of God's salvation—shows us the brokenness of human life all around us. Apart from grace, we could easily resign ourselves to the daily experiences of loss, illness, failure, injustice, malice, and evil. We could say fatalistically: "That's just the way things are in nature and the real world. What more can we expect?"

Grace, however, brings evil into the light of day, shows us how awful evil is and how unnatural it is to God's presence. The Bible links our brokenness and evil to the daily, manifold experience of death, and names it sin. Sin complicates our lives greatly, whether as

- low or mediocre expectations for living,
- moral failure,
- breakdown of nature,
- human malice,
- alienation from self and others,
- untruth,
- or death as the ultimate separation from all that is alive, beautiful, and meaningful.

Herein lies the significance of Jesus' human life and death. As one of us Jesus encounters the full measure of sin and evil in human life. On the cross he plumbs the depths of these things, and the darkness does not overcome him (John 1:5). In union with him we glimpse truth through his eyes.

So, thirdly, our union with Christ in daily life comes home with the language of justification and sanctification. In the midst of pervasive evil, suffering, and sin, how can we justify our existence to ourselves, much less to God? How can we live well with God and others, when we are daily besieged by human sin including our own? As a new creation out of death itself, union with the crucified and risen

Jesus opens up the meaning and joy of humanity in God's life-giving presence.

Calvin calls *justification* "the hinge on which religion turns"[6] (see Sidebar 7.1). Christ justifies our humanity in two ways, he says. Forgiving our sins daily *in Christ*, God releases us from the guilt of sins committed, the burden of our past sins and suffering. Clothing us *in Christ* daily, God also gives us complete access to the human excellence Christ accomplished in his own life. The ultimate justification of human existence, then, is life *in Christ*. And life *in Christ*—God with us—is the air we yearn to breathe, the water where we love to swim. Once there, we thrive in it and cannot get enough of it.

Calvin calls *sanctification* "the true turning of our life to God,"[7] or repentance unto life (see Sidebar 7.1). Living in communion with God means daily recognizing and turning away from the things that destroy life while turning toward the things that build up life. Once again, Christ is the key. Repentance unto life unites us with Christ at the full range of his defeating death on the cross and his creating new life in rising from the dead. Sanctification is our daily participation in Christ's death and resurrection.

Sanctification here does not correlate automatically with "good works," by which we usually mean acts of moral goodness. Sanctification has to do with skill, proficiency, and excellence in living. That includes but is broader in scope than moral goodness. The poignancy of moral goodness comes

---

[6] Calvin, *Institutes, op cit.*, Book 3, Chapter 11, Paragraph 1, p. 726. See also the *Westminster Confession of Faith*, Chapters XI, XII, and XIV, in John Leith, *Creeds of the Churches*, 3rd edition (Atlanta: John Knox Press, 1982), 207-209.

[7] Calvin, *Institutes, op cit.*, Book 3, Chapter 3, Paragraph 5, p. 597. See also the *Westminster Confession of Faith*, Chapters XIII, XV, and XVI, in *Creeds of the Churches, op cit.*, 209-210.

> *Sidebar 7.1. Calvin on Justification and Sanctification.*
>
> *In union with Christ, justification and sanctification are*
> > On-going, simultaneous, and overlapping,
> > > never one without the other,
> > > never one before the other,
> > > both together in our union with Christ.
>
> *Justification (accountability) entails*
> > Freedom from the burden of sin(s) committed
> > > (daily released by Christ's forgiving love)
> > > *plus*
> > Freedom to taste complete righteousness
> > > (daily clothed in Christ's accomplishment).
>
> *Sanctification (living well) entails*
> > Dying to self/Repentance unto life
> > > (daily participation in Christ's crucifixion)
> > > *plus*
> > Living to God
> > > (daily participation in Christ's resurrection)

from the fact that God is good. As Jesus says to the young ruler, *Why do you call me good? No one is good but God alone* (Luke 18:19). In the presence of God, who is good, we cannot expect to fellowship with God outside that goodness. But then, like all good things, both the goodness and the good works come from God wherever they occur. We participate in them and their goodness, but we do not create them, and their goodness is not our claim or possession. They are the work of the Spirit (Eph 2:8-10, Gal 5:23).

These reflections mesh well with the Lutheran tradition, which has no separate theme of sanctification. For Luther the vocational calling and dignity of a person's everyday labor describe the Christian life without recourse to the language of sanctification. Sanctification portrayed as doing "good works" risks falling back into the trap of works righteousness.

As understood here, however, to live well or be sanctified is to live *in Christ* fully engaged with *God's* active presence. Participating *in Christ* by grace alone, we commune with God every moment of every day.

To summarize: participating *in Jesus' crucifixion*, energized by the Spirit, we share his daily efforts to overcome our brokenness. We spend ourselves in loving service to God and others in fellowship with the crucified Jesus, not calculating the cost. We are not our own. We belong to God. To live well is to serve God and others in all that we do.

Participating *in Jesus' resurrection*, energized by the Spirit, we share in the beauty, excellence, and joy of the new creation Jesus brings daily. We embrace therein Jesus' loving energy and gracious wisdom, living for God with abandon. In fellowship with the resurrected Jesus, we discover the joy of our salvation, even in the midst of human brokenness.

Justification and sanctification belong inseparably together in our union with Jesus Christ, not one without the other, not one before the other. Jesus, after all, is his own, real person, grounded in an historical birth, life, death, and resurrection. He is the reality of God with us, daily, everywhere, and always. He is God acting as God, to forgive our sins, save us from ourselves, lift our sights, and revive our broken humanity to real life. Our faith-union with Christ makes us full participants in this reality.

Being united with Christ leads us to turn our lives to God as flowers turn to the sun. *In Christ* God's grace is *new every day* (Lament 3:23), and life, not death, has the last word (John 1:4-5).

4. *Obstacles We Put in the Way of Union with Christ.*

Union with Christ is rarely the way we hear or speak of salvation today. Modern American Christianity undermines the freedom and grace of salvation as union with Christ in two ways: (a) overemphasizing Christ in us, and (b) setting up an order of salvation.

(a) Overemphasizing Christ in Us.

Most often we hear the message of salvation today in terms of Christ dwelling in our hearts by faith, on condition of and by means of our own efforts at believing. The outcomes are predictable when the counter-balance of *us in Christ* is missing, .

When we teach our children at an early age that Christ is present with them in their hearts, we set ourselves up for a series of unwanted kickbacks. At age 12 or 13, our children are prone to wonder:
- *How much* faith do I have in me?
- *How much* does Christ really dwell *in me*?
- *How much* are humanity, moral goodness, divinity, or some combination of them really *in me*?
- *How much* faith (*Christ-in-me*) is enough to save me?

Even when our children believe, act morally, or work hard to increase their faith, the questions linger. They may conclude that, not having enough faith, they do not belong in a community of faith, and drop out mentally if not physically.

At age 18-20 or so, our youth may well perceive that, not only they but also other church people do not have much faith or goodness in them either, or that the Christ in them has not protected them from the shattering turns and problems of life. From there the step is easy, to regard the Christian Church as hypocritical, its religion hollow or self-serving, its God absent or powerless, its truth claims as something to be dismissed, and its expectations as an unnecessary burden.

These outcomes come from within, set up by a one-dimensional message of *Christ in me*. Today, many Americans with a Church background consider themselves:
- "spiritual" (focus on the inner *me*) without being "religious" (members of the institutional church),
- among the "nones" (no religious affiliation and no need for it), or
- left on their own to find meaning and authentic humanity elsewhere.

As a result, many perplexed ministers, baffled congregations, and worried parents are looking for strategies, tactics, or gimmicks that can reach youth and former church members. Some churches generate spiritual enthusiasm with contemporary worship styles, revivals, or spiritual practices. The effort takes enormous energy and resources to sustain, and the outcomes remain ambiguous and fragile at best.

(b) Setting Up an Order of Salvation, Faith Followed by Works.

Modern American Christianity further undermines salvation as union with Christ when it puts justification and sanctification into an order of salvation, a sequence of first one and then the other (see Sidebar 7.2). American Christianity typically places justification, or salvation, first in the order, focusing only on forgiveness of sins and received by faith. Sanctification, or the Christian life, comes second in the order, conceived as a vigorous striving for good works to make us actually good.[8] An order of salvation thus separates salvation from the Christian life and oversimplifies both salvation and the Christian life.

The order of salvation produces two specific outcomes. First, the Christian life becomes a striving for the righteousness Christ has already attained. If that is the case, what is the point of or need for salvation?

Second, putting salvation and the Christian life into a sequence makes one conditional upon the other, with a strong tendency to collapse one into the other. In the aftermath, these questions arise:

- Is salvation the start of the Christian life, or the conclusion of a life well lived, as life after death?
- Are good works a necessary condition for salvation, to guarantee the authenticity of our faith, as the Biblically derived catchphrase, "faith without works is dead," suggests? If so, can we ever say we are saved by faith alone apart from good works?
- Is a prior change of life, or repentance, a necessary condition for believing?

Unable to answer these questions cleanly within the paradigm of Modernism-Pietism, we step onto a treadmill of calculating what we have to do to attain salvation and live a good Christian life—by means of believing and doing good works. The Protestant Reformers call this treadmill "works righteousness." On the treadmill, salvation and the Christian life become a contract, an offer we have to accept, a burden we have to carry, a benefit we have to earn, with the threat of what will happen to us if we reject the contract.

---

[8] Goodness here may be either individual morality or social justice. As understood today, both perspectives press a striving for actual goodness.

5. Conclusion.

Christian salvation means union with Jesus Christ, a faith union in which *we abide in Christ* and *Christ abides in us*. The language of a branch engrafted into a vine could be said of a child adopted into full participation in a family, of a body member belonging integrally to the whole body, or of a building block fitting into the structure of a house. The Bible uses all these images to talk about our union with Jesus Christ and about our communion with God together *in Christ*.

Our faith—the Spirit at work—unites us with Jesus Christ, the same person who was born, lived, died, and rose from the dead 2,000 years ago, the same person who is present and active with us today on his own terms, now as well as then. Now *in Christ* by grace, the gift of a mystical union exists between Christ and us, wherever we are. Now *in Christ* by grace, we live in the covenant space where God is our God and we are God's people, in all the ups and downs of life. Now *in Christ* by grace, we live with abandon in the freedom and joy of serving God as individuals, as a community of Christians, and as a society of humans. We live by the grace of our union with Christ at every moment of every day, forever.

ESSAY 8

IS JESUS ONLY THE MEANS OF OUR SALVATION?

At some point in his missionary journeys, Paul cautions his young coworker Timothy to avoid divisive disputes and *cut straight the word of truth*,[AT 1] echoing the Old Testament refrain to make straight the way of the Lord.[2] Many disputes between Christians today seem to fall into the rut of sacrificing *the word of truth* or *the way of the Lord* to a win-lose strategy, winner take all. This essay addresses one such dispute, whether Jesus Christ is the only means of our salvation or one of many. On this issue, I believe the time has come to explore alternative ways to move ahead without compromising the Gospel or pursuing a win-lose approach.

By all accounts, Christianity along with modern culture and history are emerging from the Modernist-Pietist era (1650-2000), The main questions from this era are: who is saved, who is not saved, and by what means do you get that way? These questions not only set the agenda but also the poles of theological discussion today. In this essay, we are dealing with the third of these primary questions.

All parties agree that Jesus Christ is a means of our salvation. Both Scripture and the Reformation confessions expound at length how Jesus Christ saves us from our sins and sinfulness. *He is the expiation for our sins, and not for ours only but also for the sins of the whole world* (1 John 2:2 RSV).

---

[1] 2 Timothy 2:14-15. The KJV renders the phrase, quaintly *rightly dividing the word of truth*. The literal reading would be *cutting straight/rightly the word of truth*. The Greek word, *orthotomounta*, combines two words, *orthos* (straight, rightly) and *temno* (cut) to mean *cut straight* or *rightly*. See *Theological Dictionary of the New Testament* (Wm. B. Eerdmans, 1972), ed Kittel and Friedrich, trans Geoffrey W. Bromiley, Vol. VIII, 111-112.
[2] Isa 40:3, 35:8-10.

The total work of Christ for our redemption took place in his life and ministry among people, his teachings, his death on the cross, and his resurrection from the dead (see Essay 9).

Yet, Christians divide today over the competing questions concerning Christ's atoning work:

Is Jesus the only means of our salvation?

or

Is Jesus only one means of salvation among many?

The first question shapes the conservative perspective, which cites John 14:6: *I am the way, and the truth, and the life; no one comes to the Father, but by me.* (RSV). The second question suggests the liberal view that there are many roads to God, quoting John 14:2: *In my Father's house are many rooms; if it were not so, would I have told you that I go to prepare a place for you?* (RSV). The clash between these two perspectives contributes greatly to the divisions in the Church of our time.

1. Jesus Is More Than the Means of Our Salvation.

The two sides of the debate focus so much on each other that they overlook where they come together. They both start with Jesus Christ as a means of our salvation, whether as the only one or one of many. The fundamental agreement of the two sides on this point may be more important than the details of their disagreement.

As a mere (?!) means of salvation,[3] Jesus Christ answers well what our age says it wants from the Gospel:
- "What is useful about the Gospel?"—utilitarianism.
- "What about the Gospel actually works?"—pragmatism.
- "What do we get out of the Gospel?"—economics.
- "What about the Gospel motivates and inspires us?"—politics, psychology.

---

[3] The same considerations apply to whether Jesus is the primary means of revelation, God to humanity.

In our time and culture, the Gospel of Jesus Christ is widely touted as the best way to meet all human needs, solve every human problem, elevate humans to their best selves, and answer all human questions. Christians today—right, center, or left—freely use such calculations to gain leverage within culture, to our own advantage against our partisan opponents.

Suppose, however, Jesus Christ is *more than a means* of salvation? Suppose he is the salvation of which he is also the means? Aren't the means always subordinate to the end they are pursuing? Aren't the means to an end essentially disposable once we have used them to reach the end we seek? When we finish washing the dishes with a dish rag, do we not eventually throw the rag away?

But *Jesus is Lord*, we say. He is *much more than a mere means* to an end. He is more important than something we can use and throw away. He is greater and much less tame than our calculations of usefulness can manage.

Indeed, the issue changes dramatically when we consider who Jesus is. Without qualification, the Bible says that Jesus is God:
- God as a human being—*the Word made flesh* (John 1:14),
- *God with us—Emmanuel* (Matt 1:22),
- the *Lord—God* (Phil 2:11 and often), and
- *the Son of God*—of the same Being as the Father, in Trinitarian terms (John 20:31 and often).[4]

So, on the one hand (a): if Jesus is truly God as a human being, then to say he is the only means of our salvation doesn't say enough. For, life in union with the human Jesus Christ—life with God—is what constitutes salvation. "How can sinners be saved by Jesus Christ?" may not be the only

---

[4] "Of one Being with the Father," *The Nicene Creed* (325, 381). See *PC(USA) Book of Confessions*, 1.2.

question to ask. Sinners that we are, brought into the saving presence of Jesus Christ by the Spirit, do we not need to ask further what *God* may have in store for us for the rest of our lives?

Asking after what God has in store for us may indeed lead to glorifying and serving God[5] whatever the cost. And the cost factor bumps up against the old Calvinist question, "Are we willing to be damned for the glory of God?" Such costliness is exactly the space carved out for us by Jesus Christ,[6] and our salvation depends upon his having been just that. This very God-as-a-human-being, Jesus Christ:

- creates the space where God and sinful humanity meet,
- defines our lives by Jesus' quite historical life-death-and-resurrection, and
- governs all of life accordingly.

Salvation—union with Jesus Christ, life with God—turns out to be a daunting, untamable, rugged calling indeed!

On the other hand (b), if Jesus is truly God as a human being, then to say that he is one among many means of salvation is also not enough. By whatever measure we may apply, Jesus Christ constitutes who God is toward all humanity, indeed toward the entire universe. "God is as he [Jesus] is," says Karl Barth.[7]

Barth's quote works two ways. As Jesus is toward us, so is God toward us; *and* as Jesus is toward God, so is our humanity toward God. No earthly reality is exempt from this divine address.[8] There may be other means of salvation—

---

[5] To the question, "What is the chief end of man?" the *Westminster Shorter Catechism* answers: "to glorify God, and to enjoy him forever." See PCUSA *Book of Confessions*, 7.001.

[6] See Mark 15:34, 2 Cor 5:21.

[7] Karl Barth, *The Humanity of God*, trans John Newton Thomas (Atlanta: John Knox. Press, 1960), 51.

[8] See Matthew 28:18b and 20b, and Colossians 1:15-20.

other religions, science, great leaders, or self-help—but, because of who Jesus is, at some point they are all bound to answer to Jesus Christ.

In sum, the atoning work of Jesus Christ is *God's* act for our salvation because the incarnate person of Jesus Christ is God as a human being. This affirmation is central to both Scripture and the Church's confessions. As this human being came among us, so does God come among us even now. As God with us, we honor and worship *Jesus Christ as an end in himself* and not as someone who is merely useful to us.

Indeed, to say that Jesus Christ is God as a human being may be the most radical thing a Christian will ever say. Such a radical affirmation does not deny that Jesus Christ is the means of our salvation, but it says much more than that. This radical affirmation changes the way Christians talk with one another about Jesus Christ, God, salvation, revelation, and the current issues of the Church—in any church to which we all belong.

2. Hope in the Lord Jesus Christ

Embroiled by these questions specifically in 2001-2, the Presbyterian Church (U.S.A.) produced the excellent short treatise, *Hope in the Lord Jesus Christ*, through its Office of Theology and Worship.[9] *Hope* surveys the church's multiple creeds and confessions and reaffirms the centrality of Jesus Christ.

---

[9] The study was commissioned by the General Assembly (Louisville, KY) in 2001, and adopted in 2002 (Columbus, OH). *Hope in the Lord Jesus Christ* is available on-line, at www.pcusa.org, from Presbyterian Distribution Service, PDS No. 70420-02-004, or through the Office of Theology and Worship, 100 Witherspoon Street, Louisville, KY 40202-1396, tel. 1-888-728-7228, Ext. 5334.

The national General Assembly adopted this statement for itself in 2002 and commended it for distribution. In the course of its work, the Assembly also responded to a question posed by lifting out a paragraph that all sides acknowledged to be well grounded in Scripture and the whole range of the Church's confessions:

> Jesus Christ is the only Savior and Lord, and all people everywhere are called to place their faith, hope, and love in him. No one is saved by virtue of inherent goodness or admirable living, for *by grace you have been saved through faith, and this is not your own doing; it is the gift of God* [Eph 2:8]. No one is saved apart from God's gracious redemption in Jesus Christ. Yet we do not presume to limit the sovereign freedom of *God our Savior, who desires everyone to be saved and to come to the knowledge of the truth* [1 Tim 2:4]. Thus, we neither restrict the grace of God to those who profess explicit faith in Christ nor assume that all people are saved regardless of faith. Grace, love, and communion belong to God, and are not ours to determine.
> (Lines 155-168)

The General Assembly adopted this hope in Christ quietly, with hardly a dissenting vote. To this observer, it was the watershed moment at the 2002 meeting. With a great sigh of relief the commissioners thus united moved on to the rest of their other, sometimes contentious, business.

Affirming that Jesus is more than a means of salvation may signal something else as well. The questions of Modernistm-Pietism (who's saved, who's not, and by what means?) belong to the paradigm now coming to an end. The key questions for the new paradigm now forming may well revolve around Who is the One saving a broken humanity? Bedrock for an answer will surely be: Jesus Christ is nothing less than *Emmanuel*, which means *God with us* (Matt 1:23).

ESSAY 9

THE TOTAL WORK OF CHRIST FOR OUR REDEMPTION

The work of Christ for our redemption—atonement—is another place where Christians tend to splinter. The Bible and the Reformation identify three main views of Christ's atoning work:
- moral influence (Jesus as a good example),
- substitutionary (Jesus died for our sins), and
- classical (Jesus achieved victory over death).

We often elevate one view and set it in competition with the other two. Yet, in truth, these three views of Christ's work complement one another and together provide an amazing portrayal of the total work of Christ for our redemption. The combination lies deep within the Bible and the best of the Christian tradition.

This essay considers:
(1) The unresolved question at the heart of Modernism-Pietism, concerning Christ's work for our redemption.
(2) The three main views of Christ's atoning work in review.
(3) How these views of atonement fit and belong together.

1. The Unresolved Question at the Heart of Modernism-Pietism.

During the era of Modernism-Pietism (1650-2000), modern American Christianity typically focused on two of the three main views of atonement. With *the moral influence view,* Jesus' atoning work transforms us into good people—loving, moral, seeking justice for all, able to do good works toward God and others. Jesus shows us how to live from the example of his moral life, his deeds of love and mercy, his innocent sufferings and death, and his teachings about God.

With *the substitutionary view,* Jesus' atoning work leads to life after death, overcoming the consequences of human sin. With his sinless life, his persecution and sufferings, and his painful death on the cross, Jesus takes away the punishment we sinners deserve. That frees us up to live a healthy, loving, morally good life, worthy of the future for which Jesus has prepared us.

Within modern American Christianity, *both perspectives* envision a salvation that makes sinful humans morally good in themselves, which happens when Christ dwells in our hearts and lives there by faith. That is, *salvation takes effect in us when Christ is incarnate in us as God was incarnate in Jesus Christ.* We become an embodiment of Christ in us[1] working through us, so that we are "the hands and feet of Christ"[2] and the Church is a second incarnation of Christ indwelling its members.[3]

This view of salvation highlights the unresolved question at the heart of Modernism-Pietism from its beginnings until now: *What really happens to us when we are saved?* With Christ dwelling in us, are we united with his divinity and so are divinized like him? Are we united with his moral goodness and so are made morally good? Are we united with his perfect humanity, the image of God restored by him, and so are humanized like him? Is it some combination of these, or none of them?

The underlying question has never been clearly resolved. With growing uneasiness over a message of moral superiority, we could talk here about the self-righteousness of church members fostered by their claims to divinity, moral goodness, or perfect humanity. We could talk about the

---

[1] Alternatively, the kingdom of God or the Spirit embodied in us.
[2] The phrase originated with Teresa of Avila, 1515-1582, a Carmelite nun, mystic, and important figure in the Roman Catholic Reformation.
[3] See the book, *The Second Incarnation* (Howard Books, 1992), with revised edition (Leafwood Publications) in 2001.

tendency for some to point fingers and judge others who are not as good as they are. We could remember the public pretensions, abuses, and scandals of high-profile Christian ministers, priests, and TV evangelists over the last 50 years. We could notice the broad pull-back from the Christian Church in the West after World War II, in America since 1967.

Even Christians who are wary of a divinized humanity apart from Jesus are willing to say Christ makes us perfect human beings. Modern Presbyterians among others—liberal and conservative alike—have been quite open about the possibilities of an ideal humanity. When setting forth the Church's mission from 1983 to 2009, the Presbyterian Church (U.S.A.) *Book of Order* states that the Christian community is "the provisional demonstration of what God intends for all of humanity."[4] Here Christ is an example of moral perfection for which Christians are to strive, accompanied by an optimistic view of human perfectibility.

At this point we need to ask honestly whether divinizing us with Jesus' divinity or humanizing us with his ideal humanity may diminish Christ's saving work. On the one hand, if we are divine like him, Jesus Christ is no longer uniquely divine. He becomes for us mainly an example of how to live the divine life. For 19th Century theologian Ludwig Feuerbach (1804-1872), the Christian religion is about projecting Jesus as the deification of all humanity. People today still talk about a spark of divine goodness in every human, even after the monstrous evils committed in the name of humanity during the World Wars of the last century.

On the other hand, if Jesus humanizes us with his perfect humanity, he does not need to be more than an ideal of moral or relational perfection. Jesus does not have to be divine to accomplish this result, only divinely appointed and

---

[4] 1983-2009 PC(USA) *Book of Order*, Chapter 3, G-3.0203. The revision of 2011-13 removed this language from the *Book of Order* (see F-1).

inspired. He does not have to be a savior or lord either, for a good example may be all we need to manage the human condition ourselves. So, we should not be surprised to hear increasing doubts about Jesus' unique divinity. Doubts about his divinity make it easy to doubt his elevated humanity as well, since other heroic figures might be just as useful to self-managed self-fulfillment.

Centered on the embodiment of Christ in us, Modernist-Pietist perspectives on Christ's saving work are simply too limited. To truly engage us at the depths of the human condition, Jesus Christ has to be more than a good example or a useful means to a future life. In fact, the New Testament and the best of the Christian tradition affirm the incarnation is uniquely about Jesus Christ, who is God as a human being.[5]

As the human Jesus, *God* embraces our humanity from its highest highs to its lowest lows. As the human Jesus, *God* plumbs the depths of our humanity, precisely where we go awry. As the human Jesus, *God* experiences human life in all its living splendor, beauty, meaning, love, and joy, but also the full weight of its ambiguity, vulnerability, suffering, and finally death—the ultimate form of sinful separation. So, as the human Jesus, *God* takes on sin at its ugliest, evil at its worst, and the tragic consequences of sin for all human life. The *divinity* of Jesus makes his *human* life, death, and resurrection an act of *God* for our redemption.

God's experience of our humanity in turn is the key to our human experience of God. United with Christ, we participate as humans in Christ's divinity without becoming divine ourselves. United with Christ, we participate in the image of God and the righteousness his humanity restores—

---

[5] This is the first and primary affirmation of the Trinity. See Jürgen Moltmann, *The Crucified God* (New York: Harper & Row, 1974), and *The Trinity and the Kingdom* (London: SCM, 1981).

without possessing that righteousness, and without embodying, controlling, or dispensing that image. Once having tasted the joy and freedom of fellowship in Christ—abiding with God and God abiding with us—we cannot get enough of it. At this point, plainly, Jesus Christ is more than an example or a useful means to what we are supposed to be. That leads us to consider the three main views of Christ's atoning work.

2. The Three Main Views of Christ's Atoning Work in Review.

The primary Biblical views of atonement align with specific parts of the birth, life, sufferings, death, and resurrection of Jesus Christ (see Sidebar 9.1).

The moral influence view (Abelard, †1142) draws on Jesus' life, ministry, teachings, and sufferings unto death: *Greater love has no man than this, that a man lay down his life for his friends* (John 15:13 RSV). Jesus thus manifests God's love for humanity and inspires us to love God and live the Christian life.[6]

The substitutionary view of atonement (Anselm, †1109) encompasses Jesus' birth and sinless life, to set the stage for his vicarious suffering and death.

He was wounded for our transgressions; he was bruised for our iniquities; upon him was the chastisement that made us whole, and with his stripes we are healed (Isa 53:5 RSV).

This verse runs through the passion stories of all four New Testament Gospels. Punishment for all the sins humans ever committed against God, or ever will, is discharged into Jesus—the Son of God—agonizing on the cross at Golgotha. With this substitution, Jesus removes the legitimate conse-

---

[6] Reflected in the words to several hymns: "Jesus, the Very Thought of Thee" (11th Century), "O Master, Let Me Walk With Thee" (1879), "Lord, Speak to Me, that I May Speak" (1872), "Christ of the Upward Way" (1915), and "Where Cross the Crowded Ways of Life" (1903).

quences of God's righteous condemnation of human sin.[7] God's act cancels our debts and forgives our sins.

The "classical" view of atonement (Irenaeus, †ca. 200; Athanasius, †373; Martin Luther, †1546; John Calvin, †1564) draws mainly on the death and resurrection of Jesus Christ:[8] *Anyone who is in Christ is a new creation. The old has passed away, behold the new has come*[AT] (2 Cor 5:17).

The movement here is two-fold. First, Jesus defeats death by dying, as Hebrews 2:14 says: *that through death he might destroy the one who has the power of death*. In his dying Jesus occupies the space of death so that death and its cohorts of sin, evil, and suffering no longer have any space of their own. By his own dying Jesus:
- defeats death, *the last enemy to be defeated* (1 Cor 15:26),
- defeats the underlying problem of sin, for *the wages of sin is death* (Rom 6:23), and
- defeats all the evil and sufferings human sin brings to life, for *[nothing] will be able to separate us from the love of God in Christ Jesus our Lord* (Rom 8:35, 39).

In the second movement, Jesus recreates human life by rising from the dead, as Paul says in Rom 6:10 (RSV):

---

[7] Reflected in the words to several hymns: "O Sacred Head, Now Wounded" (ca. 1150), "Jesus Christ Is Risen Today" (14th Cent), "Ah, Holy Jesus, How Hast Thou Offended" (1834), "Hail, Thou Once Despised Jesus" (1757), "My Hope Is Built On Nothing Less" (1834), "Rock of Ages, Cleft for Me" (1776), "There Is a Green Hill Far Away" (1776), and "The Old Rugged Cross."

[8] The classical view of atonement is explicit in the *PC(USA) Book of Confessions*: *The Scots Confession*, Chapters VIII and X; *Heidelberg Catechism*, qq. 43-45; *Second Helvetic Confession*, Chapter XI (5.076); *Confession of 1967*, 9.08-.11; *A Brief Statement of Faith*, lines 20-26. See also the funeral service of *The Book of Common Worship* (Westminster/John Knox, 1993): 921 (prayer 1), 931 (mystery of faith 2), and 944 (commital prayer 6). The *Westminster Confession of Faith, Larger* and *Shorter Catechisms* set forth only a substitutionary view.

Sidebar 9.1. Jesus and the Main Views of Atonement.

Jesus	Views of Atonement		
Incarnation: Birth Life	Moral Influence: accent on life and death	Substitutionary: accent on death and life	
Death			Classical: accent on death and resurrection
Resurrection			

The death he died he died to sin, once for all, but the life he lives he lives to God.[9] Jesus' crucifixion and resurrection are two sides of the same saving act, each one inseparable from and essential to the other. The "classical" view explicitly makes the resurrection an integral part of Jesus' work of redemption.[10]

---

[9] Paul speaks often about our dying in Christ and rising with him, *e.g.*, Rom 5-6, 1 Cor 15, and 2 Cor 5:14-21. The language of these passages fits the classical view. Similarly, John links the resurrection with eternal life, *i.e.*, abiding now and forever in God's love, as in John 3:1-21, 11:1-44(25), 15:1-17, and 1 John 4:1-21(7-12).

[10] Reflected in several hymns: "Thine Is the Glory" (1884), "The Strife Is O'er, The Battle Done" (1695), "Who Trusts in God, A Strong Abode" (1572ff), "Rejoice, the Lord is King" (1746), two hymns by Luther, "A Mighty Fortress Is Our God" (1529) and even clearer "Christ Jesus Lay In Death's Strong Bands" (1524). Two recent hymns are noteworthy as well: "I Danced In the Morning" (1963) and "Christ Is Risen" (1960).

As we have seen in Section 1 above, modern American Christians largely ignore the classical view of Christ's atoning work and typically divide into two camps. We know from a life-time of controversy: *the conservative Pietist position* stresses the substitutionary view and regards Jesus' death as a divine transaction that clears the books of human wrong-doing now and always. Salvation here means living as forgiven sinners, free from the consequences of sin and certain of eternal life with God.

The liberal Pietist position elevates the moral influence view of Christ's work of redemption and takes Jesus' life of suffering love to represent the highest example of a full, obedient humanity before God. Salvation here means to live as Christ lived, in love, peace, and justice with other people and with God.

While being Christ-like is important to both positions, neither acknowledges the legitimate place of the other, and both criticize each other unmercifully. What if the total work of Christ for our redemption embraces all three views of the atonement and weaves them together, just as Jesus' life, death, and resurrection belong to a whole person?

3. How These Views of Atonement Fit and Belong Together.

To see how the three views fit and belong together, we have to disarm the criticisms of each one.

Critics of the moral influence view cite its minimal view of sin—as bad attitudes, habits, feelings, and relationships—all in the arena of the interior self. Imbedded in a particular culture or society, such sins can be pervasive and entrenched. The dynamics, however, belong to psychological or political processes. These sins don't need a radical act of forgiveness by God, say the critics. We humans can manage our sins well enough, with sound vision, support, expertise, and a little inspiration. We just need to pay closer attention to ourselves and manage the shifting norms going on around us. In this respect, what the Bible says about God and God's righteous expectations seems misplaced and irrelevant. Indeed, if it is up to us to tend to all these things, do we really need God?

This critique of the moral influence view will hold up as long as Jesus Christ represents mainly the example of an ideal humanity for which we are to strive.

On the other hand, if Jesus really is God as a human being (*Emmanuel*), his *resurrected humanity is the reality of our future life with God*. Indeed, all elements of the moral influence view fit what Jesus says about our new life in Christ, namely, in the resurrection. Participating in the resurrection of Christ brings that future into our present. Jesus provides a concrete description of the resurrected life in:

- the Sermon on the Mount (Matthew 5-7),
- his ministry of compassion and service to others,
- his strong but humble bearing,
- his devotion to God's truth and righteousness,
- his parables of the kingdom (reversal of power),
- his identification with the least among us, and
- his suffering and forgiving love.

The resurrection gives the moral influence view of atonement a significance and a power it cannot muster by itself. To dispense with this dimension of the moral influence view would seriously diminish the total work of Christ for our redemption.

Critics of the substitutionary view cite its concept of sin as individualistic and moralistic, hence often unaware of how a community's sins fall on the world at large or on its own members. Furthermore, they say, the substitutionary view is unworthy of the God of Jesus Christ. Relationship with God should highlight its warmth, mutual love, and devotion, say the critics. Instead, they say, the substitution makes God look overbearing, petty, and mean: enforcing a legal contract and exacting the gory punishment of a scapegoat to satisfy the primitive demands of a Medieval sense of honor, or worse, satisfy a law that no longer applies.

This critique of the substitutionary view will hold up as long as we take Jesus Christ mainly as the useful means of our salvation.

On the other hand, if Jesus really is God as a human being (*Emmanuel*), *God's act of forgiveness on the cross looks strikingly different*. Reconciliation with God, the injured party, happens when *God* steps into the breach and suffers the consequences. That cannot happen at arm's length, through a scapegoat or an instrument or a delegated representative. Only God's own painful act of forgiving the ones who have sinned will reconcile them.

Nor can God simply wish away the violation. Forgiveness is inherently costly. Absorbing the hard blow of the injury and suffering its consequences hurts like hell (pun intended). Only the sinned-against can forgive. Sinners can repent of the awful hurt they have caused, but they cannot forgive it and they cannot take back the brokenness they have caused. As the One most sinned against, God cannot accomplish true forgiveness without being directly touched by the sin and suffer a costly reconciliation.

On this reading of the matter, the substitutionary view of atonement is essential to *God* authentically forgiving human sin. The New Testament in fact portrays Jesus on the cross as God's forgiveness just that way. On the cross *God* absorbs the full brunt of human sin against God and removes its most tragic, punishing, and binding consequences. Those who dispense with the substitutionary view of atonement remove the forgiveness that is essential for genuine reconciliation between God and humanity.

Put together, the three views of atonement follow the stations of Jesus' birth, life, death, and resurrection (Sidebars 9.1 and 9.2).

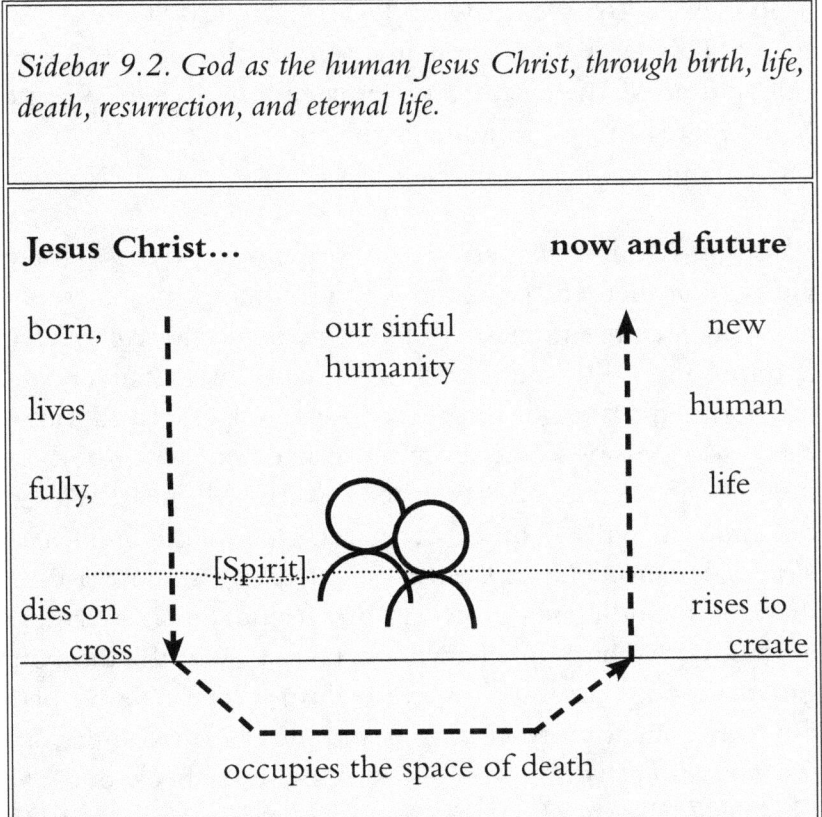

Sidebar 9.2. God as the human Jesus Christ, through birth, life, death, resurrection, and eternal life.

The "classical" view is the glue for this configuration, but each one contributes something indispensable to the total work of Christ for our redemption:
- beginning with the substitutionary view, birth to death (forgiveness, release from sin's consequences),
- moving to the "classical" view, death and resurrection (defeat of death and re-creation of life, addressing the underlying problem of sin/death), and
- adding the moral influence view, life in Christ (concretely participating in the resurrected life of Jesus Christ).

So far, I know of only three Christian theologians who hold the three views together,[11] namely, Athanasius (4th Century),

---

[11] Gustaf Aulen's important book, *Christus Victor* (Macmillan, 1969, from

John Calvin (16th Century), and Karl Barth (20th Century).[12]

This essay was originally penned during the Easter celebration of the death and resurrection of Jesus Christ. What a great time to highlight the total work of Christ for our redemption.

Postscript. Modern American culture portrays these three views of atonement powerfully and authentically but separately in specific movies. *On the moral influence view: Titanic* (Paramount, 1997) portrays a passionate love affair aboard the doomed passenger liner. As Rose says, Jack "saved me in every way possible." She promises to live her life for both of them, or, in the words of the theme song, "My heart will go on, and you will go on in my heart." *On the substitutionary view: The Hustler* (20th Century Fox, 1961) is about a pool shark, Fast Eddie, whose live-in girl friend, Sarah, sacrifices herself to give him the character it takes to win the ultimate game of pool—against those who do not love or even play the game, but want to control it and profit from the players. *On the classical view:* I am still looking, but check out *The Green Mile* (Warner Bros, 1999), which takes place on a 1935 death row, where a most unlikely and mysterious inmate, John Coffey, brings a new reality (his "gift") to death.

1931), identifies the three main theories of atonement historically as subjective, objective, and classical, but misreads all three and sets them against one another. Linking the classical view with Martin Luther, Aulen was part of a resurgence of this view over the last 100 years.

[12] See Athanasius, "On the Incarnation of the Word," sections 1-32; Calvin's *Institutes*, Book 2, Chapter 15 (the offices of prophet, priest, and king) and Chapter 16 (lays out the offices historically: the "classical" view comes up repeatedly, but especially in the descent into hell); and Karl Barth, *Church Dogmatics*, vol. IV, Parts 1 (office of priest), 2 (office of king), and 3 (office of prophet). Hymns that combine all three views are Calvin's "I Greet Thee Who My Sure Redeemer Art" (1545) and perhaps "When I Survey the Wondrous Cross" (1707), "O Love That Wilt Not Let Me Go" (1882), and "I Bind My Heart This Tide" (1907).

ESSAY 10

CHRIST AND THE GOLDEN RULE

The American Church and Nation have always been closely joined together culturally, notwithstanding the separation of church and state. For much of our history, various groups have come seeking the freedom to practice their religion. Travelling through America in 1831, Alexis de Tocqueville observed how important the churches were to keeping the nation free from the excesses of the French Revolution.[1] Indeed, turmoil in the churches has often been reflected in the Nation, and *vice versa*; and the Nation has benefited when the churches worked through their inner tensions.[2] Together, Church and Nation went through the paradigm shift from Reformation to Modernism-Pietism (1650-). They now share the turmoil of going through another one (2000-).

Both Church and Nation also have a profound stake in the Golden Rule, especially in America, as we shall see. How this plays out is the focus of this essay. Part 1 shows how the Golden Rule has shaped American political and economic life over the last centuries. Part 2 traces how the the simple message of the Golden Rule—*love one another*—works with respect to Jesus Christ.[3]

---

[1] See *Democracy in America* (Fontana Library, 1968), vol. 1, 354-381.
[2] The religious groups most affected are New England Congregationalists (the Pilgrims), Presbyterians, Baptists, Methodists, and Episcopalians. Dianna Butler Bass made this connection with the over-orderly Presbyterians at a NEXT Church Conference in Charlotte NC, 2015.
[3] Both parts draw on my earlier book, *Locke On Freedom* (Austin, 1978).

The Golden Rule, Part 1

The Golden Rule—*do to others as you wish them to do to you*—stands at the heart of the American social, political, and economic experiment from its beginning. Americans belong to the socio-political-economic tradition known as Western Liberal Democracy. The ideas came together during the revolutionary ferment of the English civil wars, 1642-1689. They stoked the Western Industrial Revolution after 1750, then the political revolutions of America and France later in the 18th Century. Dubbed "capitalism" by detractors in the 19th Century, the movement swept over the world during the 19th-20th centuries.

For its part, the Golden Rule describes a social interaction between at least two parties, "you" and "others" (see Sidebar 10.1). The interaction involves what is happening when we do something to others and they do something to us. In fact, the "as" in the middle of the Golden Rule works like an equals sign (=), so that what others do to us corresponds roughly to what we want, expect, or actually do to them ... at different levels.

1. *The Level of the Jungle.*

At one level, the Golden Rule describes our negative interactions as much as when we are kind. Indeed, if I wish people to treat me badly (as in abuse, murder, pillage), then according to the Golden Rule I should do so to them. My negative behavior soars when, shaped by bitter experience, hopelessness, or low self-esteem, my wishing turns to expecting the worst. Any further mistreatment I receive merely confirms my initial, dismal view of humanity.

An eye for an eye, and a tooth for a tooth (Lev 24:20, Matt 5:38) is how the Bible describes the Golden Rule at this level. For Englishman Thomas Hobbes, *Leviathan*

> *Sidebar 10.1. Interactions of The Golden Rule at Three Levels.*
>
> The basic Rule:
> You do to others   [AS =]   (you wish) Others do to you.
>
> The level of the jungle:
>   An eye for an eye, a tooth for a tooth.
>
> The level of give-and-take:
>   Love for love, good for good, help for help,
>   no more no less.
>
> The level of authentic community/civil society:
>   Love, do good, help, expecting nothing in return,
>   *e.g.*, love your enemies.
>
> [Here the place of the "others" is taken (a) by *God*, who guarantees our acting and frees us from the worry of self-preservation, and/or (b) by *society*, which guarantees a social fabric in which everyone actively contributes to the well-being of "others".]

(1651), bad human behavior turns into "a war of every one against everyone else," which—for Hobbes—can be subdued only by a strong-armed, centralized government. The same assessment shifts from moral to natural grounds with Darwin's theory of evolution, in *Origin of the Species* (1859). "The survival of the fittest" carries a sharp edge for individuals who stake their lives on ruthless competition in a society of unbounded economic self-interest. Operating with these expectations, some capitalists prefer to limit government so nature can take its course especially for the "others," never thinking it could happen to them.

2. The Level of Give-and-Take.

At another level of the Golden Rule, wishing others to love, do good, and help us, we act to do the same to them. Beneath the appearnace of fairness, however, lie the calculating concerns of our individual self-interest. Fair or not, we expect, even demand, to get as much from others as we give to them. The Bible notes how unexceptional this level of interaction is: *What credit is that to you? Even sinners do the same* (Luke 6:32-34).

Capitalism looks benign among competing individuals at the give-and-take level, as Ayn Rand shows, in *Atlas Shrugged* (1957). That is, intelligent, hard-working, well-trained, and self-aware individuals, can easily blend together within a self-regulating system of supply and demand. We could live at this level forever if all individuals were naturally equal in skill, training, resources, and self-awareness … and if everyone uniformly carried the same load as every other. For capitalists with these expectations, government is essentially irrelevant and often gets in the way.

Much of American political discourse today concerns what to do with individuals who are not equal or who act irrationally against their own self-interest. Do they need to be incentivized with sticks and carrots, to make them work harder? Does the existence of inherently unequal individuals perhaps require a fullblown government to establish a level playing field, equal opportunity for all, and maybe equal outcomes as well? Do they need a "safety net"? Or should we just leave such individuals to suffer the consequences of their own mistakes and misfortune? Give-and-take can go along with any of these options.

3. The Level of Authentic Community/Civil Society.

At yet another level, however, the Golden Rule goes beyond the negative or give-and-take levels. Reaching for authentic human community, Jesus says, *love your enemies* (Luke 6:27), *do good, and lend, expecting nothing in return* (Luke 6:35). The underlying idea works like "paying it forward," as in the movie by that name.[4] When we look out for the well-being of others, we (a) free them from self-concern about only preserving themselves, which then also (b) frees them to give to others without calculating the cost or demanding a return. When others act that way toward us, we gain the same freedoms.

"Paying it forward," we do not all have to do the same things for one another. Some of us will grow food, some will mill flour, some will cook, some will wait tables, some will make the chairs and tables where we eat, some will make the utensils we eat with, some will transport these things to market, some will help make the exchange of goods and services smooth (*e.g.*, money), some will invent new ways of doing things, and some will just fill our lives with joy. Businesses spring up around such activities, and together they shape the fabric of a larger society so engaged. Paul Hawken, a successful entrepreneur, shows well in *Growing A Business* (1987) how businesses arise when people come up with an idea of how to contribute to the lives of others, gather the resources to make it happen, and work diligently to bring it off. The joy and meaning of life together come from making a difference in these ways.

---
[4] Warner Brothers, 2000.

Overlapping, complementing, and even competing with one another to offer goods and services, different businesses make possible a fullness of life no individual alone could ever attain. The result is an amazingly dynamic, creative, yet down-to-earth, social interaction. We are no longer trapped in a zero-sum game, dividing up a fixed pie of wealth and well-being where one person's gain comes at the expense of another person's loss. Contrary to Karl Marx money is not at the heart of Western Liberal Democracy. People are. And, in spite of what some capitalists say today, competition is not at the heart of capitalism. Collaboration is, where people interact with one another to make a better life for all. Loving families operate the same way.

4. Locke and Civil Society in America.

Too many of us have settled for the first two levels of the Golden Rule and missed the third. The venerable (and misunderstood) John Locke, however, grounds "civil society" solidly in the Golden Rule at the level of total self-giving. In Locke's *Second Treatise of Government* (ST, 1689)[5] the three levels of the Golden Rule correspond precisely to the State of War, the State of Nature, and Civil Society. Created by God, every person is expected to preserve the life, liberty, health, limb, or goods of others AS (=) they preserve their own (ST para 6). Locke here simply restates the Golden Rule in the form of *love your neighbor as yourself* (Lev 19:18, Luke 10:27).

In Locke's civil society we pledge ourselves individually to accomplish that end collectively. But then society itself becomes the guarantor of the Golden Rule at this level—just as God is the guarantor of the Golden Rule more

---

[5] References to Locke's *Second Treatise* cite *Two Treatises of Government*, 2nd edition, ed Peter Laslett (Cambridge: At the University Press, 1967).

generally (*you will be children of the Most High*, Luke 6:35). Society (a) ensures a floor on which every individual citizen can stand, beneath which it will not allow any individual to sink, and (b) mediates between people when their interactions turn into disputes. Equality here is a matter of mutual standing and dignity:
- each person made equally in the image of God,
- preservation equally by the laws of society,
- fair and equal treatment of every individual before the law.

The role of government in this civil society is to block abusive interactions of the Golden Rule at the first two levels and provide the floor on which individuals can stand and act with maximum self-giving. Government facilitates but does not supplant the underlying social interaction among the members of society.

Locke's adaptation of the Golden Rule provided the working vision for the architects of the American Revolution. Thomas Jefferson quotes Locke almost word-for-word in the *Declaration of Independence* (1776) where it states: "all men are created equal, ... endowed by their Creator with unalienable rights, ... among these are life, liberty, and the pursuit of happiness." *The American Constitution* details these rights as the floor on which all Americans stand, beneath which no individual will be allowed to sink. *Individual rights* guarantee life itself, safety (limb), personal liberty, private property, and equal protection before the law (Preamble and Fifth Amendment). *Social rights* are stated as freedoms: of religion, speech, assembly, redress of grievances, and press (First Amendment).

Locke's focus on the basic social interaction among people contains the seeds of the current American debate over the size and role of government. Yet, the American government has always stepped in to act for the common good when individuals or private companies could not—e.g., purchase land for settlement in the West, clear the way for building transcontinental railways and roadways, break up restrictive monopolies, rescue the economy in crisis, explore outer space, and protect the nation at war.

Today the *pursuit of happiness* and *promoting the general welfare* take place in an advanced technological society that is large, complex, and rapidly changing. Because the world has changed over the lifetime of the Nation, Americans have expanded both social and individual rights, notably:

- quality education as a social right, enforced by truancy laws;
- public transportation venues as a social right, most recently in the form of the national interstate highway system and airports (previously, the railroads), with access regulated by legally-required licenses and insurance; and
- high-quality health care for everyone as an individual right, an issue now before us.

Americans have come a long way since our beginnings. We have been tested to the breaking point often and in many ways, now as much or more than ever. We have made mistakes as well, including big ones (such as: slavery, the Civil War, Jim Crow laws, monopolies, the internment of Japanese-Americans in World War II, the abuse of immigrants at the Mexican border). Yet the American experiment still holds, even for those who have suffered through its mistakes.

5. Outcomes.

I suggest several take-aways from this discussion of the Golden Rule.

First, describing the social interactions of individuals at different levels, the Golden Rule defines the day-to-day lives both of individuals and of their society together.

Second, from its origins until now, the American spirit manifests a risky, yet productive experiment at the third level of the Golden Rule. We Americans are at our best when we contribute meaningfully to the lives of others around us, when we give more and take less. All of us get stuck in the first two levels of the Golden Rule at one time or another. Personally and politically our challenge is to hold these levels at bay while pursuing the third.

Third, the assumption that human life is more-or-less an unbridled competition among individuals acting only out of self-interest traps us in a low view of humanity. This view blinds us to authentic community at the third level of the Golden Rule and to the sacrifices Americans often make for one another daily.

Fourth, when we reduce our socio-political-economic options to either a radical individualism or a radical collectivism, we lose perspective on both. Individualism coupled with unfettered competition and no government, was called Anarchism in the 19th Century. Collectivism coupled with a self-regulating industrial economy and minimal or no government, is what Karl Marx called communism. Liberal in their time, the accents on unfettered competition and minimal or no government now come mostly from the conservative side of American political discourse.

Today's liberals seem drawn to maximizing equality among individuals—not only in status but also in opportunity and outcomes. Egalitarianism, however, requires a government to regulate the interactions of people from top to bottom, to make sure that no one is "more equal" than anyone else. The result is not really liberal in the end, as we know from the French Revolution (1789). The Golden

Rule at the third level offers a positive alternative to both liberal and conservative views.

Fifth, the third level of the Golden Rule envisions an authentic community of humans, a "more perfect union" in which what happens to the least among us is as important as what happens to the greatest among us, and we interact individually with one another for the common good of all.

The Golden Rule, Part 2

The Golden Rule cannot stand on its own. Although it appears in every world religion, the different religions handle it very differently. Left as an ideal of human behavior, the Golden Rule works easily at the first or second levels outlined in Part 1, but cannot completely attain the third level. Even John Locke understood that implementing the Golden Rule at the level of authentic human community relies upon a religious grounding in God.[6] We can only deal here with the Judeo-Christian treatment in this essay.

The Golden Rule pervades the entire Bible, but in several, specific forms. Its dynamics—bad, neutral, positive, and everything in between—stretch from the Old Testament to the New Testament. The Bible in fact probes these various forms of the Golden Rule deeply (see Sidebar 10.2 on forms in the Bible). In what follows, we turn first to Jesus in Luke 6, and then to the community *in Christ* with help from the Book of Job and Paul in Ephesians 5.

On the street, people readily agree, the Golden Rule is the best way to get along with others, be successful, and be happy. Since the Golden Rule is found in all major religions throughout history, people often call it the single truth of moral life to which all religions can be reduced, after stripping away the rituals and doctrines. As the saying

---

[6] See Johnson, *Locke on Freedom, op. cit.*, Chapter 7, 145-169.

Sidebar 10.2. Forms of the Golden Rule in the Bible.

An eye for an eye and a tooth for a tooth,
   Here the Golden Rule operates at the negative level (Genesis 4:12-15; Exodus 21:24, Leviticus 24:19, Deuteronomy 19:21). Matthew 5:38 [38-48] parallels Luke 6:20-38 discussed below. The negative form shows up as part of the Lord's Prayer (*forgive us our debts as we forgive our debtors*, Matthew 5:12, explained further in 5:14f); and again in the implied threat, *whatever one sows, that will he also reap* (Galatians 6:7, 5:16-25, Matthew 16:27, Romans 2:6-11).

Do to others as you would have them do to you,
   Luke 6:31, Matthew 7:12.
   The Sermon on the Plain (Luke 6:20-49) and the Sermon on the Mount (Matthew 5-7) are extended commentaries on the Golden Rule at different levels.

Love your neighbor as yourself,
   Summarizes the Old Testament law, hence
   Leviticus 19:18/Matthew 19:19 and 22:39, with parallels in Mark and Luke;
   Romans 13:9 and Galatians 5:14; and James 2:8.

Love one another,
   Is the distinctively Johannine form of the Rule:
   John 13:34f and 15:17; 1 John 2:5f; 3:11, 23; 4:7, 10f, 12, 21.
   When phrased, *love one another as I [Jesus] have loved you* (John 13:34, 15:12), John pegs the Golden Rule to its connection in and with Christ.
   For ties to Paul and Peter, see also 1 Thessalonians 4:9 and 1 Peter 1:22, 3:8, 4:8.

goes, "just live by the Golden Rule, and everything else will take care of itself."

There is a problem, however, as we have seen above. The Golden Rule can be used as a simple give-and-take or as justification for ill-treatment, As the jokes say:
- "do to others before they do to you," or
- "those who get the gold, rule."

What we want others to do to us may be affected by our own false expectations and bad experiences of life. When we see ourselves as victims, as worthless, as damaged, or as tools to be exploited, we will likely invite others to treat us that way, and we may begin to treat them the way they treat us. Reinforcing our low expectations of others, and theirs of us, the cycle repeats itself. A vicious circle of mutually destructive attitudes and reinforcing behavior only confirms the Golden Rule negatively.

At the neutral level of give-and-take, the Golden Rule easily comes down to a well-meaning platitude without much value for life. The bad or neutral sides of the Golden Rule are enough to make a person cynical about other people, morality, religion, the institutions of society, and life in general. Recognizing these options, theologians as far apart as fundamentalist J. Gresham Machen (†1937) and liberal Paul Tillich (†1965) simply dismiss the Rule.

With full awareness of both the bad and the give-and-take sides, however, the Bible probes the positive side. More than a lesson or a platitude, *the Golden Rule rests upon Jesus Christ and entails a community living together in Christ.*

1. The Sermon on the Plain, Luke 6:29-49.

Luke 6:31 states the Golden Rule in the form, *As you wish that others would do to you, do so to them.* Jesus sets the tone with an amazing string of examples (Luke 6:22-30):

- love your enemies,
- do good to those who hate you,
- bless those who curse you,
- pray for those who abuse you,
- turn the other cheek,
- give your coat as well as your cloak,
- give to everyone who begs from you, *etc.*

Then come the questions (verses 32-35). What credit is it to you merely to love those who love you, do good to those who do good to you, or help those from whom you expect to receive as much again? *Even sinners do that*, says Jesus. These interactions confirm what we learned as children on the playground: living in a rough-and-tumble world, we have to give something to get anything back, but we expect to get something back for what we give. With keen self-awareness, we tally what, in all fairness, we earn or deserve, and what costs-and-benefits or rewards-and-punishments we can expect from our interacting with others.

Precisely in the face of our life experience since childhood, Jesus utters Luke 6:35-36: *do all these things* (love, do good, help) *expecting nothing in return*. With that, all our calculations of fairness and earning are broken. At this level, the Golden Rule entails giving of ourselves expecting *nothing* from other people. At the same time *God* guarantees a reward (*your reward will be great*, verse 35). From other people, the reward may be a slap on the other cheek, losing our coat, contempt from our enemies, and various degrees of presumption, ingratitude, or outright hatred. God guarantees, nonetheless, the stated reward of being *sons of the most high*, that is, children of God (verse 35).

The obvious, immediate, head-slapping question is, "What kind of reward is *that*?!" Do we have to give up everything in order to be a child of God? Jesus is plainly standing the whole notion of reward on its head.

In Job 1:9 and 2:4f Satana (the Adversary) asks God, *Does Job fear God for nothing?* That is, will a human serve God if there is no clear benefit, advantage, or reward to be gained from it? Will we serve God if all we get out of life is suffering, oppression, injustice, poverty, sickness, pain, grief, constant struggle for survival, or loss of human dignity? In the end Job answers the underlying question, "Yes," though not lightly. For Job, fellowship with God—life as God's children—is something we do for no higher purpose than itself, with no calculation of rewards and punishments or salvation and damnation, and with no guarantee or promise of a better, easier life.

God restores Job's fortune at the end of the story (Job 42:10-17), but not as a reward. God is God, and Job is God's creation, without standing or innocence to claim anything against God.

> *[God:] "Hear, and I will speak; I will question you and you declare to me." [Job:] I had heard of thee by the hearing of the ear, but now my eye sees thee; therefore I despise myself, and repent in dust and ashes.* (Job 42:4-6, RSV)

Jesus makes the same point in Mark 8:34f:

> *If any man would come after me, let him deny himself and take up his cross and follow me. For whoever would save his life will lose it; and whoever loses his life for my sake and the gospel's will save it.* (RSV)

At this level the Golden Rule is, above all, a reflection upon God and God's ways with a sinful humanity. For *God* is *kind to the ungrateful and the evil* (Luke 6:35d), *merciful* (verse 36), *forgiving* (verse 37), and *giving* beyond all measure (verse 38). To live according to the Golden Rule is to *share in God's own, on-going, active life.*

The problem is, we humans cannot stop calculating, "What's in it for me?" "What do I get out of it?" "What do I have to do to get the reward and benefit or avoid the cost and punishment?" Even in our closest relationships we always check, however minimally, how things are going and what we have to do for the sake of ourselves, our cause, and our tribe. When do we ever attain the Golden Rule at the level of giving expecting nothing in return? The harder we try, the more it escapes us, lying always beyond our grasp.

Jesus, speaking in the Luke 6 passage, provides the way out of this dilemma, as a participation in his accomplishment of the Golden Rule. Jesus is *the* Son of the most high God (Luke 1:32, 35; 8:28), called Son of God and Son of Man in all four Gospels. In his life, death, and resurrection, Jesus gave himself to others without counting the cost or expecting anything in return. In so doing he accomplished the Golden Rule utterly and completely, the only human who ever did. Jesus thereby secures for the rest of humanity a participation in his accomplishment.

Participation in Christ should not be mistaken as:
- an incentive—calculating cost-and-benefits,
- a capacity—restoring our ability to do good or keep God's commandments out of ourselves,
- an ideal—of striving for something always just beyond our reach,
- an example—of Jesus showing how to do what he did,
- an embodiment—the Rule working itself out in and through us,
- a partial accomplishment—of the good part, intention, or effort in place of the whole,
- a platitude—assuming anybody can and will do it, hence moralistic advice to do good.

Participation here means full fellowship with the life, death, and resurrection of Jesus Christ. As branches grafted into a root (John 15) or as children adopted into the family (John 1:12f, Gal 3:35-4:7), we are united with *Jesus' accomplishment* of the Golden Rule at its most profound level. Participating in Christ, we fellowship with God, for Jesus is God as a human being. Awakened to God henceforth, we want—and vigorously seek—to live where Christ lives, because that's where God is and where, energized by the Spirit, we want to be.

2. The Golden Rule Entails a Community of Mutual Self-giving.

At the most profound level of the Golden Rule, every member gives respect to every other person—whether earned, deserved, or not—and contributes to the wellbeing of his/her neighbors without counting the cost, as the Samaritan did toward the man who fell among thieves in the parable, Luke 10:25-37. When individually we do not have to guard our backsides by ourselves—because others are guarding our backsides, too—we are free from self-concern to contribute to the well-being of others as well as ourselves. The resulting collaboration among people is extraordinary. The increase in freedom, creative effort, and productivity for all members of the community is enormous.

Some people today focus the Golden Rule on a concern for the self, that is, love your neighbor *as yourself.* Healthy relationships, they say, involve taking care of ourselves first, to avoid being overly dependent on others, either their good opinion or their kindness. Enlightened self-interest should be the measure of how we treat others, they say, both personally and economically. This perspective, of course, pulls us right back into a give-and-take transaction and constant calculations of what we get out of the deal. Such self-concern sidesteps the authentic community of mutual self-giving and our participation in Jesus' full-blown accomplishment of the Golden Rule.

Under the title, "Of the Communion of the Saints" *The Westminster Confession of Faith* (1646) eloquently de-

scribes the Church as such a community of self-giving:
> All saints being united to Jesus Christ their head, by his Spirit and by faith, have fellowship with him in his graces, sufferings, death, resurrection, and glory; and, being united to one another in love, they have communion in each other's gifts and graces, and are obliged to the performance of such duties, public and private, as do conduce to their mutual good, both in the inward and outward man ... [—which includes:] relieving each other in outward things, according to their several abilities and necessities.[7]

Paul describes the same dynamics in discussing the community of marriage in Ephesians 5:21-33 (RSV). The Golden Rule at the third level disrupts any attempt to justify an authoritarian view of marriage and family. With echoes of *love one another,* the passage begins, *be subject to one another out of reverence for Christ* (verse 21). Then come two explicit forms of the Golden Rule.

- *Husbands, love your wives as Christ loved the church and gave himself up for her* (25, 29)—matching the Johannine form, *love one another as I have loved you.*
- *Husbands should love their wives as their own bodies* (28, 33)—matching the form, *love your neighbor as yourself.*

What does it mean for one person to submit to boundless, self-giving love practiced by another? The community of husband-and-wife here takes place entirely within the framework of belonging to Christ (*out of reverence for Christ, as to the Lord, as Christ loved the Church*), in whom alone the Golden Rule is accomplished. The unrestrained, self-giving of each to the other explodes any notion of subjugating one person to the other or a calculating give-and-take be-

---

[7] Ch. XXVI, paras I-II, quoted from *Creeds of the Churches*, 3rd edition, 222-223.

tween them, and opens the way to authentic, even extraordinary community in the context of marriage and family.

3. Insights We Can Draw from the Golden Rule.

First, the Golden Rule does not function well as a self-standing principle of morality. Operating at drastically different, mutually exclusive levels, the Golden Rule is not a fixed rule or principle that can simply be applied at will. It functions more properly to generate insight into how people interact at multiple levels, of which we have highlighted three. The first two levels reflect our usual expectations, but their limited, even destructive dynamics need to be seen for what they are. Meanwhile the third level all too often flies under our radar, and we underestimate what it takes to attain the Golden Rule at that level.

Second, the religious dimension is indispensable for coming to terms with all three levels, but especially the third. The first two levels happen on their own and require no encouragement. Without the religious dimension, however, the third level is simply unattainable. Notably for Christians, the Golden Rule cannot reach its full depth without participation in Jesus Christ. In fact, the Golden Rule at the third level goes to the heart of what it means to be Christian,
- living in fellowship with Jesus Christ (*Emmanuel, God with us*), hence in fellowship with God,
- *in Christ* living with fellow Christians, and—
- still *in Christ*—living with all humans.

All humans do not thus become Christian, but *in Christ* all Christians will honor all humans.

Third, the Golden Rule points to where authentic community is to be found for the Church as well as for the Nation. This point bears directly on the congregational life of Christian churches in dissarray during a time of paradigm shift. The same point bears equally on the deep divisions of the American social fabric. Perhaps we can see why the straightforward wholeness of the churches may be essential for authentic community in the American experiment.[8] In a society of indescribable diversity, community comes not from what we get out of it but from what each person, each family, each group, contributes to the whole at the point of a shared unity. For Christians the point of unity is Jesus Christ. A similar point of unity—*e pluribus unum,* "out of many one"—centers in the *American Constitution,* a rule of law before which every citizen has equal standing.

Authentic human community comes from its core unity and cannot be imposed from the rim. Operating at the rim, we will debate endlessly *who is in* and *who is out. Who is in* entails some kind of uniformity or sameness of person, and creates a new class of undesirables, no matter how widely the net is cast. The results diminish authentic community for both those *who are in* and those *who are out.*[9] Authentic human community comes from a common unity in something other than the people themselves— for the Church, Christ; for the Nation, the *American Constituution.*

From its core unity, the American practice of the Golden Rule has shaped the Western socio-political-economic world for the last 400 years (see Part 1 and Sidebar 10.3). The same goes for American Christians, who have engaged society both as church members and as citizens for all these years. Even when our practice of community is

---

[8] This was Alexis de Tocqueville's observation in the 1830s. See *Democracy in America*, vol 1 (New York: Fontana Library, 1968), 342-390, discussing religion under the heading of "The Main Causes Tending to Maintain a Democratic Republic in the United States."
[9] The demand for uniformity lies behind de Tocqueville's warning against "the tyranny of the majority." See *ibid.*, 304-322.

distorted or overreaching, in both Church and Nation, the Golden Rule provides a God-given path forward.

Sidebar 10.3. The Golden Rule over Time.

Beginning at least with the *Corpus Juris Civilis* (the *Institutiones, ca.* 530) by Justinian I (†565), a Christian Emperor of Rome, the Golden Rule was widely perceived in the West as part of the law of nature. The same perception ran through the Middle Ages, the Protestant Reformation, and the beginnings of the scientific-industrial age in the 17th-18th centuries. After Kant restates it as the "categorical imperative," *ca.* 1800, the Golden Rule disappears from direct consideration except as a moral principle or platitude, found with slight variations in all world religions and moral philosophies.

Indirectly, however, the equivalencies established in the Golden Rule at all levels parallel those in:
- modern mathematics (*e.g.*, the equals sign in algebra),
- commerce (mutual exchange of labor, goods, and capital),
- the rule of law (equity, regulating social interactions),
- civil society (fair provision for all people),
- religion (grace, interactions with God and one another), and
- science (interactions between cause and effect, as in the 3rd law of thermodynamics—for every action there is an equal and opposite reaction; or interactions between matter and energy, as in the theory of relativity, $E = mc^2$).

ESSAY 11

THE MARKS OF THE TRUE CHURCH

The authenticity of the Church's connection to God is imperiled when:
- the Christian community is deeply confused or divided over its basic message and reason for being;
- Church leaders are floundering for a spark of energy, confidence, clarity, and direction going forward; and
- members and congregations talk openly about separating from Church or denomination.

All these dynamics are now in play for Western Christian churches, notably in the United States and Europe.[1] Previous ways of establishing authenticity around worship, organization, mission, or theology no longer work for the contemporary church. The Church of our time is struggling to locate its peace, unity, and purity.

Where, then, shall we find the true, authentic Church? Amidst the diversity of members and the confusion of truth claims at the present time, how can we even talk about a "true Church"? To find a way forward, this essay considers the historic marks of the true Church. The essay:

(1) reviews marks of the true Church in different eras (Early Church, Reformation, Modernist-Pietist),
(2) discusses where we stand on them today, and
(3) shows how Jesus Christ may be moving us beyond our current impasse.

---

[1] Since 1950 such breaks have happened in every major American Protestant segment, including Lutheran, Episcopalian, Presbyterian, Methodist, Baptist, and Pentecostal—in spite of vigorous efforts within the Ecumenical Movement, both left and right. Since 1950 the Presbyterian Church (U.S.A.) alone has gone through two mergers (1958, 1983) and three splits (1973, 1981, 2011), plus spinoffs into megachurches, while dealing with a host of theological, governance, and social issues.

1. A Review of Historic Marks of the True Church.

Over time Christians have identified the Church's authenticity with three sets of "marks of the true church." [2]
- The true Church is *one, holy, catholic, and apostolic*—from the early Church (33-600).[3]
- The true Church is *the place where the Word is purely preached, the Sacraments are rightly administered, and church discipline (or discipleship) is exercised*—from the Reformation era(1350-1650).[4]
- The true Church engages in *mission*—from the Modernist-Pietist era (1650-2000).[5]

---

[2] All the confessions listed below can be found in the collection of Jaroslav Pelikan, *The Christian Tradition: A History of Development of Doctrine,* 5 vols. (Chicago: Univ. of Chicago Press, 1971-1989). The current *PC(USA) Book of Confessions* (*BC*) contains all three sets of marks; the current *PC(USA) Book of Order* (*BO*) reviews them in F-1.0302-1.0304.

[3] From the *Nicene Creed* (325 and 381ce). "The holy catholic church" is also part of the Apostles Creed. See *PC(USA) 2011-12 BO* F-1.0302.

[4] For the Reformation marks of the true church see the *Augsburg Confession* (1530), Art. VII; *Scots Confession* (1560), Chapter 18; *Heidelberg Catechism* (1560), questions. 65, 67, 83-85; *Second Helvetic Confession* (1566), Chapt. XIV para. 5, Chapt. XVII paras. 11-12; *Westminster Confession* (1646), Chapt. 25; *Shorter Catechism* (1646), questions. 86, 88-91; *Larger Catechism* (1646), questions. 154-161; *Barmen Declaration* (1934), Sect. II no. 3; the *French Confession* of 1559, Chapters 23-38, esp. 25-29; and PC(USA) *BO* F-1.02, 1.0303). *The Declaration of Barmen* uses the Reformation marks of the Church to resist Nazi efforts to turn the Church into an arm of the State.

[5] For Presbyterians, mission is explicit in the *Confession of 1967* (*BC* 9.06) and *A Brief Statement of Faith* (1996, *BC* 11); in the 1903 chapters added to *The Westminster Confession of Faith* (*BC* 6.051-58); and in 2011-2013 PC(USA) *Book of Order* F-1.01 ("God's Mission") and F-1.0304 ("Six Great Ends of the Church").

a. *One, Holy, Catholic, Apostolic (Sidebar 11.1).*

The *Nicene Creed* (325, 381) states plainly, "we believe in one holy catholic and apostolic Church." Following Paul (1 Cor 12:27), the early Christians said that the Church is the mystical body of Christ. In the *Nicene Creed* they agreed:
- Since the body of Christ is *one*, the true Church has to be one, a unity within itself, unique and authentic as the repository of God's truth and saving grace.
- Because Christ is *holy*, the true Church united with Christ must also be holy, set aside as the realm of God's work and pure in belief and morals.
- Since the risen Christ knows no geographical limits, the true Church is *catholic* or universal in the scope of its truth and in its applicability to all people.
- The true Church will always follow after the Biblical prophets and apostles, hence *apostolicity*, whereby the chosen leaders preserve the truth of the Gospel against falsehood and misdirection.

The weight of these marks falls upon church leadership to establish and enforce. As Cyprian said (†258), followed closely by Augustine (354-430)[6] and others: "Where the bishop is, there is the Church" (see Sidebar 11.1).

Sharing the mystical body of Christ, however, meant different things for Eastern and Western Christians, even in the Early Church. For Eastern Christians, mostly Eastern Orthodox today, the accent falls on the believer participating in the divinity of Jesus Christ, notably at the point of worship. For most Western Christians, the

---

[6] Augustine's views came out in his controversy with the Donatists and in his major work, *The City of God*. Adolph Harnack reviews his perspective on the Church and its four marks in *History of Dogma*, 3rd edition (New York: Dover Publications, 1961—German original, 1893), Volume V, 143-168.

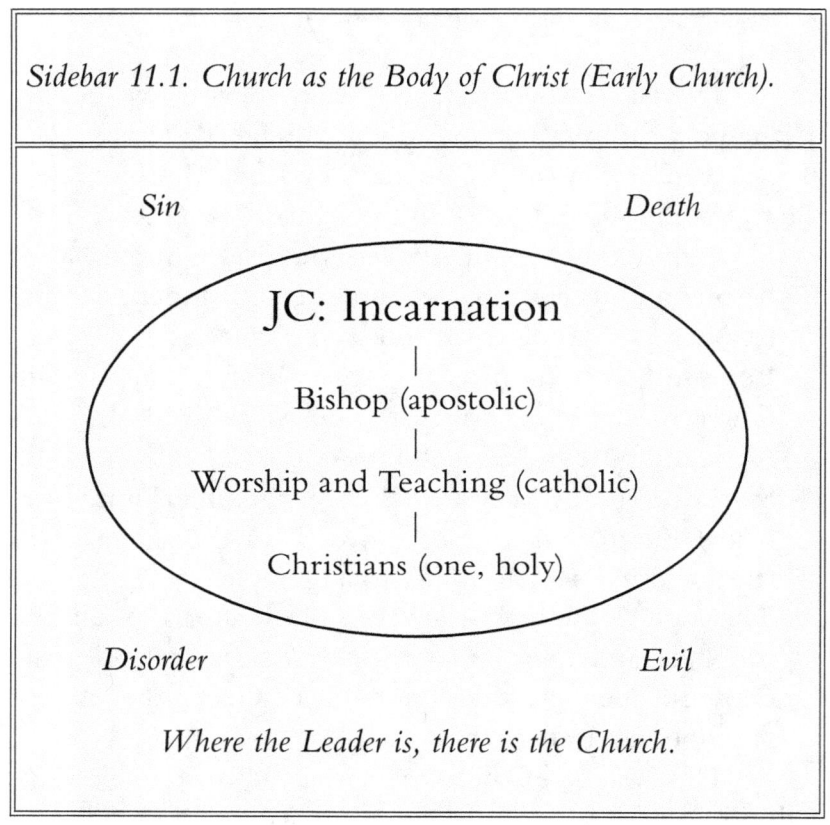

divine Jesus enters into, dwells in, transforms, and works through Christians individually and collectively. The Reformation offered an interlude to this view in the West.

During the Middle Ages, 600-1350, the Western sense of embodiment extended to the whole Church—its leaders, its people, its rituals, its property, and its actions. More and more the Bishop of Rome, or Pope, centered the leadership of priests and bishops hierarchically in himself. The instrumental means of grace expanded to include seven sacraments that covered human life from cradle to grave.[7] A

---

[7] Baptism, confirmation, penance, communion (Mass), marriage, last rites, and priestly ordination. These were formally adopted at the Council of Florence (1438-45). See Leith, *Creeds of the Churches*, 60-61.

merit system helped to quantify the amount of grace embodied, which invited strong comparisons between:
- the sacred (divine) and the secular (merely human),
- the supernatural (miraculous) and the natural (ordinary),
- the moral (good) and the immoral (bad), and
- the immortal (eternal life) and the mortal (eternal death).

These developments took place within the framework of the Early Church marks of the true Church (one, holy, catholic, apostolic). They set the backdrop for reform in the Western Church, which led Protestants to declare a new set of marks for the true Church altogether.

b. Word Preached, Sacraments Administered (Sidebar 11.2).

Although they did not turn away from the Church, the Protestant Reformers of the 16th century turned away from the embodiment of Christ in the Church and sharply criticized the abuses of the sacramental system through which it operated. The leading figures—Lutheran, Reformed, and Anglican—preferred the more Eastern view of the Church as participation in the presence and activity of Jesus Christ. The true Church, they said, centered in worship as an interactive event between God and God's people gathered around the proclamation of the Word and the celebration of the Sacraments (Baptism, Lord's Supper).

In worship, the spoken Word derives from Scripture, points to Jesus Christ, and addresses the issues of daily life for the gathered worshipers. Christ thus redefines our lives by his life, and his forgiving love sets our lives into the constant presence and activity of the living God. The Spirit moves us to take God's Word to heart in living every moment of every day.

The Sacraments build on the Word proclaimed. In Baptism and the Lord's Supper we act out the Gospel in all its simplicity. The Sacraments sift the human proclamation, then confirm, consolidate, and seal the true faith stirred up by the Word.

Standing at the center of the worship event, Jesus Christ gathers Christians together and governs the assembled believers directly and immediately, in Spirit and in truth. Reformed churches add a third mark at this point, the exercise of ecclesiastical discipline (root word, "disciple"), in which the service of worship extends into the service of discipleship for our common lives.

A number of crucial elements flow together around these marks of the true Church:

- Jesus Christ is Savior and Lord over all of life.
- Jesus exercises power from the bottom up, not the top down, as he says: *whoever wants to become great among you shall be your servant, and whoever wants to be first among you shall be your slave.*^AT (Mark 10:43-44)[8]
- Scripture exercised in worship establishes the authority of the Bible by its function in that setting.
- The worship of God is an end in itself; it does not derive importance from its "usefulness" but from God's power *Jews demand signs and Greeks seek wisdom, but we preach Christ crucified, a stumbling block to Jews and folly to Gentiles, … Christ the power of God and the wisdom of God.* (1 Cor 1:22-24, RSV)
- The covenant community is gathered together in Jesus Christ (*in his name*, Matt 18:20, Phil 2:10-11), united with him in the faith stirred by the Spirit (I Cor 12:3).
- Those so united *in Christ* share in his priesthood, and so they priest for one another ("communion of the saints").
- Engaging Christ in worship fosters a vigorous discipleship, both corporately and individually participating in his active presence wherever he leads.
- Jesus Christ is the true governor of the Church, at worship above all, and derivatively in church councils, gatherings, and individual lives (*the government will be on his*

---

[8] See also 1 Cor 1:17-30 and 2 Cor 12:9.

shoulders, Isaiah 9:6, RSV. See also Isa 42:1-4). The structures of church governance flow around Christ's activity.

With these marks in play, the worship event is the place where Christ governs the Church directly and immediately, energized by the Spirit. The resulting church structure looks like an upside-down pyramid (see Sidebar 11.1), where the point is down and the long edge—the local occasions of worship and service—are the primary locations of governance. Church councils function in a serving or support role. Reformation theology and practices all revolve around these elements, making the structures of governance a matter of conviction, not convenience. For the Re-

---

Sidebar 11.2. Church as Participation in Christ's On-going Life (Reformation).

[providence]   [history]

Jesus Christ
alive
[Word, Sacraments, shared community]

congregations

councils

Where Christ is, there is the Church.

All power in heaven and on earth have been given to me.
Lo, I am with you always, to the end of time.
Matthew 28:18, 20

formers Martin Luther, John Calvin, as well as for modern theologians Karl Barth, Dietrich Bonhoeffer, and Jürgen Moltmann, "Where Christ is, there is the Church."

c. Mission (Sidebar 11.3).

The Modernist-Pietist era, 1650-2000, elevates mission as a singular mark of the true Church. Pietism came into its own in the 18th century concern for who is saved, who is not saved, and how do we get saved? Salvation is the goal, and mission sets up the useful means to attain it.

For the Modernist-Pietist era as a whole, Jesus Christ is the principal means of our salvation. By his birth, deeds of love and mercy, teachings, and sacrificial death on the cross, God redeems us for eternal life and/or entry into the kingdom of God. By faith Christ dwells in our hearts[9] and transforms our lives from the inside out.

So, for Modernism-Pietism preaching, worship, and personal witnessing are highly prized, useful tools to communicate the Gospel and stir faith among believers. God gathers the saved into the Church as an association of believers, leaving the unsaved at large in the World. People are the Church, not the buildings, organization, or doctrines. So, "Where the believers are, there is the Church."

The mission of the Church arises at this point. In and through the believers, the Church is to carry out God's saving and transforming purposes in and to the World:
- outreach to the unsaved,
- liberation for the oppressed,
- manifestation of the kingdom of God on earth, and
- exhibition of goodness.

Mission takes place as an interaction between Church and

---

[9] Instead of Christ, some put the kingdom of God or God the Spirit dwelling within.

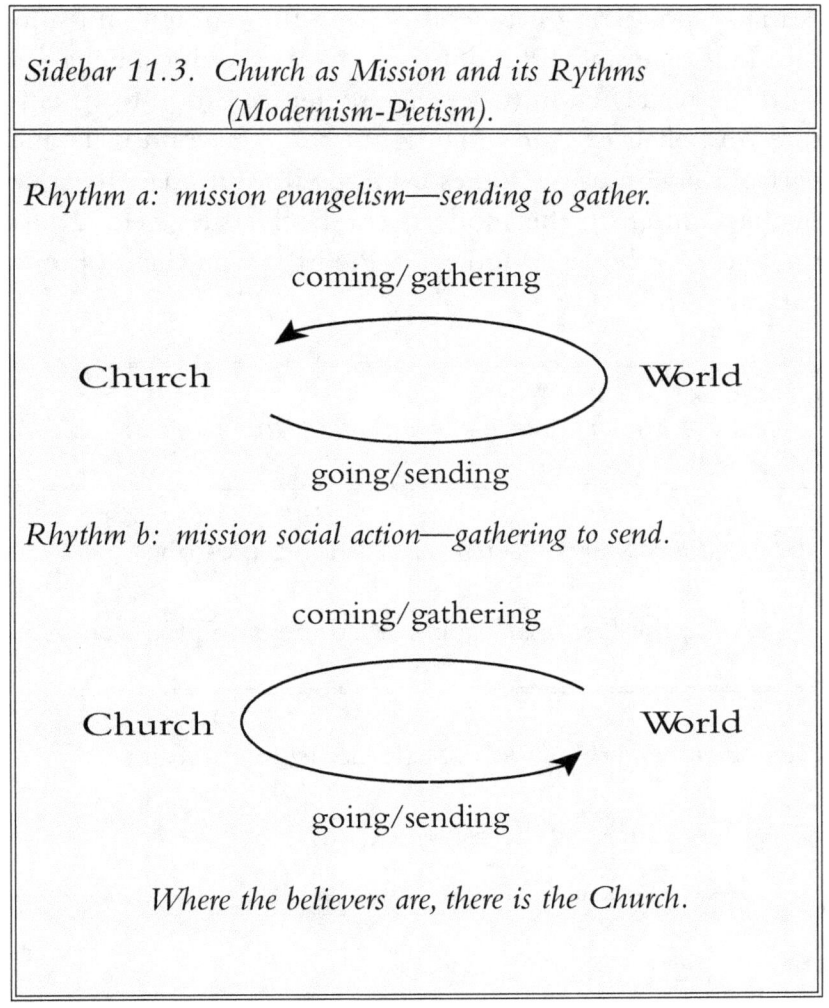

Sidebar 11.3. Church as Mission and its Rythms (Modernism-Pietism).

World, in a rhythm of coming and going, gathering and sending (see Sidebar 11.3). For Modernism-Pietism, the Church is unthinkable apart from its mission to the World.

2. Where We Stand on These Marks of the Church Today.

Two issues arise when we sift and discuss where we stand in relation to these historic marks of the true Church.

A major, polarizing issue comes from the Church's mission: should it be evangelistic outreach (to save souls on behalf of God) or social action (to engage society and transform culture on behalf of God's loving justice)? A second issue and part of the confusion comes from the institutional character of the Church in the modern era. Both issues belong distinctively to the late Modernist-Pietist era on the cusp of a paradigm shift.

Side 11.4. Emphases in the Marks of the True Church.

Early Church marks—one, holy, catholic, apostolic

Where the bishops/leaders are, there is the Church.

Reformation marks—Word, Sacraments, Discipleship

Where Christ is, there is the Church.

Modernism-Pietism marks—mission

Where the believers are, there is the Church.

---

a. *Mission as Evangelism or Social Action.*

Division over the Church's mission comes from the substance of the Gospel. Does the Gospel pertain to the salvation of individuals or to the well-being of people in community? These two perspectives entail complementary rhythms for going and coming as the Church engages the World. These rhythms involve the same dynamic of sending and gathering, but they bring out different outcomes.

One rhythm involves sending evangelists out into the World to bear witness to the Gospel, and, when people believe in Christ, gathering them into the Church to celebrate and nurture their salvation (Sidebar 11.3a). The other rhythm involves gathering people from the World into the Church to be equipped and inspired, then sending them back into the World for self-giving love and service to all who have needs (Sidebar 11.3b).

When one rhythm is separated from the other, both rhythms risk losing perspective on the Gospel that enfolds them. Sending people out to ingather others will eventually take on an institutional flavor, with provisions for buildings, finances, belief systems, and organization essential to keep the operation going. Gathering people in to send them out in selfless service will eventually immerse them in the causes they serve and risk losing the Christian identity and motivation that got them there.

The two rhythms complement each other quite well. The first rhythm keeps Christians grounded in Christ. The second rhythm keeps Christians honest, serving others selflessly in Christ's name. Both rhythms have been part and parcel of Pietism from its beginnings in the 17th Century. American revivalism hit its stride in the 18th, 19th and 20th centuries, while the Social Gospel Movement has been alive in this country since at least 1870. The institutional character of churches increased dramatically throughout the 20th Century, creating a countermove to become more self-giving. For Americans the watershed years are probably 1966-68, when membership peaked and the churches began to lose their youth. When taken separately, the two rhythms advance competing views of the Gospel which divide, even split apart churches and denominations. This pattern of division in the name of purity is distinctive to the Modernist-Pietist era of the Church.

b. The Church as Institution.

Recent discussions of Church and mission seek to return to a simple, apostolic vision of the Church.[10] According to these discussions, the Church became "Christendom" when the Emperor Constantine declared Christianity the official religion of the Roman Empire in 318 CE. Allied with the State, the Church took on an institutional responsibility for civil society. For some people today, that compromised the Church in the process, a mistake that persists down to our own time. In their view, the pressures of modernity are now breaking up "Christendom" and the "institutional church," identified with formal, doctrinal, or organized religion of any kind. We live in a post-modern, post-denominational, post-Christian era, they say, and the Church must recover the simple Gospel and mission from an earlier time.

These recent discussions envision a close link between *mission*, the Modernist-Pietist mark of the true Church, and the marks of the pre-Constantinian, Christian Church—*one, holy, catholic, and apostolic*. Especially important is "apostolicity," whose root meaning is "to send out."

Of course, the root meaning of "apostolicity" is not how the Early Church used the term as a mark of the true Church. At that critical time, with the Church facing serious

---

[10] See David J. Bosch, *Transforming Mission: Paradigm Shifts in Theology of Mission* (Maryknoll, NY: Orbis Books, 1991) and books published in *The Gospel and Our Culture Series*, 1998ff, notably, Darrell L. Guder, *The Continuing Conversion of the Church* (Wm. B. Eerdmans, 2000).

distortions from both without and within, "apostolocity" dealt with whether the message was authoritatively in line with the prophets and apostles. This word has to be totally redefined, to fit the mission accents of Modernism-Pietism.

Left unexamined in these discussions is why the Early Church and Modernist-Pietist eras of the Church both assume such a strongly institutional character. From the beginning, the Western rendering of *one, holy, catholic, and apostolic* invites Christians to view the Church as an embodiment of Christ and themselves as extensions of Christ's incarnation.[11] Such perceptions cannot avoid rigorous, often self-serving, institutional expectations and claims.

Modernism-Pietism fares no better with its emphasis on *Christ in me*, or the Church as the people of God, in and through whom God's mission gets carried out. Like the Early Church in the West, this view assumes that Christ is embodied in the believers both individually and collectively. Whether early or modern, the embodiment notion of the Church inherently fosters an institutional outcome.

Missing altogether from these recent discussions are the Reformation marks of the true Church. Coming to the Word and Sacraments largely from a Modernist-Pietist perspective, American Christians today typically regard them as tools for mission and the Church itself as the primary means of doing God's work in the World, whether evangelism or social

---

[11] The convergence of views by modern Roman Catholics (stemming from the Western, Medieval rendering of Early Church marks) and modern Protestants (stemming from the Modernist-Pietist accent on mission) is remarkable. The Roman Catholic Vatican II (1963-65) affirms that the laity, gathered together in the People of God, "make up the Body of Christ under one Head." (see Leith, *Creeds of the Church*, 3rd edition, 482). Protestants today often refer to the Church as a "redeeming community" (as in the current United Methodist *Book of Discipline*) or as "the second incarnation" (as in the book so entitled, by Rubel Shelly and Randall Harris, 1992, 2001).

action. Accordingly, church worship, order, and doctrine are measured for their utilitarian, institutional effectiveness, *i.e.,* how well people are saved and transformed through them, and whether we get anything out of attending to them. Pietism simply redresses the Reformation marks in missional garb and misses their original, even revolutionary impact.[12]

The corporate, institutional features decried for "traditional churches" in America today apply nonetheless to the successful churches of late Modernism-Pietism. The big-scale rallies, revivals, media operations, and community-based megachurches all require the same attention to organization, buildings, money, a self-perpetuating staff, and membership in large numbers. A way forward for the Church today probably entails recovering the Reformation marks of the true Church centered *in Christ*.

3. Jesus Christ as the Way Forward.

The accent on Jesus Christ in the Reformation marks of the true Church changed everything at the time. The lead statement for the Reformation says, *Where Christ is, there is the Church*. It does not say the reverse, "Where the Church is, there is Christ." Christ plays a vital role in all marks of the Church we have considered. Jesus Christ, energized by the Spirit, establishes the marks of the true Church, whether:

- Unity—in Christ,
- Worthiness—in Christ's righteousness,
- Universality—in Christ's lordship over all things,
- Leadership—in Christ's person,

---

[12] Accompanying the Reformation marks are (a) the inherent reversal of values (God's power made perfect in weakness), (b) a conciliar or democratic bent toward governance, and (c) the expectations and precedents they require to operate, namely, the freedoms of speech, religion, assembly, press, and redress of grievances—the same elements outlined as human rights in the First Amendment to the *American Constitution*.

- Mission, evangelism or social action—in Christ's active presence,
- Worship—of Christ as God with us (*Emmanuel*), or
- Discipleship—following Christ in all of life.

The Reformation marks of the true Church can help us in several ways at the present time.

First, the Reformation confessions[13] have a distinctive take on grace and salvation. Faith, they say, is the result of our salvation, not the cause of it. The chief end of the Christian life is to glorify and enjoy God forever, not to be saved for its own sake (see Mark 8:34-35). To glorify God is to serve God in all of life, whatever the cost. To enjoy God is to commune with the living God at every moment of our daily lives. These accents often led our forebears to expend themselves selflessly and heroically in following Jesus Christ.

Second, emphasizing Jesus Christ at the center of the Church's worship, energized by the Spirit, the Reformation confessions highlight a key, Biblical insight. The mission of the Church really is the mission *of* Jesus Christ. As God with us (*Emmanuel*) Christ both utters the Great Commission (Matt 28: 19-20a) and carries it out. Just prior to the Great Commission Jesus says: *All power [exousia] in heaven and on earth has been given to me*[AT] (Matt 28:18). Just after the Great Commission Jesus says: *Lo, I am with you always, to the end of the age*[AT] (28:20b). *Therefore* (28:19) we go, baptize, and teach, more as participants in Christ's activity than as his instruments or agents. *Therefore also* the gates of hell will not prevail against the Church (Matt 16:18), because Christ cannot fail.

Third, the Reformation marks of the true Church point fundamentally away from an incarnational or embodiment notion of the Church. Christ at work in the power of the Spirit does not set up the Church as a repository for

---

[13] See the confessions listed in Footnote 4 above, and Essay 13, "What Does it Mean to be a Confessional Church?"

the saved. The Church cannot contain, funnel, or otherwise domesticate and dispense the grace of God. When amazing things happen in the Church—which they certainly do!—they still belong to God. Serving Christ is our greatest joy in life wherever it may lead. Being touched by the Spirit, we want to be where Christ is manifestly at work and nowhere else. That is the case whether as the Church gathered or as the Church sent.

The *PC(USA) 2011-2013 Book of Order* attempts to weave all three sets of marks together. In the process it
- adds a new section on the mission of God (F-1.01);
- strengthens the hallmark Reformed emphasis on Jesus Christ as the only Head of the Church (F-1.02);
- presents the Church as the body of Christ (F-1.0301), a community of faith, hope, and love;
- elaborates separately each of the three sets of marks of the true Church (F-1.0302-1.0304);
- highlights the Spirit's role in all its work (F-1.04).

The same *Book of Order* combines the Reformation and Modernist-Pietist marks into the operational fabric of governance (G-300), which is a real accomplishment.[14]

God has not finished with the Christian Church today, in spite of its confusion, disarray, misdirection, and frequent unfaithfulness. Jesus Christ, our Lord at the center of both Church and World, remains the key to our future.

---

[14] Unfortunately, the revised *Book of Order* still functions like a top-down, institutional rule book or manual of operations instead of a covenant enabling constitution, and that keeps it from being a breakthrough model of its kind.

ESSAY 12

IS AUTHENTIC CHRISTIAN COMMUNITY EVEN POSSIBLE?

Western Christianity faces a dire situation today. The modern, secular World, created largely by the Christian West, has "come of age,"[1] *i.e.*, grown up enough to take responsibility for itself. Many people confidently believe they can meet their own emotional, physical, and spiritual needs very well without divine assistance. For such a World, the Church is unnecessary at best, useless at worst, and generally disposable as a matter of consumer choice. From where, then, does authentic Christian community come, what holds it together, and what keeps it going?

In truth, God creates the Christian community. So, the answer to these questions must lie with God. This essay makes three points.

(1) Authentic Christian community starts with Jesus Christ.
(2) The usual quick-fixes will not reverse an increasing separation of American culture from Christianity.
(3) Christ in fact brings otherwise self-isolated, unique individuals together.

1. Authentic Christian Community Starts with Jesus Christ.

Faced with a "world come of age" in the extreme turbulence of Nazi Germany, 1933-1945, Dietrich Bonhoeffer came to a simple insight: Jesus Christ is the reality

---

[1] Dietrich Bonhoeffer's phrase, from his time in prison, 1943ff. See his letters of 8 June and 16 July 1944, plus his "Outline for a Book" in *Letters and Papers from Prison: Dietrich Bonhoeffer Works*, Vol. 8, *op cit.*, 424-432, 473-482, 499-504.

of *God with us* (Matthew 1:23). Living together within this reality, Bonhoeffer says, all Christians take their cues *from Christ, through Christ*, and *in Christ*.[2]

a. *From Christ.*

Life with God comes *from Jesus Christ*, the Word of God incarnate. The Word of God pronounces us guilty and righteous before God even when we do not feel guilty or righteous. God puts this Word of life— truth and salvation— into the mouths of others. "Therefore," says Bonhoeffer,

> Christians need other Christians who speak God's Word to them. ... They need them solely for the sake of Jesus Christ. The Christ in their own hearts is weaker than the Christ in the word of other Christians. Their own hearts are uncertain; those of their brothers and sisters are sure.[3]

"The Christ in [our] own hearts" cannot and does not stand alone. The Christ in us is rooted in the reality of Jesus Christ as his own person. "The Christ in the word of other Christians" is part of the priesthood of all believers that conveys Christ to us tangibly. Bonhoeffer is here blending *Christ in us* with the larger term, *us in Christ*.

b. *Through Christ.*

Christians come to one another only *through Jesus Christ*. Reconciling us with God, Christ also reconciles us to one another. That binds us to forgiving those whom he has forgiven, loving those whom he loves, serving those whom he serves, and living with those who live with him. Christ thus mediates our relationships with others.

---

[2] *Life Together/Prayerbook of the Bible: Dietrich Bonhoeffer Works*, Volume 5, *op cit.*, Chapter 1, "Community," 27-47.
[3] *Ibid.*, 32.

Bonhoeffer calls the ideal of unmediated relationships a dreamwish. Unmediated relationships present an ideal or goal for us to pursue person-to-person and with all the love, intimacy, and trust we can muster. Such direct relationships, however, are demanding without relief; finding and keeping them at all costs often becomes all-consuming, a hot house that takes on a life of its own. If we can attain these relationships on our own, God is unnecessary. For this reason, says Bonhoeffer, "God's grace quickly frustrates all such dreams."[4] Authentic Christian community is grounded in God's forgiving love, defined and mediated by Jesus Christ, and energized by the Spirit (1 John 4).

c. *In Christ.*

Our life together takes place *in Christ.* Jesus Christ defines the Church by his life, death, and resurrection. The Church and Christians do not thus embody Christ, as if we could incarnate either Christ's divinity or his perfect humanity. Christ lives in us as part of what it means for us to live more fully in Christ. Fellowship *in Christ* is the aim of salvation. *In Christ* we fellowship with GOD up to and including eternal life. *In Christ* we fellowship with all others who are in Christ, past, present, and future. *In Christ* we participate in a mystical community that is greater than the sum of its parts.

In worship, the life blood of Christian community, Christ stands at the center of the Church. Christ forms, transforms, and re-forms Christians together, wherever the Word is preached and the Sacraments are celebrated—based on Scripture and empowered by the Spirit. Jesus Christ himself stands there before us and speaks his life-giving Word.

---

[4] *Ibid.*, 35.

Christ also stands at the center of the World. No matter how undeveloped, disfigured, or depraved humans may be, each person brings us face-to-face with the image of God made by God and re-created in Jesus Christ. God thus makes a claim upon our lives with every person we meet, and the way we deal with them one-by-one is the way we deal with Jesus Christ. We cannot know that everyone we meet is saved, but we do know that *God* stands before us and around us at every moment of every day.

2. Unworkable Quick Fixes for Culture vs. Christianity.

American culture is *de facto* separating itself from Christianity today. What are we to do as Christians? We seemingly have no ground on which to stand. The easy way out is to take matters into our own hands. Three quick-fixes lie close at hand. None of them are workable in the end.

Quick Fix One.

Seeking authenticity without culture supports, one quick-fix might be to dispense with the trappings of organized religion altogether. Why not start with a blank sheet of paper and cultivate a pure, individual, inner spirituality? Then we could dispense with formal worship, organization, rules, doctrine, maybe even one-sided sources of revelation like the Bible. Without the formalities of religion, we could also get rid of the church politics, doctrinal disputes, denominations, and sectarian traditions that divide us from one another. Would it not be great to mingle only with pure, unvarnished truth and authentically spiritual individuals?

The trouble is, we cannot start from scratch. We are dealing with real people, including ourselves, as 21st century American Christians. Starting elsewhere invites false hopes, mistakes, and abuses in the name of what is new and free. "New" and "free," however, do not guarantee authenticity.

Further, do we really want to separate ourselves from our forebears in the faith? Surely they were not totally ignorant, misled, corrupt, or unfaithful. Even in their ambiguities and mistakes, they bear witness to Jesus Christ, and for that we can be thankful (Phil 1:15-18). In the name of authentic Christian community it makes no sense to isolate ourselves from the "great cloud of witnesses" (Hebrews 12:1), try to be Christian alone, or otherwise separate ourselves from God.

Quick Fix Two.

Another quick-fix might be to re-establish ourselves as useful instruments to the world around us, restoring our relevance and mission. Western culture already adapts the Gospel for its own purposes of meeting human needs as in modern psychology, medicine, technology, and the marketplace. So, why not redouble our efforts to be useful, like a wrench whose instrumental purpose lies in turning nuts and bolts? Then we can go on making "useful" contributions to people's lives and infusing culture with our religious vision.

The trouble is, as the World also knows, making the Gospel or the Church "useful" merely turns the Gospel into a commodity and secularizes the Church. Is that not already a problem for the Church?

Furthermore, instruments used to fix things make no real claims upon us and may be self-justifying. On their face they appear clean, pure, and self-contained. A wrench is simple and clear in its purpose, to turn nuts and bolts. We may argue over how the wrench is designed and used, but not over its inherent usefulness. To be a wrench in the hands of God seems to give us a free pass, a justification of ourselves as we are, a declaration of some kind of innate goodness.

The wrench, of course, is not immune to either defects or misuse. More importantly, the Christian Church cannot justify itself in terms of its inherent usefulness to God any more than through good works. Authenticity for the Christian Church comes from connecting to its source, to God alone. *In Christ* God sets the Church in motion, makes it unique and precious, and sustains it beyond all usefulness.

Quick Fix Three.

A third quick-fix could come from casting our nets more widely to include an endless diversity of different people in the Christian community. With maximum inclusiveness, maybe we can grow the Church to the far reaches of creation itself. Isn't everything and everyone good just as God made them? Would not such openness re-establish our place in the World?

The trouble is, radical diversity—different individuals utterly unique in their person, story, and present circumstances—in fact presses the very questions of authentic Christian community with which we are wrestling. What makes our differences an asset instead of a liability? How can we communicate and collaborate across our differences? What draws us together? What holds us together?

The Church cannot be concerned only for itself, its own kind, the "saved." Nor can we limit the "saved" to our view of who is in and who is out, nor confine the people of God to those whom we think God loves or serves. Diversity for its own sake, however, does not guarantee authenticity. The novelty of major differences wears off quickly unless our relationships are mediated through Christ and we are centered in something other than ourselves.

Furthermore, a community cannot long survive merely on a loving disposition, unspecified openness, or tolerance secured by the lowest common denominator. Real diversity entails an equal concern for what unites us. The only solid basis for an authentic Christian community lies with the God Who—*in Christ*—brings and holds together very different, unique individuals.

3. Christ Brings Self-isolated, Unique Individuals Together.

The alternative to these quick-fixes for Bonhoeffer is Jesus Christ "existing as community."[5] The words of the Gospel remind us constantly that we are *from Christ, through Christ,* and *in Christ.* We belong to God by God's own action, *from Christ.* Our relationships to God, the World, and all others are mediated *through Christ.* Being *in Christ* together encompasses all our relationships with others and the World around us. *From Christ, through Christ,* and *in Christ* we become something we could never be, left to our own devices. The Church, on the other hand, participates fully *in Christ,* and *through his uniqueness* overcomes the inherent isolation of diverse individuals.

Above all, focusing on Christ gives us an openness to fellow Christians that doesn't rely on either self-limiting sameness or unlimited diversity. Only *in Christ* can we recognize the authenticity of one another's Christian experience of God. Only *in and through Christ* can we bridge unique, individual differences rendered infinitely diverse.

The following list is only a beginning for what goes into our individual, unique life experiences with God:
- age,
- gender,
- background,
- life situation,
- time in history,
- ethnicity,
- culture,
- socio-economic standing,
- education,
- expectations,
- politics,
- self-understanding, and ... more.

---
[5] *Act and Being: Dietrich Bonhoeffer Works,* Vol. 2, op cit., 112.

On our own, we struggle to communicate across such differences. With authenticity on the line, how, indeed, can we be a Christian community?

Tolerance and mutual acceptance have their breaking points, so merely striving for these ideas in our common life is not enough. Christian commmunity operates at another whole level when we value, celebrate, carefully listen to, and learn from another person's life experiences *in Christ*. Notice the ascending engagement in that sentence. We venture there only when each person we meet presents us with God's claim upon us, as the image of God restored—*from Christ, through Christ, and in Christ*. Authentic Christian community comes from sharing the depth and range of one another's unique life experiences with God, *in Christ*.

The face of Christ is not limited to members of the Christian community. We will look for Christ beyond the Church as well. By grace alone God leads us, sinners that we are, to take seriously the image of God on the face of every human we meet. We do not thus baptize people outside the Church as anonymous Christians. We do, however, seek their well-being, peace, and justice as fellow humans for whom Christ died and rose again. Christ mediates these relationships as well, and the Gospel itself leads us to them. *In Christ*, then, we also share authentic community with those outside the Church.

Is authentic Christian community even possible today? I believe it is. The Christian community—including my own church and others—has indeed found authenticity in the past. I also believe such authenticity will be found going forward, because *in Christ* God's grace to us is *new every morning* (Lament 3:23).

ESSAY 13

WHAT DOES IT MEAN TO BE A CONFESSIONAL CHURCH?

The title "confessional church"[1] arose in striking fashion when a small band of Christians resisted Nazi efforts to take over the Protestant Church of Germany in the 1930s. The Confessing Church of Germany declared a *status confessionis*—a crisis moment when the Gospel itself was at risk. With *The Declaration of Barmen* (1934) these Christians affirmed, bore witness to, and gave public testimony to the Gospel in that situation. Although interest in similar historic statements had been growing for some time,[2] *Barmen* proved to be a watershed moment that inspired other hard-pressed Christians and churches to write a new confession.

The Confessing Church dispute took place at a critical point in the Modernist-Pietist era (1650-2000), well known for opposing "creedalism" and relying on personal experience as the basis of truth.[3] How indeed does professing the faith with a formal creedal statement coincide with faith from the heart? Confessional churches face this question from within their own ranks as much as churches who have no formal confessions. At a time of paradigm shift, creeds and confessions deserve another look.

Sidebar 13.1 lists major, written confessions over the years. They are most striking in the creeds of the Early

---

[1] "Confession" is also used to ask for forgiveness, as in "confessing our sins," but derives this meaning from the truth that illumines the place where we stand.
[2] See *Creeds and Confessions of Faith in the Christian Tradition, Vol III: Modern Christianity*, ed Pelikan, Hotchkiss (Yale Univ. Press, 2003), 18-21. For the worldwide explosion of confessions after 1925, see 437-888.
[3] *Creeds and Confessions*, 5-12.

Sidebar 13.1. Major Written Confessions of Faith.

ca. 180	*Apostles Creed* (held by most Christians)
325, 381	*Nicene-Athanasian Creed* (by most Christians)
451	Council of Chalcedon (by most Christians)
529	Council of Orange (Western Christians)
1525	*Luther's Small and Large Catechisms*(Lutheran)
1530	*Augsburg Confession* (Lutheran)
1546-63	Council of Trent (Roman Catholic)
1560	*Scots Confession* (Reformed-Presbyterian)
1563	*Heidelberg Catechism* (Reformed)
1566	*Second Helvetic Confession* (Reformed)
1571	*Thirty-Nine Articles* (Anglican-Episcopalian)
1677	*Formula of Concord* (Lutheran)
1619	Synod of Dorts (Reformed)
1546-48	*Westminster Confession of Faith, Larger and Shorter Catechisms* (Reformed)
1575	*Helvetic Consensus Formula* (Reformed)
1869-70	First Vatican Council (Roman Catholic)
1925	*Baptist Faith and Message* (South Baptist/Ref)
1927, 1937, and 1948	Faith and Order (World Council of Curches)
1934	*Declaration of Barmen* (Lutheran-Reformed)
1962-65	Second Vatican Council (Roman Catholic)
1967	*Confession of 1967* (Reformed-Presbyterian)
1982	*Confession of Belhar* (Reformed)

For a broad list, see *Creeds and Confessions of Faith in the Christian Tradition*, 3 volumes, edited by Jaroslav Pelikan and Valerie Hotchkiss. (New Haven: Yale University Press, 2003).

Church (33-600) along with the confessions and catechisms of the Reformation era (1350-1650). Written confessions are largely absent from the Middle Ages (600-1350) and most of the Modernist-Pietist (1650-2000) era. The surge in confession writing since 1925 suggests we are entering a new era. Rediscovering the value of a confessional church may be an important step into the future God has in store for us.

This essay considers:
(1) The crucial role of confessions of faith for Christians.
(2) What confessions do when the Gospel is at risk.
(3) The cycle of non-confessional dynamics, 1650-2000.
(4) Confessing the faith when the Gospel is at risk.

1. The Crucial Role of Confessions of Faith for Christians.

The New Testament is clear in what it seeks, namely,

In the name of Jesus every knee shall bow in heaven and on earth and below earth, and every tongue shall confess that Jesus Christ is Lord into the glory of God the Father.[AT 4] (Phil 2:10-11)

When you confess with your lips that Jesus is Lord and believe in your heart that God raised him from the dead, you will be saved.[AT] (Ro 10:9)

Whoever confesses that Jesus is the Son of God, God abides in him, and he in God.[AT] (I John 4:15)

So, confessing the truth of the Gospel goes to the heart of Christianity:
- Confessing the truth of the Gospel pertains to the individual as well as to the community of believers.
- Confessing the truth of the Gospel pertains to the act of believing as well as to the words of what is believed.

---
[4] A superscript [AT] denotes the author's translation from the Greek.

- Confessing the truth of the Gospel is trustworthy only when grounded in Scripture: creeds and confessions are simply shorthand statements of the Gospel in the Old and New Testaments, and they send us back to the Bible.
- Confessing the truth of the Gospel is the challenge of every moment, whether of worship or of daily life, when and where, by grace, we live into God's activity with us.

A vibrant, confessing church holds all these aspects together.

How, then, does a confession of faith help us function as a Christian Church and live as intentional Christians? In every age and situation "faith seeks understanding."[5] The destruction of the World Trade Center on September 11, 2001, for example, drives faith to make sense out of an utterly senseless act. The everyday experiences of life—birth, growth, marriage, dramatic change, success and failure, death—all drive people of faith to understand each moment in the light of the living God. Written confessions of faith help give us language to do that.

A confession of faith functions like the anchor of a ship. An anchor centers the ship and keeps it from foundering when it gets too close to shore. A confession centers on the Gospel. When we drift or the currents pull us away from that center, the confession pulls us back. But in order to work, especially in rough seas, an anchor needs enough slack or space for the anchor to dig into the sea bottom and hold the ship no matter which way the current and wind are blowing. Like an anchor, a confession of faith provides the Church both a secure center and, around that center, space to move.

Because the confessions remind us of the Gospel at its heart, we do not have to cling too tightly to the past, resist the changes of the present, or fear the future. God does not

---

[5] From Anselm, †1109. Similarly, "I believe in order to understand," Augustine, †430.

stand still, but, like grace, is *new every morning* (Lam 3:23). Listening to previous confessions and confessing the truth with their lives, a community can live confidently in the present. Shaped by these confessions along with regular worship by Word and Sacraments, a community can be confident of Christ's presence and navigate the issues of our daily lives. With a cultivated discernment they will read and hear the Biblical witness to Jesus Christ on the one hand and the daily news on the other. Stirred by the Spirit, such an intentional community of faith is indeed "the Church reformed, always to be reformed according to the Word of God."[6]

2. What Confessions Do When the Gospel Is at Risk.

The most important confessions of faith arise in moments of crisis (*status confessionis*) when the Gospel itself is at risk. Although the Christian movement may feel the press of hostile circumstances or major change, the crisis comes mainly from within the Christian community.

For example, *The Apostles Creed* (ca. 180 AD) was used for adult baptisms to define a Christian's core identity in a pagan culture. Especially during the 2nd Century, facing the distortions of Gnosticism, the early Church struggled with urgent, internal questions about who Jesus Christ is and what the Scriptures tell us about redemption in his name: Is Jesus merely a useful means of creation, divine wisdom, and salvation? *Or*, is Jesus really God as a human being—the creating, revealing, saving reality of *God with us* (*Emmanuel*) (Matt 1:23) breaking into our midst? These issues came to a head 150 years later, when the Church drew on Scripture to confess publicly in *The Nicene Creed* (325, 381): Jesus Christ is God as a human being (*homoousios*).

---

[6] *Ecclesia reformata semper reformanda secundum verbum Dei*; 2011/2012 PC(USA) *Book of Order* F-2.02.

Similarly, the 16th Century Reformation confessions and catechisms were beaten out in a time of turmoil in the West, between Protestants and the Church of Rome (see Sidebar 13.1). Even as late as mid-17th Century England, when the Protestant gains of the Reformation seemed at risk, the Westminster Assembly was convened in London and confirmed the five *solas* of the Reformation era:
- Christ alone,
- Scripture alone,
- Faith alone,
- Grace alone,
- The Church reformed.[7]

In the 20th Century *The Declaration of Barmen* (1934) arose when some church members were willing to replace the Gospel with the social and cultural agenda of Nazi sympathizers. *Barmen* drew its main lines of resistance from Scripture read through the lens of Reformation confessions. Similarly, in the midst of American culture, *The Confession of 1967* emerged at a critical moment of confusion, social change, and growing secularism, which called into question the Gospel itself. In South Africa, *The Belhar Confession* (1982) faced a racial ideology within the Church that denied the inherent unity Christians share in Christ.

At a moment of crisis, a confession of faith is as important for what it does as for what it says. We can identify three steps.

---

[7] *The Westminster Confession of Faith* and catechisms (1646ff) were produced for the Church of England and adopted by the Church of Scotland. Adaptations for other churches include the *Declaration of Savoy* (Congregational, 1658); the *London Confession* (Baptist, 1677, 1688); and many Baptist spinoffs in the 19th Century. See John H. Leith, *Creeds of the Churches*, third edition (John Knox Press, 1982), 334ff, and Thomas J. Nettles, *By His Grace and For His Glory* (Baker Book House, 1986).

The first step is to recognize and declare a crisis of faith—a *status confessionis*—a situation in which the Gospel is at risk. Christians did that in their own times for every confession reviewed above.

The second step is to redefine the moment in terms of Jesus Christ, the Word of God made flesh, using simple, clear, straightforward language. When Jesus walked by the Sea of Galilee, he said *follow me* to the fishermen there (Mark 1:17), and redefined their lives by his own present and future journey. The confession *Jesus is Lord* recurs throughout the New Testament. The Early Church creeds and Protestant confessions listed above do the same for their own times, places, and situations. For Christians Jesus Christ is *the way, the truth, and the life* in our walk with God (John 14:6).

The third step is to rally all Christians everywhere and for all time to share this new confession. Having confessed the Gospel anew in the midst of a crisis, a confessional church addresses and enlists the *great cloud of witnesses* throughout history (Hebrews 12:1) to join in confessing the truth of the Gospel for that time, that place, and that situation, using the language of that confession.

All three steps toward an authentic confession of faith are manifest in the recent jewel, The Belhar Confession (1982), of the Dutch Reformed Mission Church of South Africa.[8]

Notice: a confession of faith does not say everything, only what is pertinent to the Gospel at risk in that moment. Even taken all together, the confessions do not cover all the topics of systematic theology.

Notice further: a confession of faith aims to state the truth of the Gospel for all Christians everywhere and for all time. Authentic confessions are not partisan documents, written to support a sectarian cause or defend a particular

---

[8] The Accompanying Letter is crucial to the meaning of *Belhar*.

denomination. They speak to and for the entire Christian community. The best ones do that.

The confessions join us with very different moments in time, as they arose in the history of the Church, each one centered in the Gospel of Jesus Christ. The aim is not to make the old confessions relevant to us in our own language, but for us to enter into the language of the confessions and affirm the Gospel at the times, places, and settings of their origins. That is how confessions shape our insights into the heart of the Gospel and prepare us to see when and where the Gospel may be at risk in our own time.

We often—mistakenly—try to reduce all the confessions to a short list of fixed, abstract, seemingly timeless principles of theology. Several problems attend such a move:

- The sheer effort to sift all the confessions for their "essential tenets"[9] is enormous. We will invariably have trouble agreeing about what to include and what to exclude on such a list. Even if we succeed, we risk replacing the original confessions with a composite statement, a confession within the confessions.
- Trying to enforce certain ideas as legal demands for correct belief, we risk separating what we believe in—our closely held theological convictions—from the act of believing that gives them their authenticity for life.
- Seeking agreement on ideas and principles, we tend to press for uniformity among believers instead of reaffirming our basic unity together in Christ.
- Focusing on the past, we may miss the need to confess the Gospel faithfully in our own time.

---

[9] The phrase, "essential tenets," is used in the current *PC(USA) Book of Order*, W-4.0404c. See also F-2.03-2.05 on lists of themes in the *Book of Confessions*. Arguments over the "essential tenets" are part of the polarization now taking place in the PC(USA), which throws this church into a non-confessional turmoil.

While Jesus Christ himself is timeless, we daily confess the truth of the Gospel for our own lives as we live them. So, confessing the Gospel is always bound to its own time and will not wander far from its center, *in Christ*.

3. The Cycle of Non-Confessional Dynamics, 1650-2000.

Non-confessional churches dominate the era of Modernism-Pietism (1650-2000), spilling over into the present. The Lutheran and the Anglican-Episcopalian churches, traditionally confessional, produced no new confessions after the 1570s (see Sidebar 13.1). Similarly, Reformed churches produced no major confessions between *The Helvetic Consensus Formula (*1675) and *The Barmen Declaration* (1934). The Anglican-Episcopal and Roman Catholic churches largely side-stepped confessional issues by emphasizing worship (liturgy, sacraments) and church order (the infallibility of the Pope) during this time. The Pietism of John Wesley (†1791) and the Methodist Church, of course, came out of the Anglican Church of England in the 1700s. All modern Christian churches (and Judaism), however, have gone through a Pietistic phase, and they reflect the resulting tensions within.

The drift to non-confessional dynamics came with two developments during the 17th Century. One was the demand for a uniform orthodoxy in the aftermath of the Protestant Reformation. This typically took the form of making the confessions legaling binding for the state churches of Europe and Britain. *The unity of the Church was perceived as a uniformity of agreement with the confessions.* The expectation of uniformity traveled to the New World and became a feature of American confessional churches.

The other development was a separation between the act of believing and what is believed. What started as a convention of Protestant theology in the 17th Century opened the floodgates of reaction to the largely rational bent in the Protestant churches of the day. The movement known as Pietism began (1650-) with an accent on the inner self, notably the private, individual acts of believing (Baptist), loving (Methodist), or experiencing the Spirit (Pentecostal). Faith was located in feeling or experience, not in thinking.[10] Pietism unleashed an enormous amount of energy going forward and established the non-confessional dynamics of the whole Modernist-Pietist era.[11]

During the Modernist-Pietist era, however, *the demand for uniformity among confessional churches spilled over into the non-confessional churches as well.* How does this take place? When facing particular moments of need, challenge, or distress, non-confessional churches lean toward catch phrases. Catch phrases provide a simple content in a uniform language held with strong feeling. For example,
- "the Bible alone is enough,"
- "all we need is faith from the heart and love,"
- "faith without works is dead,"
- "the Bible is inerrant,"
- "diversity and inclusiveness," or more recently,
- "God is in control."

Close-knit groups assume that all right-hearted Christians agree on essentials, and they expect everyone to repeat these catch phrases verbatim. The group typically uses peer pressure to enforce its stance. Those who do not readily agree may find themselves outside the group, even ostracized. This kind of group control is very effective, as we

---

[10] Jonathan Edwards (†1758) documents the exeperiential side of the First Great Awakening in his *A Personal Narrative of Surprising Conversions* (1740). Friedrich Schleiermacher (†1834) locates Christian faith in feeling, not in either thinking or doing.

[11] William G. McLoughlin outlines four "Great Awakenings" to date, in *Revivals, Awakenings, and Reform: An Essay on Religion and Social Change in America, 1605-1977* (Chicago: U. of Chicago Press, 1978).

know from the peer pressure of our teenage years, from de Tocqueville's warnings about "the tyranny of the majority," and from popular cultural or political sentiments that sweep through a community (now intensified by social media).[12]

The struggle for uniformity in both Pietism and Orthodoxy pervades the entire history of Presbyterians in America. From colonial times until now Presbyterians have repeatedly divided and reunited, notably,
- New Side vs. Old Side (1741 split, 1758 reunion),
- Cumberland Presbytery vs. the broader Presbyterian Church (1810 split, 1896 reunion of most but not all),
- New School vs. Old School (1837 split, 1864 reunion in the South and 1869 reunion in the North),
- Northern vs. Southern (1861 split, 1983 reunion),
- Liberal vs. Conservative (splits: OPC, 1936-; PCA, 1973-; EPC, 1981-; ECO, 2011-; with no reunions in sight).

When demand for uniformity was strongest, the Presbyterians divided. When they realized a unity *in Christ* beyond themselves, they reunited. The disruptions almost always came from non-confessional demands for experience, practice, or purity that disturbed the confessional consensus. One side demanded uniform agreement in doctrine, the other side demanded uniformity of feeling or experience. Both sides mistook uniformity for unity, which triggered a cycle of division and reunion.

Regional differences doubtless complicated the reunion of American Presbyterians after the Civil War. But competing demands for uniformity in both Northern and Southern branches delayed the eventual reunion. *e.g.*, the

---

[12] Ostracism as a form of church discipline is called the ban, in which church members are not allowed to speak to or have normal contact with the person ostracized. This form of church discipline is practiced quite effectively by modern Anabaptist churches (Amish, Mennonite).

spirituality of the Church in the South[13] and the modernist-fundamentalist controversy in the North.[14] Like uniformity, purity demands perfection and does not tolerate even minor differences well.

Non-confessional dynamics favor strong feelings, spontaneity, and quick changes. Non-confessional movements spread quickly and often bring about significant change in a short time for both religion and culture.[15] Recent examples are "the Jesus Movement," "the church growth movement," "the seeker church," the "non-denominational/community" church (often mega-church), and "the emergent church" (now in progress). After making their mark, these movements often end as quickly as they began, to be replaced by the next point of urgency and its catch phrase.

Non-confessional dynamics are not inherently anti-intellectual. The best schools of 18th Century Europe were Pietistic. Out of these schools came such watershed philosophers as Immanuel Kant and G.W.F. Hegel and theologian Friedrich Schleiermacher. The language and idiom of modern discourse—relation or relationship—grew out of Pietistic roots[16] and extend to modern science. Yet, the era

---

[13] See Ernest Trice Thompson, *The Spirituality of the Church* (John Knox Press, 1961) and *Presbyterians in the South*, volumes 1-3 (John Knox Press, 1963-74)

[14] The earlier dates above coincide with the First and Second Awakenings, as covered in McLoughlin's book, cited in Footnote 11. The modernist-fundamentalist controversy, 1896-1937, is well documented in Lefferts A. Loetscher, *The Broadening Church* (Univ. of Pennsylvania Press, 1954) and Bradley Longfield, *The Presbyterian Controversy: Fundamentalists, Modernists, and Moderates* (Oxford University Press, 1991).

[15] McLoughlin's book, *op cit*, shows the cultural as well as the religious impact of the four "Great Awakenings".

[16] See Merwyn S. Johnson, "The Three-Legged Stool: Pietism and Post-Modern Theology," *Theology between East and West*, ed Macchia and Chung (Wipf and Stock Publishers, 2002), 33f, 317-340.

of Modernism-Pietism is marked by deep-seated conflicts between faith and reason as well as religion and science. Non-confessional dynamics today have fostered retreats from science, reason, or fixed systems of any kind.

The current assault on organized religion in America has all the hallmarks of late, non-confessional Modernism-Pietism coming to a head. Those who cry for a "Christianity after religion"[17] also announce "the end of church" as defined by confessions. The same people call for "the birth of a new spiritual awakening" based on the uniform human experience of relationships in community, as found in non-confessional churches. Neither the cry nor the call are new. The movement simply repeats the underlying concerns that stirred the 17th Century Modernist-Pietist paradigm at its start—and the same demand for uniformity.

American Church and culture today are both stuck in a deep-seated polarization. The roots of this polarization are clear enough: the Enlightenment-Pietist separation of head from heart coupled with the demand for uniformity on both sides, often carried to extremes. The simpler distinctions between liberal and conservative no longer work here, because partisans of all stripes share the same dynamics.

4. Confessing the Faith When the Gospel Is at Risk.

The question very quickly becomes, How can we combine the act of believing with what is believed? For John

---

[17] The quoted phrases in this paragraph all come from *Christianity After Religion: The End of Church and the Birth of a New Spiritual Awakening* (HarperCollins, 2012), by Diana Butler Bass. See p. 69 for the contrasts drawn here. Bass separates the act of believing from what is believed at the start, then uses social science categories (believing, behaving, belonging) and survey data (from 2008) to argue the end of the old and the birth of the new. Authors in the "emergent church" movement like Phyllis Tickle, Brian McLaren, and Tony Jones make similar arguments.

Calvin, faith is

> a firm and certain knowledgte of God's benevolence toward us, founded upon the truth of the freely given promise in Christ, both revealed to our minds and sealed upon our hearts through the Holy Spirit, [18]

A true, living faith for Calvin is an act of the whole person, with the head, the heart, and the spirit each working together, not alone. The Scripture passages cited at the beginning of this essay do not separate head, heart, and spirit, either, nor do the dynamics of a confessional church outlined in Sections 1 and 2 above. The question going forward is: How can we recover this kind of wholeness when the prevailing paradigm leans heavily in a non-confessional direction?

When not burdened by demands for uniformity, confessional dynamics can be remarkably adaptive and vigorous. They cultivate a lived faith, secure in its foundations, open for constructive dialog with its surroundings, and free to roam within a range of faithful possibilities. Confessional dynamics, centered and united in Christ, do not see differences and diversity as a threat but as a source of energy and liveliness. They offer considered reflection to the issues and turns of event at the present moment.[19]

---

[18] *Institutes*, 3.2.7, p. 551.

[19] The 9/11/2001 terrorist attack on the World Trade Center in New York provides a good example to showcase confessional and non-confessional dynamics at work. The catch phrase "God is in control" comforted many Christians at the time. The phrase, however, says both too much and too little. If God is really in control, why did this terrible event happen in the first place? At the time some Christians said God was punishing America for its sins. Others said God was permissively letting it happen for the sake of enabling human freedom. Neither explanation is satisfying.

A confessional church asks for more than a catch phrase. The question is not whether God is in control, but what was God actively doing in the midst of this evil? Only Jesus Christ on the cross can help us with this question. Jesus on the cross is where God's love and power

American Presbyterians moved in a confessional direction when they created and adopted *The Confession of 1967*.[20] By all accounts, 1967-68 was a watershed moment for American Church and culture, and the insights of *C67* have worn well. That church also adopted a book of confessions coming from different times. The collection highlighted the value and benefit of the confessions without tying them to uniformity of belief.

Since then, it must be said, the Presbyterians have slid back into old habits. Their reunion of 1983 produced *A Brief Statement of Faith* (adopted 1996), which reads more like a uniform agenda than an earnest confession of faith, and it breaks no fresh ground. When serious polarization emerged in the 1990s, the General Assembly authorized the Peace Unity and Purity Task Force, which met 2000-2006. The Task Force modeled for everyone how a confessional church can be open, lively, and nimble. Likewise, the General Assembly authorized a small, interim statement, *Hope in the Lord Jesus Christ* (2001-2002), which passed the Assembly overwhelmingly, showing how different confessions point to authentic unity beyond the demands for uniformity.[21]

---

come together without one canceling out the other. That is, God remains at work in places where we least expect to find God. Without fail—and without ever justifying what is simply awful—God powerfully brings life, love, and goodness out of death, evil, and destruction. That is what God does on the cross of Jesus and in the moments of our greatest pain or distress.

[20] The adopting church was the United Presbyterian Church (USA), a merger of the former PCUSA and UPONA in 1958. When this body merged with the PCUS in 1983, completing the post-Civil War reunion of Presbyterians, both *C67* and the *Book of Confessions* carried over into the newly formed Presbyterian Church (U.S.A.).

[21] The statement draws on the Scriptures and *The PCUSA Book of Confessions*. and confesses plainly the heart of the Gospel:

> Jesus Christ is the only Savior and Lord, and all people everywhere are called to place their faith, hope, and love in him. ... *[cont'd]*

Alas, these several activities were overshadowed by the church dispute over the role of gays and lesbians (see Sidebar 18.3).[22] When the far right and the far left both demanded uniformity in their competing policies, the center could not hold the two sides together. In 2011, the PC(USA) split again,[23] perhaps to be reunited later, in God's time.

So, *is the Gospel itself at risk in America today?* I offer the following observations, to answer with a resounding *"Yes!"*:

- The prevailing paradigm, Modernism-Pietism, has left us with truth claims and a demand for uniformity that are neither workable nor sustainable as a Church today.
- Christians today are unsure of who Christ is, what if anything God is doing, what connection Christ has to life all around us, and where authenticity and community are to be found in the context of Christian faith.
- The secularism of culture—at least partly of the modern Church's own making—demands honesty, simplicity, and clarity for Christian faith, but completely changes the Church's self-understanding and role in such a culture.
- Living in a rapidly expanding, advanced technological society, complicated by worldwide climate change, presents specific, unexplored challenges to Christian faith and life.
- The Christian Church today is polarized within itself to the point of paralysis, and ways of being Christian in the Modernist-Pietist paradigm no longer work well.

In the providence of God, all indications point to the Gospel at risk in America at the present moment.

No one is saved apart from God's gracious redemption in Jesus Christ. (*Hope*, lines 155, 160f).

[22] The church's polarization also overshadowed efforts in 2006-2011 to revise the 1983 *PC(USA) Book of Order*. The revision strengthens the confessional basis of Presbyterian church govenance but also leaves in place a form of majority rule that stresses uniformity, so the *Book of Order* functions more as a manual of operations than a constitution.

[23] The Evangelical Covenant Order of Presbyterians formed in that year.

What would a confession of faith look like today? A confession can take many forms but most urgently will place Jesus Christ at the center of our reality today. Christianity without Christ is nothing but jibberish. On the other hand, any or all of the following affirmations stand out:

i. If indeed, as Christ says (Matt 28:18), *All power in heaven and earth has been given to me;*[AT] then no power lies beyond Christ's reach, and these earthly powers measure themselves by how they serve those who have no power, namly, *the least among us* (Matt 25:40,45).

ii. If indeed, as Christ says (Matt 28:20), *I am with you all the days until the end of time;*[AT] then we are in the presence of Christ at every moment, and *nothing ... shall separate us from the love of God in Christ Jesus our Lord* [AT] (Rom 8:39).

iii. If indeed, *God was in Christ reconciling the world to himself*[AT] (II Cor 5:19), then Christ mediates not only between God and us, but also between us and every human we meet, and between a sinful humanity and a creation upset by massive climate change.

- *In Christ* our mediator—*the way, and the truth, and the life* (John 14:6)—we participate in what the crucified and risen Christ is actively doing among us here and now.
- *In Christ* our mediator we find our unity no matter how diverse we are, our reconciliation no matter how deep our divisions, our strength and courage no matter how great the obstacles against us, our endurance no matter how much our shortfall or our suffering.
- *In Christ* our mediator we find our hope no matter what the future may bring.

iv. If indeed, God's forgiving love alone brings us to the truth of God in whom *we live and move and are*[AT] (Acts 17:28); we will find ourselves *in Christ* by God's grace, we will know the truth while doing the truth, and *the truth shall make you free*[AT] (John 8:32, with 8:31 and 3:21).

v. When indeed by God's grace we *abide in [Christ's] love* (John 15:10), we will find ourselves daily in the covenant space, where God abides with us and we with God and others, and where indeed *without [Christ] [we] can accomplish nothing [fruitful]* ᴬᵀ (John 15:5).

vi. When indeed we are *in Christ*, we meet and celebrate the image of God restored on the face of every person we meet (Gen 1:26-27), whether they are Christian or not.

vii. When indeed Christ is *before all things, and in him all things hold together*ᴬᵀ (Col 1:17), we respect all people, value truth wherever we find it, seek excellence in all things, and praise God every moment of every day.

viii. In sum, following the Biblical promises of God's covenant with David (God: *I will be a father to [your son], and he shall be a son to me,*ᴬᵀ 2 Sam 7:14), we confess for our time what Christians—*the great cloud of witnesses* (Heb 12:1)—have believed for all time, that

◊ Jesus Christ is the Son of God (John 1:14, 18; 20:31),

◊ Jesus Christ is Lord of all even as Servant of all (Phil 2:11),

◊ Jesus Christ is God as a human being (Matt 1:23, John 20:28), hence we *baptize into the name of the Father, and of the Son, and of the Holy Spirit* ᴬᵀ (Matt 28:19).

Each of these affirmations locates Christ at the center of life as we face it today, sometimes in extreme situations. That is where we will find points of universality for the Gospel in our time. That is where a new Reformation will begin, in God's time. That is where a confession of faith needs to take us. Maybe the most fitting way to end this essay is in such a place as this, playing with the building blocks of a living confession of faith.

ESSAY 14

ARE WE PARTICIPANTS IN OR INSTRUMENTS OF GOD'S MISSION?

This question poses a watershed issue in the Christian Church for our time. Does the Church's appointed life and work of Christian mission center on human participation in and with what God is doing—*missio DEI*—or does Christian mission focus on what humans do as the instruments in and through whom God is acting—*MISSIO dei*? The first position lies closer to Scripture and to the streams flowing from the Early Church and the Protestant Reformation. The prevailing Church culture today, however, presses an instrumentalist language and approach to mission.

Raising and clarifying this issue bears directly on the divisions now within the larger Christian Church, as in particular churches and denominations. This essay considers

(1) the origin of mission in the Modernist-Pietist era,
(2) the instrumentalist approach to mission and its problems,
(3) the Biblical-historical accent on participation in God's mission,
(4) why the two cannot be easily combined.

1. The Origin of Mission in the Modernist-Pietist Era.

Mission is the watchword of most American churches today. That's a good thing. Out of sincere love and committed devotion to Jesus Christ, faithful Christians engage in a whole range of creative efforts. The classic statement of "Six Great Ends of the Church" traces the Church's mission from "the proclamation of the gospel for the salvation of humankind" (evangelism) to "the promotion of social righteousness" (social justice).[1] The American Presbyterian *Confession of 1967* adds,

> God's reconciling work in Jesus Christ and the mission of reconciliation to which he has called his church are the heart of the gospel in any age.[2]

Mission is a distinctly modern idea for the entire Christian movement. Fully engaged in spreading the good news of the Gospel, the Early Church (33–600 CE), does not mention mission by name. Instead the *Apostles* and *Nicene* creeds define the core truth of the Gospel in terms of Trinitarian language. When the early Christians refer to "apostolicity" as a mark of the true Church, they are concerned with how faithfully the Church's message followed that of the New Testament apostles, *i.e.*, the chain of authority.

The Protestant reformers, 1500–1650 CE, also do not talk about mission as such.[3] They were fully engaged in reforming the Church they inherited from the previous era. The Reformation confessions deal with the five *solas* of the Reformation:
- Christ alone,
- Scripture alone,
- Faith alone,
- Grace alone, and
- The true Church (but not as mission).

---

[1] The other four "Ends" are the
- "shelter, nurture, and spiritual fellowship of the children of God;
- maintenance of divine worship;
- preservation of the truth; and
- exhibition of the Kingdom of Heaven to the world."

These "Ends" were first set forth in 1910 by the United Presbyterian Church of North America. Quoted from *Presbyterian Church (USA) 2011/2013 Book of Order*, F-1.0304; in previous years G-1.0200.

[2] *PC(USA) Book of Confessions*, 9.06.

[3] See the all-Reformation Lutheran *Book of Concord* (1577) and the *PC(USA) Book of Confessions* (mostly from the Reformation era).

Of course, all eras of the Church saw outreach efforts for the spread of the Gospel, including the Middle Ages. Not until the Modernist-Pietist era, 1650-2000, does mission take center stage and appear as such in Church confessions.[4] Even here mission is typically put into the larger framework of the triune God, and mission engages in what God is doing among us. This development occurs among Protestants in all its denominational streams during this era.

America Presbyterians offer a case study. For their first 200 years they fought, divided, and reunited over issues of mission *vis à vis* accents they brought over from Europe.
- Should Presbyterians focus on mission-evangelism or on espousing correct doctrine (New Side vs. Old Side, 1741-1758)?
- Should Presbyterians focus on mission-expansion or on building up established churches (Cumberland vs. PCUSA, 1810-1906; New School vs. Old School, 1837-1864/69)?

Mission won each of those disputes over time. These disputes helped position the vigorously mission-oriented Methodist and Baptist movements in America during the 18th-20th centuries, when mission has permeated all denominations.

For the last 100 years or more, the issue has become defining mission more closely. Is mission

saving souls/evangelism/foreign missions?

or

social Gospel/social action/justice/local missions?

Along with the Six Great Ends of the Church, Presbyterians over the last century generally agree that mis-

---

[4] David J. Bosch talks about "The Pietist Breakthrough" in his important book, *Transforming Mission: Paradigm Shifts in Theology of Mission* (Maryknoll, NY: Orbis, 1991), 252-255. Mission appears in a Reformed-Presbyterian confession first in the 1903 chapter additions to *The Westminster Confession of Faith*, then regularly in *The Confession of 1967*, *The Belhar Confession* (1986), and *A Brief Statement of Faith* (1996).

sion-evangelism and mission-social action are vital companions, and we cannot have one without the other. The agreement has not kept partisans from taking sides and causing splits: in the 1930s (Orthodox Presbyterian Church), in the 1970s (Presbyterian Church in America), in the 1980s (Evangelical Presbyterian Church), and again in the 2010s (Evangelical Covenant Order of Presbyterians). These divisions seem to have no end in sight.

With the accent on mission came the related concerns for usefulness or effectiveness. While the instrumentalist approach has historical antecedents,[5] it is distinctive to the Modernist-Pietist era. Note well: mission-evangelism and mission-social action share an instrumentalist approach to the Church and to the Christian faith.

2. The Instrumentalist Approach to Mission, and Its Problems.

Modernism and Pietism form two lines of historical development that merged in the 18th Century. The religious line, Pietism, probes the experience of God in the hearts of Christian individuals as they engage in various relationships with God, other people, and nature.

The secular line, Modernism, embraces the Enlightenment ideal of a self-sufficient, rational humanity. The great interest in nature led to dramatic developments in science, technology, and useful ways to meet human needs. At the same time, an increasing awareness of history with all its particularities focused on the individual, the individual's social

---

[5] Important antecedents are the Arian position at the Council of Nicaea in 325 and the priestly role of the Church and its Sacraments during the Middle Ages, 600-1350. In 1534, reacting to the Protestant Reformation, Ignatius of Loyola (†1556) founded the Society of Jesus and initiated an instrumentalist approach to mission that heavily influenced Protestant thinking and practice from the 17th Century onwards.

context, the human experience of things around us, and the changes that take place over time. That in turn opened up new, expansive, and distinctively Western political and economic institutions.

The Pietist line is usually underestimated in this mix, though the overlap between Pietism and Modernism is perhaps clear from what has been said already. Both were reacting to the rigid, hierarchical, essentially timeless, dogmatic systems of church and society they inherited from the 17th Century. But the people who shaped the Modernist agenda and its critical categories in fact came from strong Pietist backgrounds, including, notably, Immanuel Kant, G.W.F. Hegel, Jean-Jacques Rousseau, and perhaps Adam Smith.[6] The Pietist allowance for manifesting God's holiness and goodness—as in John Wesley's "entire sanctification"—made the perfectibility of the human compelling also for Modernism.

Sharing the Pietist concern for the inner self, Western culture had to work out anew how the inner self (subjective) relates to the outer self (objective) of nature. The task reached into every area of human endeavor—
- human capabilities *vs.* natural and historical necessity,
- feeling and experience *vs.* thinking with doctrinal ideas,
- workers *vs.* industrial machines,
- family relations *vs.* an industrial economic system,
- the individual person *vs.* the group, organization, and rules.

The driving questions of Pietism were and still are, "Who is and who is not saved, and by what means?" The lead questions are personal. The impersonal, instrumentalist part comes last but is indispensable to the outcomes. For Pietism, the primary instrumental means of salvation—Jesus Christ—extends to the believer. As Christ embodied

---

[6] See my essay, "The Three-Legged Stool: Pietism and Post-Modern Theology," *Theology Between East and West* (Wipf-Stock, 2002), 317-340.

God, so believers are to embody Christ (or the Spirit) in their hearts and practice their faith in all their relationships. Now as God's instruments—God in them working through them—they are to save souls for eternal life, bring in the kingdom of God, and meet human needs.

To its credit, the instrumentalist call to mission appeals to excellence, high energy, and commitment—even perfection—matching God's. The calling is to do God's work on God's behalf. If God is embodied in these believers, the response of other people to believers must be their response to God as well. Embodying God in mission takes the form of:
- willing evangelists,
- true missionaries,
- social change agents,
- bearers of God's love to a sin-sick world,
- a redeemed and redeeming community, and
- a demonstration of what God intends for all people.

The embodiment of God in the inner self, however, raises some urgent questions about the instrumentalist—and Pietist—approach to mission. The following questions stand out:

a. With God embodied in us working through us, can we so express God's love or grace to other people that it actually saves their souls, redeems them from their sins, or brings in God's kingdom? Can we control when the love or grace of God flows through us and when it cannot?

b. If we really do God's work for God, do we risk replacing God in the process or at least confusing *ourselves as instruments* with *God* who is coming through us?

c. Is there any room for sin in the instrument? If God is in us working through us, how can we sin? If we do sin, what becomes of us and of God's mission through us? Does God fail if we fail?

d. Does the mission of the Church—God in us working through us to transform the World—put Christians in the untenable, even imperialist stance of striving to rule the World on behalf of God? With this kind of thinking the missionary movement allied itself closely with Western colonialism during the 19th and 20th centuries.
e. Is the aim of being Christian, with God embodied in us, to make humans good, right, and successful? If so, how much is enough—of faith, of works, of goodness? Can such a view avoid works righteousness, even self-righteousness, when we compare our faith and good works to those around us?

Too much of contemporary Church life, conservative or liberal, Presbyterian or other, reflects the dynamics of these questions in their most troublesome aspects.

3. The Biblical-Historical Accent on Participation in God's Mission.

Participation in God's mission begins with the Great Commission (Matt 28:18-20). At the start Jesus says:

(18) *All power [or authority–exousia] in heaven and on earth has been given to me [Jesus].*[AT]

At the end Jesus says:

(20b) *Lo, I [Jesus] am with you always, to the end of time.*[AT]

Sandwiched between these two verses is the following:

(19-20a) *Going therefore, disciple all the nations, baptizing them into the name of the father and of the son and of the holy spirit, teaching them to be keeping everything I have commanded you.*[AT]

The commission here not only tells us what we are to do but more importantly what Christ is doing. Jesus Christ is the primary actor here, the one who exercises the power and authority, the one who is present at all times. Jesus is also doing what he calls us to do. When we actually do what Jesus calls for, we commune with Christ while he is doing the same things.

We do not thus act on behalf of Christ or in a delayed response to him. We act simultaneously with Jesus Christ, in fellowship with him, going to the nations, pursuing discipleship in all of life, baptizing into the name of the triune God, and teaching others to do what Christ is doing. The intense closeness with Christ makes everything we do, say, think, feel, and choose more important, not less, because we are acting in the presence of Christ at the moment.

Stirred by the Spirit, our faith drives us to understand every moment, situation, relationship, and activity in relation to God.[7] Also brought to life by the Spirit, the Bible presents patterns of discernment that point to Jesus Christ, without whom there is no participation in God.

Foremost among these patterns of discernment is the Trinity. As the Bible portrays it, the Father is all-powerful ("almighty"), the Son is all-weakness (the story of a vulnerable human birth, life, suffering, death, and resurrection), and the Spirit is the unity of the two together. But, the three are inseparable: no Father without Son, no Son without Father, and the Spirit as the bond between them. Together therefore, they make the lowly, vulnerable Jesus Christ (Son of God) the touchstone of God's power, a *power [that] is made perfect in weakness* (2 Cor 12:9).

By God's action, then, the first shall be last and the last first, the servant of all will be the greatest of all, and the cross will be foolishness to some and a stumbling block to others. By God's action the measure of all power—economic, political, military, personal—will be the way real power serves those who have none. The Bible speaks plainly of:

---

[7] Faith seeking understanding, from Augustine, Anselm, Luther, Calvin, Schleiermacher, Barth, the Niebuhrs, and Moltmann.

- Jesus' identity with the least among us,
- The reversal of values (proud and humble, rich and poor, strong and weak, sated and needy),
- God's hospitality to the stranger and the lowly,
- God's justice as saving mercy to the sinner,
- God's kingdom as a new creation in Christ,
- God's providential care for all creatures and creation,
- God's commandments pointing to who God is and what God is doing (hence occasions for communing with God), and
- God's Word defining every moment in terms of God.

Jürgen Moltmann captures this Biblical sense of God's constant presence and activity in his discussion of the three persons of the Trinity interacting among themselves:[8]

- sending (as in mission: the Father as the sender, the Son as the one sent, the Spirit as the sending itself),
- suffering love (as in forgiveness: the Father who suffers the loss of the Son, the Son as the one who suffers being lost, the Spirit as the suffering itself), and
- glorifying (as in God's aim: the Father as glorifier, the Son as the one glorified, the Spirit as the glory itself).

From the Trinity, then, we get a remarkable picture of the missio DEI. With a profound sense of God at work in the ordinary events and concrete relationships of human life, *we participate with God here and now.* Enlivened by God's own Spirit, we are driven to seek God at every turn.

Participating this way in God's mission leaves God free to be God and humans free to be human. God alone creates and provides for every moment of our lives—past, present, and future. We don't have to. God alone in Christ alone recreates our humanity in the image of God. We don't have to. Fellowship with God does not require us to be

---

[8] See Jürgen Moltmann, *The Trinity and the Kingdom* (London: SCM Press, 1981; Minneapolis: Fortress Press, 1993).

semi-divine or perfect humans apart from Christ. God acts more often in spite of us than because of us. Yet *in Christ* by God's own action, we participate in a constant, running, communion with God. To live thus with God is an end in itself, with no higher goal than to glorify and enjoy God forever.

Our communion with God hinges on God's grace and its gift character. Yet the joy of walking with God draws Christians into a vigorous style of living. By all accounts, the accent on grace among early Lutherans and Calvinists fostered a strikingly dynamic cultural, ethical, and even missionary vigor.[9] Convinced that they were in God's hands at all times, many found the vision, strength, and courage to stand up for the truth when it was at risk; to explore hitherto unknown lands across the oceans; to engage new horizons in science, politics, commerce, learning, and outer space; or to stand up to evil in its modern forms.[10]

4. Why the Two Cannot Be Easily Combined.

Why not just combine the instrumentalist and participatory approaches to mission and get the best of both worlds? That is the most-asked question I get on this topic.

---

[9] Adolf Harnack brings out the revolutionary dimensions of Luther's reform movement centered in grace, in *What Is Christianity?* (New York: Harper Torchbooks, 1957. Original, 1900), 268-281. For early Calvinism, see Ernst Troeltsch, *The Social Teaching of the Christian Churches*, (George Allen & Unwin, 1931); Max Weber, *The Protestant Ethic and the Rise of Capitalism*; (Allen & Unwin, 1930); and Michael Walzer, *The Revolution of the Saints* (Harvard Univ Press, 1965). According to Lutheran Roland Bainton, early Calvinism bred "a race of heroes," in *The Reformation of the Sixteenth Century* (Boston: Beacon Press, 1952), 117.

[10] Modern day examples include Dietrich Bonhoeffer and the courageous members of the Confessing Church from 1933-45.

The two do converge at a certain point. Instruments participating in God's mission surely commune with God. God surely uses participants as instruments of mission. The dynamics of the two, however, differ greatly, and it is not obvious that we can get to the middle from both directions.

The participatory approach strives diligently to discern and engage God's redeeming love and operations wherever they happen all around us. The aim of participation is a shared life, which we embrace eagerly once we have tasted it. When authentic participation does take place, however, it comes as a gift, a specific act of God's grace.

The instrumentalist approach, on the other hand, binds us to our intention to be divinely useful and effective. To do that, we have to empty ourselves of any self-claims, so that what comes through is God alone. Good intentions will not suffice, however, nor will strenuous effort by itself. In truth, we cannot attain full instrumentality any more than we can attain humility. Any sin or incompleteness in the instrument poses an insurmountable barrier, for, sinners that we are, our own efforts to overcome our sin only compound it into a self-righteousness that no longer relies upon God. Being an instrument of God is finally up to God, not to us. So, if we claim to be instruments of God, we probably are not.

When the New Testament speaks of our instrumentality, it grounds whatever we do in what God is doing at that moment. Ephesians 2:8-10 begins with grace and ends:
for we are [God's] workmanship, created in Christ Jesus for good works, which God prepared beforehand that in them we walk[AT 11]

---

[11] *In them* is a statement of location; *walk* is subjunctive (hence *would* or *might walk*) but the sense is not imperative (*should walk*, RSV and KJV) or permissive (*may walk*). NIV and NRSV mistranslate the phrase as setting up a way of life for us to accomplish.

John 3:1-21 ends the same way:

The one doing the truth comes to the light that his/her deeds might manifest that they are wrought in God.^{AT 12}

When Jesus sends out the disciples to act on his behalf (Matt 10; Mark 6:7-13, 30; Luke 9:2-6, 10:1-24), he always grounds their activities in God, whether in Jesus' own power (Luke 9:1), the Spirit (Matt 10:20),[13] or Jesus' name, (Luke 10:17)—just like the Great Commission. These passages all end with Jesus feeding the five thousand or walking on water ... and the disciples participating therein.

Paul also talks about the matter directly. Speaking of the cross, he says,

Since, in the wisdom of God, the world did not know God through wisdom, it pleased God through the folly of what we preach to save those who believe. (1 Cor 1:21, RSV)

The cross is folly to some and a stumbling block to others (1:24). At best, then, the effectiveness of our words to produce faith does not rest in our wisdom, eloquence, or charisma as instruments, but solely in God's power (1 Cor 2:5).

The passage 2 Corinthians 5:18-20a seems to carry a mantra of instrumentalism, God in us working through us:

18 All these things [are] from God having reconciled us to himself through Christ and having given us the service of reconciliation; 19 that is, God was in Christ reconciling the world to himself, not counting their trespasses against them and having placed among us the word of reconciliation. 20 On behalf of Christ, therefore, we are spokespersons as of God making his appeal through us.^{AT}

Let me elaborate this passage at several points, to show how it does not rule out and may in fact prefer a focus on participation:

---

[12] Verse 21, which corresponds with verse 8: *The wind blows where it wills and you hear the sound of it but do not know from whence it comes or where it is going; so is every on born from the Spirit.*^{AT}

[13] Greek: "in you" (KJV), not "through you" (RSV, NRSV, NIV).

i. In the verses before and after this passage Paul highlights *us in Christ* instead of *Christ in us*:
   5:17 *Whoever is in Christ [is] a new creation.*^AT
   5:21 God *made him to be sin who knew no sin, so that we might become the righteousness of God in him.*^AT
ii. The passage says twice that the reconciliation of sinners takes place through Christ (18-19), not through us. So *the service [diakonia] of reconciliation* (18) and *the word [logon] of reconciliation* (19) are both rooted in Christ as a participation in his death and resurrection (14-15).
iii. The phrase, *God was in Christ reconciling the world to himself* (5:19a), lends itself to a participatory as easily as an instrumentalist sense. Here, as for Paul generally, *in Christ* readily refers to the place where we participate in God's covenant, as 5:17 and 21 say. In that case, we are participants in *Christ's* instrumentality above all (*God making his appeal through us*, 20).
iv. For Paul here and elsewhere, *us in Christ* is the basis of *Christ in us*, not the other way around. Let the reader compare these two phrases anywhere in Paul! A merely instrumentalist reading typically ignores the difference and collapses the first phrase *us in Christ* into the second phrase *Christ in us*.

The participatory and instrumentalist approaches to life with God do converge in the Bible. Both approaches depend upon God. Where they diverge is when we become intentional about doing them. *As participants*, recognizing our sinfulness, we can only rely on the reality of God with us—*in Christ*—to make itself known at the moment, and we participate in that reality by God's grace alone.

As instruments, we focus on what we bring to situations, with our God-given talents and opportunities. For that reason, the instrumentalist accent falls on what we can accomplish for God and on generating the energy to do it.

But to be an authentic instrument requires that we humble ourselves so that what comes through us is nothing but God. As sinful human beings, we cannot do that out of ourselves. On the other hand, when God does humble us and draw us into what God is doing—often in spite of ourselves—we are first and foremost participants in God's on-going, active life.

On solid ground, the deep accents of the Reformation point to mission as participation in the sovereign activity of the triune God, *missio DEI*. The time has come to reconfigure our current language about mission.[14] Maybe this is a way out of our current divisions. Maybe *in Christ* the Spirit will free us to embrace with joy and eager anticipation where God is taking us—all together—into the future.

Postscript: The issues raised in this essay are front and center in the flagship book of my dear colleague, Darrell L. Guder, *The Continuing Conversion of the Church* (Wm. B. Eerdmans, 2000). Guder locates the *missio Dei* in the Trinity, which bears witness to God as the principal actor in mission. When the Church "translates" the Gospel into each culture where it resides, the Church risks confusing the Gospel with the forms of culture that embody it. The Church today, he says, needs to free itself from its inherited captivity to the institutional forms of "Christendom" and recover both its message and its mission to a modern, secular society. I find much of Guder's analysis insightful. When he yields to an "incarnational ministry" for the Church, however, he does not avoid the dilemmas of an instrumentalist approach to mission and the urgent questions posed by the unresolved difficulties of Modernism-Pietism.

---

[14] The revision of the PC(USA) *2011-2013 Book of Order* actually makes this move in the opening section of F-1.01, "Of God's Mission," albeit with lingering vestiges of instrumentalism.

ESSAY 15

CHURCH AND WORLD

Church-and-World sets up the primary language for the Church's mission in the Christian Church today. The Church calls people out of the world to be reconciled or saved, then sends them back into the world, whether for mission-evangelism or mission-social action or both (see Sidebar 11.3). The language and theology belong to the era of Modernism-Pietism (1650-2000), which by all accounts is now giving way to another paradigm. This essay explores:
(1) What Pietism contributes to the Modernist-Pietist era,
(2) How the separation of Church and World has reached its limits today, and
(3) Modern efforts to overcome the separation of Church and World and move beyond Modernism-Pietism.

1. What Pietism Contributes to the Modernist-Pietist Era.

The word pair, Church-and-World sets forth the Pietist concern for personal salvation from sin through Jesus Christ. The Church is the place where people saved from sin reside, says Pietism, and the World is where sinners reside—unsaved-but-potentially-saved. The mission of the Church is to rescue sinners from the World, so they too can belong to the ranks of the saved. As a community of saved people, the Pietist Church is to reflect in its own life the same transformation to goodness it seeks to impart to the World.

More particularly, Pietism focuses on the inner self and the experience of the self in its relationships with God, with other people, and with nature. To be saved, or reconciled, is to get those relationships right, both individually and collectively. For Pietism, the means by which all this takes place is Christ dwelling in the heart by faith, an incarnation of Christ in the believer.

The Reformed theologian Friedrich Schleiermacher (1768-1834) is a watershed figure here. He transposed the Reformation and Orthodox theology of earlier centuries into the categories of Pietism. The Christian faith, he says, is "the feeling of absolute dependence."[1] This feeling is more basic than doctrine (thinking) or ethics (doing) but infuses both of these and makes them authentically Christian. The feeling cannot be self-generated without losing its absolute dependence upon God, from whom it comes as a gift. Such a feeling is less an emotion than a relationship with an orientation to God. In Jesus Christ the "feeling of absolute dependence" becomes available to humankind. The society of Christians, or Church, exists to share Jesus' "God-consciousness" among themselves. Schleiermacher was above all a churchman: he preached weekly for 40 years, even while he lectured on theology.

Other figures helped usher in and foster the era of Pietism. The eminent Lutheran Pastor Phillip Jakob Spener (†1705) initiated the movement in Europe with his pamphlet, *Pious Yearnings* (1675).[2] Following in his footsteps, Count Nicolaus Zinzindorf (†1760) started a community of the pious (*Herrnhütern*) in 1722, which spawned other communitarian movements. These included the Moravians in Germany (which deeply influenced Wesley and Schleiermacher) and extensive social experiments in America, notably, the Shaker, Oneida, Amana, Fourier, and Mormon communities.

Pastor-theologian Jonathan Edwards (†1758) and the

---

[1] See Friedrich Schleiermacher, *The Christian Faith*, German in 1830, English in 1928 (Edinburgh: T & T Clark, 1928), 12-18.

[2] *Reclaiming Pietism*, by Roger Olson and Christian Collins Winn (Wm. B. Eerdmans, 2015), gives a succinct overview of Pietism at its origins.

great preacher John Whitefield (†1770) used revival meetings to stir up a Great Awakening in the American colonies, in 1740 and after. They marked a tradition of revivalism that included John Wesley (†1791) in England, Ebeneezer Erskine (†1754) and his brother Ralph in Scotland, and a string of Americans throughout the 19th and 20th centuries. The remarkable blending of American church and culture can be well understood in terms of a cycle of mass Awakenings,[3] down to and including the great Billy Graham (†2018).

In the 19th-20th centuries Pietism focused more on
- the individual, the inner self of each person,
- experience, with emotional revivals, and
- an emphasis on free will.

Overall, Pietism is one of the most successful eras of the Christian Church. In percentage and raw numbers the 19th century saw the greatest expansion of Christianity since the first century.[4] The Pietist transformation has pervaded modern, Western culture ever since.

Within the Pietist ethos, new fields arose to explore the inner self, notably psychology and psychiatry. Focusing on the inner self and its relationships elevated individual rights and capabilities. Pietism brought out a consciousness of history with inherent relational concerns for situational context in time and community dynamics (sociology). Relational patterns of thinking spilled over into:
- macro-economics and modern "capitalism,"
- Einstein's theory of relativity, which enabled the atomic bomb and nuclear energy,

---

[3] See the important book, *Revivals, Awakenings, and Reform: An Essay on Religion and Social Change in America, 1607-1977*, by William G. McLoughlin (University of Chicago Press, 1978). McLoughlin identifies four awakenings, including one in progress as of 1978.

[4] See Kenneth Scott Latourette, *A History of the Expansion of Christianity*, 7 volumes (New York: Harper & Bros., 1945).

- field theories of quantum physics, the basis of advanced technology, and
- the inter-connectedness of everything, embracing personal relationships, social systems, international affairs, and the far reaches of the universe.

For its part, the Pietist churches modeled the utilitarian concern for all things useful, effective, and efficient in their functional role of carrying out God's mission to the World. We are listening to a Pietistic mind set when we hear the constant, pop-cultural advice to "follow your heart" or "let your conscience be your guide" or "go with your gut"—in novels, sitcoms, dramas, movies, and self-help books.

In his book, *Christ and Culture*,[5] H. Richard Niebuhr brilliantly describes five different ways Christians historically have worked out the impact of the Gospel upon culture, *i.e.*, the relation between Church and World, in the era of Modernism-Pietism:

- *Christ-above-culture* (Roman Catholic), comes from the Medieval and Reformation eras;
- *Christ-and-culture-in-paradox* (Lutheran), comes from the Reformation era;
- *Christ-transforming-culture* (Reformed-Calvinist) also comes from the Reformation era;
- *Christ-and-culture* (accommodationist, liberal); and
- *Christ-against-culture* (anti-cultural, conservative).

The last two are distinctive to the Modernist-Pietist era. For himself, Niebuhr prefers *Christ-transforming-culture*, but he shows how each approach has made a significant contribution to the modern era. All these options have gone through a Pietist phase. Pietism's accent on personal transformation has clearly been the engine for the entire Modernist-Pietist era, in both Church and culture.

---

[5] Harper and Brothers, 1951.

2. The Separation of Church and World Has Reached its Limits.

The very success of Christian Pietism, however, jeopardizes its future from within. The distinction between Church and World suggests a certain dualism, each term defining itself by its opposition to the other. If Church is the saved people of God, then the World is, simply, people who are unsaved. Beyond this primary difference, however, the lines begin to blur. Outside of and other than the Church, what is the World, really? The societal, historical, cultural milieu that always surrounds the Church? The realm of evil, which is unregulated and at odds with God? The created universe? But isn't the Church also part of the World in all these ways? Indeed, is everyone in the Church saved and everyone in the World unsaved? With the success of Pietism, such questions press upon us more urgently.

As the era has gone by, the distinction between Church and World has become drawn more sharply. In some circles, the Church is the place of God, a foretaste of heaven, and/or a provisional demonstration of what God intends for all humanity. The World by contrast is the place of evil, injustice, constant temptations, and repeated falls from grace.

Focusing on salvation and the transformation of sinners, the Church under Pietism has increasingly distanced itself from salvation's sister theme, creation. Creation is now widely regarded as a neutral ground for the battle between saints and sinners, God and the Devil. The message of late Pietism often presents itself
- as an escape from the harsh realities of life,
- as a place of feeling instead of thinking,
- as a realm of private opinion that can disregard the hard facts of natural science, and/or
- as a concern for one's future destiny while disregarding the present.

Most risky of all, the late Pietist distinction between Church and World may actually point to a place where God is not sovereign and Christ is not Lord. The World in that sense is the very definition of the secular.

Notice that the increasing secularism of the Christian West comes from within Pietism. For over 350 years Pietism has given status to the very thing it has named and opposed as its enemy. As a place separate from God, from the perspective of prevailing Pietism, the World has no binding connection to God unless Christians and the Christian Church make it happen. So, under Pietism in its late stages: joining Church and World together comes down to human effort. For Christians living in a secular world which they have helped create, the situation has become a crisis of relevance, mission strategy, and energy for the Church.

The vigor and impact of the Church during the era of Modernism-Pietism are undeniable. The Church has taken seriously the task of bridging the gap between Church and World. Earlier in the era Christians understood mission as our participation in what God does to save people, transform societies, and bring history to its God-appointed ends. In late Modernism-Pietism, however—including the latter half of the 20th Century—the weight shifted away from the mission of *God* over to the embodiment of God in the Church working through *human instruments* of mission to transform the World.

With the rising instrumentalist role of the Church under Pietism come large demands upon Christians. The saved of the Church become God's appointed means for transforming the World. As God's appointed instruments, good Christians are now held responsible for
- converting the unsaved,
- regulating society and culture, and
- bending nature to serve humankind.

The Church's expansion in fact coincides with 19th century imperialism, the Western World's drive to develop colonial empires and harness nature for human purposes. Acting out these impulses for itself has put the Church on the World's turf, playing the modern World's game.

In the meanwhile, the World—successfully defined over against the Pietist Church—has taken on a life of its own, now broadly rooted in nature taken as an objective, morally neutral, *i.e.*, sinless realm. With amazing scientific, medical, financial, military, and other technological accomplishments, the modern World has become truly interpersonal, international, and universal in its reach, power, and scale. Increasingly self-sufficient, the modern World no longer needs the Pietism that made it what it is. To use Bonhoeffer's language, the World has "come of age" and has no place for a "fixit god" to make up for human shortcomings.[6]

3. Efforts to Overcome the Separation of Church and World.

The Protestant Reformers of the 16th century had to overcome a similar separation between the sacred and the secular, and they can help us do the same today. The Reformers broke through this word-pair in two ways.

First, they said that the fall of humanity infected all creation with sin. The grip of sin is so strong that grace has to free creation itself from sin. In the saving work of Jesus Christ God both defeats death (and sin) and re-creates the universe (1 Cor 15). So, Martin Luther left the monastery, elevated marriage-and-secular-work to a Christian vocation, and proclaimed the Gospel to a sinful creation.

---

[6] See Dietrich Bonhoeffer's letters of 29 May, 8 June, and 16 July, 1044, in *Letters and Papers from Prison: Dietrich Bonhoeffer Works*, Volume 8, op cit., 404-408, 424-432, & 473-482. See also the "Outline for a Book" on 499-504.

Second, Jesus Christ alone is Lord over all creation, history, and life. For John Calvin, sinful humans united with Jesus Christ become disciples who seek and follow Christ in all of life. Energized by the Spirit, they hear Christ's voice while at worship, in Word and Sacrament, and they meet Christ providentially at every moment of every day.

Borrowing heavily from Luther and Calvin, 20th century theologians Karl Barth (†1968) and Dietrich Bonhoeffer (†1945) broke through the Pietist separation of Church and World. They did so in different but complementary ways.

God is God, says Barth (see Sidebar 15.1), different in kind from any creature. God transcends all that God has made, whether Church or World. Both Church and World stand closer to each other than either one stands to God. The sinfulness of the Church stands alongside the sinfulness of the World, and the Church discerns in God's creating and re-creating activity with the World the point of its own life (Sidebar 15.1a). But further (Sidebar 15.1b), Christ is our mediator, reconciling both Church and World to God vertically and reconciling them to each other horizontally. So, the Church's confession, *Jesus is Lord*, cannot be imperialistic, for the almighty power and forgiving love of God joins us to Jesus on the cross and to life in fellowship with the risen Christ.

Bonhoeffer pondered the question throughout his ministry: What is the concrete reality and command of God at any given moment? Bonhoeffer was certain that Jesus Christ is the reality of God with us (*Emmanuel*). *In Christ*, he says, we belong to God and one another. The Church hears the clear voice of Christ speaking at worship focused on Word and Sacraments and as a community of believers constantly priesting for one another.

> *Sidbar 15.1. Barth on Church and World.*
>
> *a. God as God is more different from both Church and World than Church and World are different from each other.*
>
>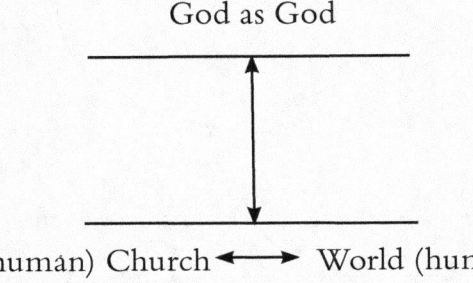
>
> *b. In Christ God reconciles and binds Church and World to each other as well as to Godself.*
>
>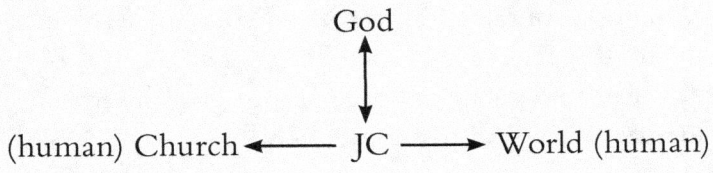

Consigned to a Nazi prison during World War II, Bonhoeffer found himself in the World, cut off in every way from the Christian community he cherished as much as life itself. His dire situation—hopelessly trapped in the bowels of a hellacious prison, in the middle of a war zone—forced him to ask further: Was he also cut off from Christ? Finding himself still *in Christ* even there, he could affirm Christ at the center of the World as much as Christ at the center of the Church (see Sidebar 15.2). He no longer needed a supernatural, "fixit" god

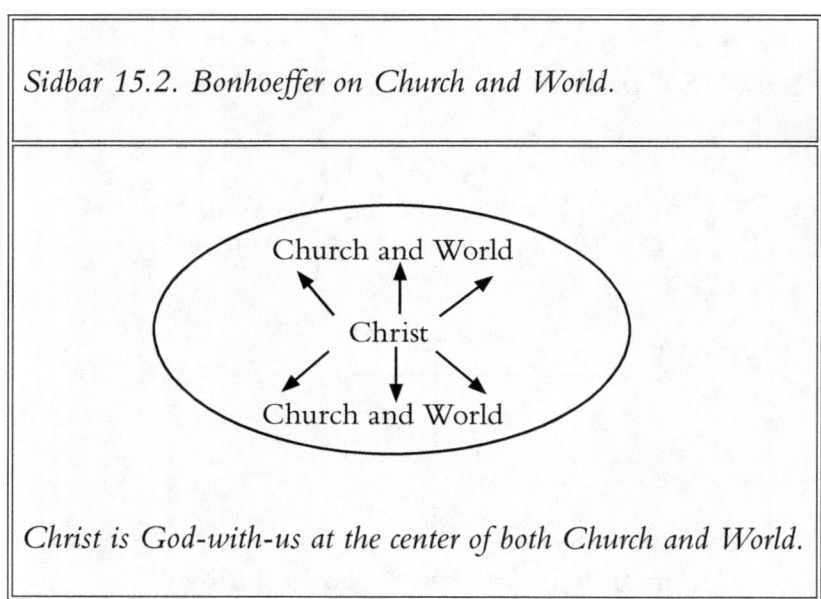

Sidbar 15.2. Bonhoeffer on Church and World.

Christ is God-with-us at the center of both Church and World.

to get him out of a jam. *In Christ,* God lovingly and powerfully reconciles the World as it is to God's self. *In Christ,* that is, God embraces the sinful, self-sufficient World in which we live and reconciles Church and World to each other as well as to the reality of God. So, *in Christ*—according to the report of his execution by hanging—Bonhoeffer walked confidently with God to the very end.

Church-and-World is one of the defining elements of modernity, indeed of the Modernist-Pietist era. As we have seen, the era has been one of the most successful in the history of Christianity, fostering a vigorous culture as well as a thriving religion. Curiously, both Church and World seem to have forgotten where they came from. The Christian faith has been and remains one of the creative engines of modern secular society. The World, however, has taken on a life of its own as a secular realm where relationships and instruments are measured by their usefulness without any reference to

God. And the Church, having painted itself into a corner by separating iself from the World in the first place, tends to adopt the World's language of usefulness for itself, in order to maintain its standing next to the World. As Darrell Guder and others have pointed out, we can scarcely tell the difference between the two any more.[7] The secular World is at risk of losing its soul, and the Church is at risk of losing its Way.

Today, however, the separation of Church and World has reached its limits, and with it the paradigm of Modernism-Pietism, 1650-2000 extending into the present. The dichotomy is collapsing of its own weight. This reality now affects all American Christian churches directly—right, left, or middle—and will simply by-pass anyone who ignores it.

Maybe the time has come for the whole Christian Church to reaffirm the simple Gospel centered in Jesus Christ, and restate the Church's mission accordingly. Christ indeed redefines all of life in terms of himself, World as well as Church, and reconciles the two together in him who is the reality of God with us.

---

[7] See *The Continuing Conversion of the Church* (Wm. B. Eerdmans, 2000), Part II, 71-141, where Guder discusses the challenge of "translation" in mission. When translated into the lives of real people, the Gospel becomes embodied in cultural formations and risks being reduced to cultural norms in the process. For Guder and his circle, Christians need to recover the Gospel—and Church—as it was before "Christendom" welded Christianity to culture under Constantine (318). As solid as Guder's analysis is in so many ways, it does not escape projecting a late Modernist-Pietist version of the Gospel back into the Early Church.

ESSAY 16

THE UNIVERSALITY OF THE GOSPEL

The Gospel is about truth, and truth is about God's faithfulness. That is the unwavering testimony of Scripture:

Hear, Israel, the Lord our God, the Lord is one. And you shall love the Lord your God with all your heart and with all you being and with all your might.[1] (Deut 6:4-5)

For the Lord is good; his steadfast love endures for ever, and his faithfulness to all generations. (Psalm 100:5, RSV)

The righteous shall live by my [God's] faithfulness.[AT] [2] (Hab 2:4)

Whence then comes wisdom? And where is the place of understanding? ... God understands the way to it, and he knows its place. (Job 28:20, 23, RSV)

And the Word became flesh and dwelt among us, full of grace and truth. (John 1:14, RSV)

God is spirit, and it is necessary for those worshipping him to worship in spirit and truth.[AT] (John 4:24)

The one doing the truth comes to the light, that it may be manifest his deeds are wrought in God.[AT] (John 3:21)

Let God be true, though every human be false.[AT] (Rom 3:4)

---

[1] Translation from Robert Alter, *The Five Books of Moses: A Translation with Commentary* (New York: W.W. Norton & Co., 2004), 912.

[2] Based on the *Septuagint* (285-247 BCE), the earliest translation of the Old Testament Hebrew into Greek, as used by the early Church. The superscript[AT] indicates the author's translation from Greek to English.

> *"I am the Alpha and the Omega," says the Lord God, who is and who was and who is to come, the Almighty.* (Rev 1:8, also 22:13, RSV)

The time and culture in which we live puts truth in the eye of the beholder, or, as it were, in the heart of the believer. The Modernist-Pietist emphasis on the inner self brings all assessment of truth down to the individual's view from within his/her personal history at the present moment.[3] We can expand our reach by talking with other people, cooperating with them, or reading their thoughts from different times. We can even buttress our truth claims by appealing to how widely others agree with us and we with them or how our truth gets support from experts and authorities in science or religion. But in late Modernism-Pietism truth comes down to what is true for me as an individual in isolation from all other individuals, to the point where truth is whatever I say it is.

These dynamics are on full display in contemporary American religion, culture, and politics. They make it easy to discount any truth we cannot verify for ourselves. So, we reject traditional concepts or sources of truth, insisting that they answer to us. We lose thereby our confidence in the truth of the Bible, the Christian Church, even God's Spirit.

Truth, however, by its very nature cannot be truth in isolation. Truth reaches across every divide, connects us with reality beyond ourselves, and wants to be shared. That is emphatically the case with Christian truth, which is rooted in God, centers in the person of Jesus Christ, and entails loving one another. Such truth will always be personal to "me," *i.e.*,

---

[3] The Spanish-American philosopher, George Santayana (1863-1952) calls this "the solipsism of the present moment." See *Scepticism and Animal Faith: Introduction to a System of Philosophy* (New York: Dover Publications, 1955), 35 and elsewhere.

a reality to which my faith connects me. My faith also looks for a universality that makes the Gospel true for everyone everywhere all the time, whether they believe it or not. Such universality at specific points helps me value, celebrate, and live confidently in the truth of the Christian faith.

This essay looks for points of universality in which the truth of the Gospel stands out today, in a rapidly changing, rough-and-tumble, advanced technological world, namely,

(1) The universality of creation and re-creation,

(2) The universality of Jesus Christ, and

(3) The universality of the Gospel at five specific life points.

1. The Universality of Creation and Re-Creation.

God creates all that was, is, or ever will be. Faced with many religions and challenges in their own time, the Biblical authors are constantly repeating this refrain. God made all things at the beginning (Genesis 1-11). God establishes them moment-by-moment and guides them to specific ends.[4] God even makes the hands that make the idols.[5] God is God for all people, whether they know it or not.

More than a concept or an idea, the truth of creation resides with the Creator, not the creature. To the question, *Where shall wisdom be found?* the Bible answers, *Where God is* (Job 28:12-28). Therefore, *the fear of the Lord is the beginning of knowledge* (Proverbs 1:7 RSV, Job 28:28). God alone exercises the wisdom to create and govern all things. So, from God comes all human knowledge or science.

Likewise, all humans bear the image of God who made them, whether they know it or not. According to Calvin the way we deal with people who bear the image of God—no matter how sinful, corrupt, or unknowing they

---

[4] Job 37ff, Psalm 104, and elsewhere.

[5] See Isaiah 44-47, Jeremiah 10, and elsewhere.

may be—is the way we deal with the God in whose image they are made.[6] The Hebrew word for truth, *amun*, traces *God's* faithfulness—toward creation and God's chosen people—as the touchstones for all people down through history.

The New Testament speaks of Jesus as the beginning of a new creation, continuing the accent on creation. Jesus Christ is the Word of God through whom all things were made (John 1:1-3). *All things were created through him and for him . . . and in him all things hold together* (Col 1:16-17 RSV).[7] The human Jesus is Lord—God acting among us (Matt 2:23, John 1:14, Phil 2:6-13), the One around whom God shapes the rest of creation. The human Jesus is to the divine Creator as family—Son to Father—and through him all humanity has access to God's familial presence.

Jesus' resurrection makes salvation itself a re-creation. *As in Adam all die, so in Christ shall all be made alive* (1 Cor 15:22 RSV, Rom 5-6). With the resurrection of Jesus Christ, God re-creates the image of God among humans, which is the beginning of re-creating everything.[8] So, anyone in Christ is *a new creation* (2 Cor 5:17). Centered in Jesus Christ, the new creation marks the kingdom of God now and forevermore (Matthew, Mark, and Luke). Whether as creation or re-creation, we are dealing here with a point of universality.

2. The Universality of Jesus Christ.

We come thus to the truth of Jesus Christ, where the *amun* of Hebrew becomes the *amein* of Greek and the shout *amen!* of English. The glory, majesty, power, and truth of God for all time, all creation, and all people settle decisively on

---

[6] Calvin, *Institutes, op cit.*, Book 3, Chapter 7, Paragraph 6, pp. 696f.
[7] Similarly, Hebrews 1:2f, 1 Corinthians 8:6, and Ephesians 1.
[8] 1 Corinthians 15:35-57, Romans 8:19-23.

one, particular person, Jesus, who "was born . . ., suffered under Pontius Pilate, was crucified, dead, and buried ... and rose again from the dead" (*Apostles Creed*).

This poignant claim belongs to a moment in time, from which we are separated by more than 2,000 years. That sets up the "ugly, broad ditch"[9] of time which the Enlightenment—and still today—we struggle to bridge. How can you get universal truth from a one-time, historically-bound, unique person or event? One person can teach a timeless truth and exemplify it. But to be truly universal, does the truth not have to rise above the historical moment in which it occurs? How, then, can we state a universal truth in historical terms?

For the Bible and the Reformation confessions, Jesus Christ combines the universal truth of the Gospel within his own particular humanity. Commissioning the disciples just after his resurrection, Jesus uses "all" four times in Matthew 28:16-22.

- All *power/authority [exousia] has been given to me in heaven and on the earth*[AT] (18b).
- *Going, therefore, disciple* all *the peoples*[AT] (19a).
- *Teaching them to be keeping* all *I have commanded you*[AT] (20a).
- *I am with you* all *the days until the end of the age*[AT] (20b).

The first and the last of these are statements Jesus makes about himself—he has been given universal power-and-authority (18b); and he will be with us every step of the way (20b). Jesus sandwiches his commission to the disciples (19a-20a) between these two benchmarks. Jesus himself is doing what he tells his disciples to do. *Jesus* is on the move, going. *Jesus* is discipling the peoples. *Jesus* is baptizing them into the *Trinitarian name of God*, which includes himself as Son. *Jesus* is teaching—and doing—everything he has commanded us to do.

---

[9] So said Gottfried Lessing (†1781) during the 18th Century. This phrase remains one of the most widespread in modern theological literature.

The Great Commission describes Jesus more than it prescribes what the disciples are to do, and God binds the disciples to Jesus. Drawn by the Spirit to participate in what he is doing, they fellowship with him directly in the doing and from him they receive their energy and accomplishments. Those awakened by the Spirit will not want to be anywhere else or doing anything else, except what puts them into that communion with Jesus Christ.

Pointing to Jesus, the Commission points to *God* keeping what *God* commands. The birth, life, death, and resurrection of Jesus are *God* keeping God's own commandments. The commandments describe the place where *God* lives and where, by grace, we fellowship with God in our own time. Joined with this time-bound Jesus Christ, we come into fellowship with the God of the whole universe. So, in the human Jesus Christ God establishes the pre-eminent, authentic point of universality for all creation.

3. The Universality of the Gospel at Five Points of Life Today.

Jesus' universality embraces modern humanity at the heart of Western culture today. He does so by occupying the space where we invest ourselves most deeply, at five specific points. The following items match these points of deep cultural concern with corresponding points of universality centered in Jesus Christ. In occupying this space, Jesus engages our world and claims it for himself. Note well: nowhere in this essay is universality in Christ the same as universalism, in which everyone is saved.

a. Jesus the Individual as a Point of Universality.

Western, especially American, culture focuses on the unique, particular, human person, the individual who can be or do anything she/he sets her mind to. The sky is the only limit. The opportunities set up in an advanced technological society make such aspirations seem well within the reach of our humanity. This accent on individualism comes in the midst of a world-wide population explosion and migration.

To occupy the space of radical individualism Jesus has to be more than an example. He has to be the pivotal individual in whom and through whom all people find the God-given truth of their own human individuality.

The key insight here comes from how Karl Barth portrays the theme of election in and through Christ.[10] As this one particular human, Jesus is the elected human (Son of Man), and Jesus includes all humans in his individual humanity. As the Word become flesh, dwelling among us full of truth and grace, Jesus is the electing God (Son of God), and he manifests in his individual humanity God's entire activity toward sinful humans. In other words, the way this *one human Jesus* acts toward humans is the way *God* acts toward them. The way this *one human Jesus* acts toward God is the way all humans act toward *God*. Jesus thus carries in his individuality the universal truth of ours.

Jesus reinforces this universality further by identifying with *the least among us* (Matt 25:40, 45). No one is beneath him, not even the most helpless, needy, poor, or depraved individual. Individuals who attain greatness, wealth, power, skill, or some high human achievement—cannot subsume all humans in themselves, because not all humans can reach the higher levels of attainment. But everyone *can* descend from the heights where they are to a lower station in life. In his life, ministry, and death on the cross Jesus descends to *below* the least among us, so that in himself he encompasses every individual human being.

---

[10] See *Church Dogmatics*, Vol 2, Part 2, § 33, on the election of Jesus Christ; and Vol 4, Part 2, § 64, on Jesus Christ as "the royal Son;" and *The Humanity of God* (John Knox Press, 1960), 37-65

We put ourselves at risk if and when we look down on those more lowly than we. The point of the Matthew 25 passage is just this: the way we regard and treat the least among us is the way we regard and treat Jesus Christ. Jesus' universality as an individual stands, nonetheless, regardless of how the rest of humanity feels about either him or those below them. When the Spirit unites us with Christ as individuals, we are united also with all other individuals in him, beginning with *the least among us*. And that is a point of universality for him and for us.

b. Excellence as a Point of Universality.

Modern American culture focuses on success, namely, human achievement at the highest levels. Such achievement is on full display in an advanced technological society. The American way of life is a story of how a person can start from nothing and by dint of hard work become quite successful, whether in wealth, power, influence, or status.

To occupy the space of human achievement at the heights, Jesus Christ has to do more than show examples of where he enjoys good food and wine or delivers on promises made for salvation based on our faith and good works. A huge part of human endeavor involves high levels of skill development, athletic prowess, things that cultivate the mind or imagination, and the sheer enjoyment of all things beautiful. To occupy such space Christ has to extend himself to such matters in their excellence.

In a remarkable passage, Philippians 4:4-9, Paul urges his friends to *rejoice in the Lord always* (4:4). At a certain point he expands on what it means to be *in Christ*,[11] where *the*

---

[11] Chapter 4 has at least 9 references to *in Christ* and uses some variation of "all" 27 times! The imperatives in the passage rest on the foundation of Paul's indicatives, which he spells out at every turn.

peace of God that surpasses all understanding will keep our hearts and minds^{AT} (4:7). Continuing, Paul describes what opens up specifically *in Christ*.

> *Whatever is true, whatever is grand [or majestic], whatever is just, whatever is good, whatever is friendly [or winsome], whatever is well-spoken [or uplifting], if there is any excellence, and if there is anything praiseworthy, consider these things.*^{AT} (Phil 4:8)

Paul does not say we are to value truth, beauty, justice, and excellence just because Christians do them. We value these things because *in Christ* God values them wherever they show up. They are part of the image of God given to humanity at creation and again at our re-creation in Christ Jesus. They are gifts from God wherever we find them.

We are not dealing here with mere optimism or wishful thinking. We hardly expect to find joy or excellence or beauty, *etc.*, amidst humans beset on every side with suffering, sickness, lying, evil, injustice, mediocrity, failure, and people tearing one another down. Yet, to our great surprise, excellence and its companions do appear in the messiness of life. Whenever they do show up, they belong to the reality of God with us, even when our expectations are low. *In Christ* the universality of the Gospel is at hand when we recognize, value, and seek excellence among us.

c. Forgiving Love as a Point of Universality.

American and Western culture elevates human subjectivity—which, at its deepest, is love. Yet we live in a sea of de-humanizing objective systems coming from modern institutions, whether of science, business, society, or religion, The question modern culture raises is whether love has the same hard, truth value as, say, the fact-based objectivity of science, the cost-benefit analyses of business, or efficiency measurements of human usefulness in social and political systems. Does human—or divine—love ever rise above the level of subjectivity, private feeling, personal belief, or fleeting emotion? Can the truth for "me" ever match the truth for the universe around or beyond me?

For Jesus to occupy the space of love, he has to do more than just model it for us to copy or shower us with love, even salvation, to elicit a response of love from us. He has to raise love to a level that embraces both the natural and the supernatural, both the momentary and the eternal. Jesus has to make love part of the reality of all existence.

God's love for humanity and creation runs through the whole Bible. God chose to make something other than Godself—creation—and preserve it alongside God. That is love. God also chose to rescue a people from captivity, repeatedly, as well as save us from a whole range of human foolishness. That, too, is love. But salvation entails a different kind of love, namely, mercy in the face of wrongdoing and a love that forgives sin.

Forgiving love goes to the heart of the Gospel of Jesus Christ. John not only declares that *God is love* (I John 4:8) but also renders it as forgiving love: *In this is love, not that we loved God but that God loved us and sent his Son to be the expiation for our sins* (4:10). We could add as well: *not for our sins only but also for the sins of the whole world* (2:2. See also John 3:16).[12]

Now, as the Bible portrays love, whether God's or humanity's, it comes from the heart, yes, but always focuses on the beloved as well. In love we cherish people who are dear to us, and we accept our beloved as they truly are. Such love is itself a reality statement, like a mirror, in which the beloved can see themselves in truth.

---

[12] These passages point to the universality of God's forgiving love, but do not require universalism.

But forgiving love goes a step further, accepting our unworthiness, paying the cost of our brokenness, and fixing our broken relationships. Forgiving love loves with eyes wide open, sees the wrong of constant sinning, knows the depths of evil, suffers the hurt of love refused, and loves anyway. On the cross, Jesus Christ manifests God's forgiving love and in the process bathes all reality in its truth. God's forgiving love deals with not only the salvation of sinners but also the universal truth of things as they really are. Out of such forgiveness God re-builds our humanity and re-creates our world, which makes this dimension of the Gospel an authentic point of universality.

d. Suffering as a Point of Universality.

Human suffering today seems to be pervasive and unending. It is world-wide in scope, massive in its impact, and poignant in the extent to which our experience leaves us unprepared to handle it. The modern question of suffering asks, How can a truly good, loving, powerful God allow people to suffer?

For Jesus Christ to occupy the space of human suffering, he has to go beyond sympathizing (holding our hands), patronizing (patting our heads), or moralizing (teaching us lessons). He has to embrace suffering and transform it.

The cross of Jesus Christ asks not only, Why does God allow people to suffer? but also, Why does God allow *God* to suffer? Jesus, after all, cries out from the cross: *My God, my God, why hast thou forsaken me?* (Mark 15:34). As Jürgen Moltmann makes clear, this question and the problem of human suffering only make sense within a Trinitarian understanding: [13]

---

[13] This is Moltmann's argument in *The Crucified God* (London: SCM Press, 1974). See also *The Trinity and the Kingdom* (San Francisco: Harper

- *God the Son*, precisely as the human Jesus on the cross, plumbs the depths of human suffering—of rejection and betrayal, condemnation and injustice, failure and defeat, physical pain and death, and worst of all, total separation from God the Father.
- *God the Father* experiences for himself everything the Son goes through.
- *God the Spirit* unites Father and Son across the uttermost separation between them, on the cross.

Only as the human Jesus, who suffered and died, could God come near enough to the human condition to save a sinful humanity.[14] With the Spirit, God's power is exercised—and made perfect—in weakness (2 Cor 12:9), at the point of Jesus on the cross. So, Jesus' humanity is no less important than his divinity for our salvation today, and salvation in him encompasses the suffering of all creation (Rom 8:22). The cross of Jesus establishes a point of universality for the Gospel in relation to human suffering.

e. The Future as a Point of Universality.

Amidst the threats of global warming, nuclear war, population explosion, and constant conflicts both local and international, we face an uncertain future in the world today. We can add the ups and downs, bumps and bruises, or successes and failures, of everyday life. Modern Americans assume we create the future for ourselves out of our present actions and as such we must face the consequences of our mistakes. As the saying goes, "If it's to be, it's up to me."

For Jesus Christ to occupy the space of the future, he has to do more than tell us how to behave for the best

---

and Row, 1981), and Arthur C. McGill, *Suffering: A Test of Theological Method* (Philadelphia: Westminster Press, 1968).

[14] See John Calvin, *Institutes, op cit.*, Book 2, Chapter 12-17.

outcomes or make suitable provisions for life after death. He has to be part of the future reality that is drawing us into itself. From the future, he has to define the present moment in terms of himself.

The Bible concerns itself as much with the end of creation as with its beginning. The future pertains to the whole universe and its inhabitants, without exception. For the Bible, Jesus Christ is clearly the anticipation of the future Messianic Kingdom of God in the line of David. Initiating, tending, and completing the kingdom, Jesus turns our world upside down. Identifying himself with the weak, the poor, the humble, the needy, the sick, the child, he makes treatment of the lowliest humans the measure of God's future kingdom.

The New Testament portrays Jesus Christ in just these ways. His life, ministry, death, and resurrection mark the beginning of the kingdom of God, which defines the present moment now and for all time.

Jesus came into Galilee, preaching the gospel of God, and saying, 'The time is fulfilled, and the kingdom of God is at hand; repent, and believe in the gospel' (Mark 1:14-15, RSV). Jesus will come again to meet us as we draw near to the future.

Then they will see the Son of man coming in clouds with great power and glory. (Mark 13:26, RSV)

We do not know what the future will look like, but we know our future will be shaped by Jesus Christ, keyed to the new creation in his resurrection, just like our present moment.

- *As in Adam all die, so also in Christ shall all be made alive.* (1 Cor 15:22, RSV. See the whole of chapter 15)
- *Whoever is in Christ is a new creation; the old has passed away, behold, the new has come.*^AT (2 Cor 5:17)
- *Beloved, we are God's children now; it does not yet appear what we shall be, but we know that when he appears we shall be like him, for we shall see him as he is.* (1 John 3:2, RSV)

The reality of this future stands out above all. The future is: not a dream wish for better days, nor high ideals for which we are to strive, nor what we can make out of the present moment. What is uncertain for us is not uncertain for Jesus Christ. His certainty is as real as he is in time.

This lens on the future comes through when the Bible sets forth the so-called messianic banquet.[15] The banquet refers to a great feast that will take place when the Lord has been victorious over all enemies, including death, the ultimate scourge of humanity. As Isaiah puts it:

On this mountain the Lord of hosts will make for all peoples a feast of fat things, a feast of wine on the lees, of fat things full of marrow, of wine on the lees well refined. And he will destroy on this mountain the covering that is cast over all peoples, the veil that is spread over all nations. He will swallow up death for ever, and the Lord God will wipe away tears from all faces, and the reproach of his people he will take away from all the earth; for the Lord has spoken. (Isa 25:6-9, RSV)

The universality of this passage shows up in the repeated references to "all." The hope for this future emerges at many points throughout the New Testament. Most poignantly, this feast is anticipated in the Last Supper of Jesus Christ. Each time we celebrate the Lord's Supper we participate in its future reality, accomplished already by God in the life, death, and resurrection of Jesus Christ. But the truth of this future in Christ pertains to everyone, everywhere, all the time, whether they believe it or not. And that is a point of universality for the Gospel in our time.

Our confidence in the truth of the Gospel hinges on its universality. Only with confidence in its truth will we live for the Gospel, die for it, or hold our own amidst the

---

[15] See Dennis E. Smith, "Messianic Banquet," in *The Anchor Bible Dictionary*, vol 4 (Doubleday, 1992), 788a-791a.

tall trees of other world religions and competing notions of truth. Only with confidence in the Gospel will we stand fast amidst an epochal shift in Church and culture today. Only with confidence in the Gospel will we share the message with others, and act boldly in love, justice, or random acts of kindness. Only with such confidence will we give ourselves over to doing God's will with abandon.

Universality or not, our confidence in the Gospel is first and foremost a gift, God the Spirit at work uniting us with Jesus Christ, who is *the way, the truth, and the life* (John 14:6). So, we do not have to prove the truth of the Gospel. Nor is the Gospel true because we say it is. The Gospel is true because God is true, and God is faithful to God's own truth.

Because Jesus Christ bears the universality of the Gospel on his shoulders, the burden is light and the yoke is easy, and we can take confidence in its truth. Thanks be to God!

ESSAY 17

HISTORICAL CHRISTIAN PARADIGMS AND THE CURRENT PARADIGM SHIFT

The history of Christianity divides readily into four periods, each with a distinctive constellation or paradigm of beliefs and practices gathered around a primary focus (see Sidebar 17.1 below). Every paradigm, it must be said, strives to be faithful to the Gospel in its own time. The framework of a paradigm actually allows for a lot of variations to develop, co-exist, and even compete with one another. The variations all share the same space until the ambiguities and conflicts become too big to handle. Then the old paradigm teeters and a new paradigm forms. That is what the history of the Church shows us from age to age. The question now is: Are we in the middle of a paradigm shift today?

To answer that question, we will look at previous paradigms and paradigm shifts, but especially whether the issues and ambiguities of the prevailing paradigm today are at a tipping point. The four paradigms covered here are:
1. First Century and Early Church (33-600);
2. The Middle Ages in the West (600-1350);
3. Reformation in the West (1350-1650); and
4. Modernism-Pietism mainly in the West (1650-2000), where the current paradigm shift is taking place.

1. The Early Church (33-600).

From the beginning, Christians were considered a threat to the established orders of religion and government. In Christ's name Christians endured direct persecution for three centuries, often to the point of martyrdom. But the struggle of the first 5-6 centuries was to define the Gospel when everything was on the line—against the full weight of paganizing cultural, religious, and political forces. The biggest challenges came from attempts to infiltrate and redirect the fledgling Christian movement.

Gnosticism, rooted in paganism and pervasive in the ancient world, posed the most immediate threat.[8] To this pseudo-religion Jesus fit the profile of a Gnostic teacher who conveyed a secret wisdom (*sophia*) for those privileged to receive it. This wisdom or "salvation" revived the inner light of divinity in believers, freed them from the prisonhouse of their physical bodies (the flesh), and enabled them to escape from this evil world. Such an instrument of divinizing wisdom could be more than human but not fully God. Humanity so divinized has no need for God as God, who at most remains at a distance. As an instrument of Gnostic wisdom, Jesus would be only one instrument among many.

These views became prominent in Christian circles during the second century and remained a constant point of debate through the fifth century. The key issue revolves around the question, who is Jesus Christ? Is Jesus really *God with us* (*Emmanuel*, Matt 1:23), as close to us and our humanity as this one human being? Is Jesus, then, an incarnation of God in human flesh, as when John says, *the Word became flesh* (1:14)? Or, when dealing with the flesh-and-blood human Jesus, are we dealing with a delegate, a representative, an instrument, a prophet of God? In other words, are we dealing

---

[8] The most balanced treatment of Glosticism remains Hans Jonas, *The Gnostic Religion*, 2nd ed enlarged (Boston: Beacon Press, 1963). A treasure trove of ancient Gnostic documents was discovered at Nag Hammadi, northern Egypt, in 1945: see *The Nag Hammadi Library in English*, rev ed (San Francisco: Harper and Row, 1988). These documents have made Gnosticism an option for modern Christians, invited and encouraged by the prevailing paradigm, Modernism-Pietism, in its late stages.

authentically with God as God, nothing less than God, and the fullness of God altogether? On the face of it, the truth about human salvation rests upon whether Jesus—human born, crucified, and risen—is authentically God at work.

Sidebar 17.1. Historical Paradigms of Christian Theology.

Church history divides roughly into the following periods:
i. 33-600, Early Church:
    Focus on God's Incarnation in/with Christ.
ii. 600-1350. Middle Ages:
    Focus on God's Grace in/through the Church/Sacraments.
iii. 1350-1650, The Reformation:
    Focus on God's Grace in/through Christ.
iv. 1650-2000, Modernism-Pietism:
    Focus on God's Incarnation in/through the Believer.
v. 2000-, Next era, focus not yet specified.

- The Church of the Middle Ages divided at 1054, when the Eastern and Western branches went separate ways.
- The seven sacraments became widespread practice in the Western Church, *ca.* 1215-1250, linked with the theology of Thomas Aquinas (†1274), formally adopted at the Council of Florence, 1438-45, and codified for the Catholic Reformation at the Council of Trent (1546-1563).
- The Renaissance and Protestant Reformation, 1350-1650, overlap and feed each other as parts of the same paradigm.
- Martin Luther posted his 95 Theses on October 21, 1517, starting the Protestant Reformation. The same issues—of Bible, faith, Church reform, rejection of indulgences—were raised by John Wycliffe and Jan Hus over 100 years earlier.

For the theological patterns and dynamics of each paradigm listed, see Merwyn S. Johnson, *Resource Materials for the Study of Christian Theology and Ministry* (Charlotte, 2016), 7-11.

The same questions about Jesus were in play when Constantine adopted Christianity as the official religion of the Roman Empire in 318:
- Was Jesus merely human (unlike God)?
- Was Jesus merely an instrument of God's purposes (like God, more than human but not fully God)? or
- Was Jesus fully God (God as a human being)?

At the Council of Nicaea (325), the Early Church answered "yes" to the last question, preferring Scripture over and against the Gnosticism hiding in the first two questions.[9] The Church's answer—Jesus is fully and authentically God—immediatedly raised the next question: Is Jesus fully and authentically human? To accomplish the salvation of humankind, the humanity of Jesus is as important as his divinity. The early Church understood it well.

The early Christians had to debate all these questions in the public forum of the whole Roman Empire, with regular interference from the highest political figures, notably successive Emperors. The period from the Council of Nicaea (325) to the Council of Chalcedon (451) is one of the most contentious in the history of the Church. *Athanasius* (†373), long-time Bishop of Alexandria, was exiled five times by State forces allied with the party which had opposed him at Nicaea. Long years later, *Augustine* (†430), Bishop of Hippo in North Africa for 35 years, was still contending vigorously with those who would spiritualize the Gospel, water down God's grace, or undermine the centrality of Jesus Christ.

---

[9] Whether or not Jesus Christ is fully divine lies at the heart of the Trinity. If Jesus is God as a human being, we cannot talk about God without talking about Jesus Christ—any more than we can talk about a parent (or, Father) without talking about its child (or, Son), and *vice versa*. The two are bound and work together in a common Spirit, hence the third person of the Trinity. Matthew 28:19 combines the three into the name, or reality, of God as Father, Son, and Spirit

For these Christians, the Gospel message centered in the incarnate Christ who defeated death (and sin with it) and brought eternal life with God. The theological paradigm of the Early Church settled into its worship, notably the liturgy of John Chrysostom (Patriarch of Constantinople, †407). At worship the believer participates in the living, active presence of the incarnate Christ. That liturgy sustains Eastern Orthodox churches today.

2. The Middle Ages in the West (600-1350).

When Constantine became Emperor (324), he moved the capitol of the Roman Empire eastward to the newly built city of Constantinople (modern Istanbul, Turkey). The city of Rome, together with the Western Empire and the Western Church, languished for the next 200 years. In the 500s, invading forces from the north (the Goths) largely gutted the city of Rome. From Constantinople, Emperor Justinian I (†565) sent military forces to rescue Rome from its immediate foes but then left the Western part of the empire to fend for itself. So, Western Christians had to assume a greater burden of care for the culture as well as for the Church. Their efforts came together around Gregory the Great (†604), a former administrator of Rome who became Bishop there (590-604). Gregory in turn aligned himself with the Rule of Benedict (540-), part of the emerging monastic movement that carried Western Christians through the Middle Ages.

Christians everywhere faced threats to their very existence during the Middle Ages. In the East the largely Christian, Byzantine Empire endured for over a thousand years, only to succumb (1453) to the mass migrations pressing in from further east.[10] In the West Christians faced extinc-

---

[10] It started with the Mongols under Ghengis Kahn (†1127) and reached the Mediterranean with the Mongol-Turks, now Muslim,

tion from:
- warring tribes coming out of the north and east;
- militant Islam coming across North Africa through Spain (711) and up the Balkan Peninsula (1354);
- a formal split that took place in 1054, between the large, strong, Greek-speaking church of the Byzantine Empire centered in Constantinople and the smaller, weaker, Latin-speaking church centered in Rome; and
- repeated outbreaks of the plague (cataclysmic in 1350).

In spite of the threats arrayed against it, the Western Church not only survived but expanded.[11] The spiritual vigor of the age came mainly from monastic startups during this time, notably, the Benedictines at Cluny (910-), the Cistercians (1098-), the Franciscans (1209-), the Dominicans (1216-), and the Augustinians (1254-). They sought a supernatural realm of grace, specifically the vision of God promised by the beatitude, *Blessed are the pure in heart, for they shall see God* (Matt 5:8). To get there, they developed spiritual practices around a sacramental system that engaged people from the cradle to the grave, including:
- baptism (at birth), confirmation (at maturity), marriage (and family), and extreme unction (at end of life); plus
- confession of sins (in preparation for the mass) and daily mass (eucharist),
- and ordination (for priests only).

The sacramental system became standard practice in the West before it was formally adopted and required for the

---

under Tamerlane (†1405). The Ottoman Turks continued this pattern, capped by the conquest of Constantinople in 1453 and with it the end of the largely Christian, Byzantine Empire. Vikings and Germanic tribes were also migrating from northern Europe during this time.

[11] A key figure in this expansion was Charlemagne (†814), a warrior king who consolidated much of Europe under the banner of Christianity.

faithful.[12] The Dominican monk, *Thomas Aquinas* (†1274) gave the system staying power by elaborating it forcefully *vis à vis* the Muslim onslaught.[13]

The seven-sacrament system expressed well the distinctively Western view of the Church as an extension of the incarnation of God in Christ. When administered by the Church's sacramentally ordained priests and bishops, each sacrament conveys a measure of grace that elevates the faithful from their natural condition in a sinful, chaotic world to a state above nature, where the pure in heart can see God.[14] The sacraments helped Western Christians withstand the forces that threatened to annihilate them. The sacramental system and Thomist theology remain at the core of the Roman Catholic Church today.

3. Reformation in the West (1350-1650).

The impulses to a different, Christ-centered paradigm began in the 14th Century, aided by the Renaissance impulse toward a recovery of ancient languages, authors, and insights. *John Wycliffe* (†1384) and *Jan Hus* (†1415) both sought a return to Biblical foundations, a grace-based proclamation of the Gospel, and a preference for councils instead of popes for church governance.

---

[12] The Fourth Lateran Council (1215) required confession of all believers and declared the dogma of transubstantiation (*i.e.,* the bread and wine of the mass are transformed into the actual body and blood of Jesus). The whole system was ratified at the Council of Florence (1438-1445) and again at the Council of Trent (1545-1563).

[13] Aquinas' great *Summa theologiae* (*The Highest of Theology*, 1273) developed out of his earlier *Summa contra gentiles* (*The Highest against the Pagans*, 1265) and sought to counter the vigorous Muslim use of Aristotle by transposing Christian theology into Aristotelian thought forms.

[14] See also Dante Alighieri (†1321), *The Divine Comedy*, which describes Dante's journey through Hell, Purgatory, and Paradise, and climaxes when he looks into the face of God.

When *Martin Luther* (†1546) triggered the Protestant Reformation in 1517, he was an Augustinian monk. He experienced the sacramental system first hand and where it broke down. The grace conveyed by sacraments was easily confused with the sacramental means of conveying it and was often manipulated by the people (clergy) managing the sacraments. The result was a loss of authenticity, widespread superstition, and abuses of power from top to bottom. The Church badly needed reform.

So, Luther left the monastery and sought to make the monastic life of walking with Christ an everyday reality for all believers. The Protestant reform came together around him. Luther recognized only two Biblically-authorized sacraments, not seven. The Protestant Gospel revolved around key "solas:" Christ alone, Scripture alone, faith alone, grace alone, and the Church as the community of these "solas."

Meanwhile, the unsettling dangers of the Middle Ages persisted throughout the 15th-17th centuries. The plague recurred with great devastation, and the threats of outside invasion continued.[15]

Within the Church, the same forces that burned Jan Hus at the stake arrayed themselves against Martin Luther 100 years later. *John Calvin* (†1564) lived his entire adult life exiled from his homeland in France, subject to death if captured. Pitched battles between Catholics and Protestants lasted until the end of the Thirty Years War which ravaged Europe, 1618-1648, from north to south. Meanwhile, in the English Civil Wars, 1642-1648, Protestants struggled to maintain their hand on the till of the English church and nation.

---

[17] The Ottoman Turks reached the gates of Vienna in 1541, when Calvin went to Geneva, and the plague struck the city of Geneva with great force in 1542. Both threats would not be resolved until 1688.

Reform also took place within the broader Western Roman Church. Responding to developments in Protestant lands, Pope Paul III called for a council as early as 1537, which met off-and-on as the Council of Trent (1545-1563). Trent reaffirmed the seven-sacrament system and opposed the Protestant understanding of justification with distinctly non-Augustinian views of original sin and free will. In 1540 Ignatius of Loyola (†1556) received the go-ahead to establish a new monastic order, the Society of Jesus, along the lines of a highly disciplined military. The Jesuits pressed the interests of the Roman Church with fresh and aggressive energy.

As late as 1685, the French Catholic King, Louis XIV, triggered a mass exodus of Protestant Huguenots from France when he revoked a long-standing policy of religious tolerance. America became the destination of choice for Protestant groups seeking the freedom to practice their religion. Protestants found their focus in Christ wherever they stood, even when the whole world was shaking beneath their feet. Vestiges of the Reformation can be found in Lutheran and Reformed (Presbyterian, Congregational) confessional churches today.

4. Modernism-Pietism Mainly in the West (1650-2000).

By 1650 the Reformation message had begun to lapse into orthodox formulas and dry, rational debates. So, Protestants retreated into themselves. They began to talk less about Christ, more about the believers in whom Christ is incarnate (*Christ dwelling in our hearts by faith*, Eph 3:17), and more about the experience that accompanies that indwelling. So we arrive at the Modernist-Pietist paradigm, the strenuous efforts to establish it in the early days (1650-1800) and the years of its great success (1800-1960). Note well: the ambiguities and problems were there from the beginning.

Five points delineate the Modernist-Pietist paradigm as practiced in America over the last 350 years:
- The basic question is: who is saved (going to heaven when we die), who is not saved (going to hell), and how do you get that way?
- The focus is on the inner self, notably the feelings and experience of Christ dwelling in our hearts by faith, radiating outward to all our relationships.
- A distinctive accent falls on being a good Christian, the moral goodness, which salvation seeks as its outcome.
- The paradigm envisions a separation of Church and World such that the mission of the Church is to rescue people from the World and transform the World in the process.
- The Church and its individual members are the instrumental means through which God works.

This paradigm converges remarkably well with that of the Middle Ages. Accordingly, Western Christians, mainly Protestant but also Roman Catholic, took this message all over the globe. The message may have invited, but surely supported the colonization of Third World countries by European powers during the 19th Century. In the upshot, it must be said, that as a movement and as a paradigm Modernism-Pietism is one of the most successful eras in Christian history—in raw numbers, in the extent of its reach, and in cultural and political impact.

The remarkable effectiveness of this paradigm can no longer hide its ambiguities. Foremost among those ambiguities is the question, what happens to us when we are saved? When united with Christ by faith: Are we divinized by his divinity dwelling in us? Are we rendered morally good by his essential righteousnes in us? Are we humanized by his perfect humanity in us? Is it some combination of these three, or none of the above? Over the last 350 years Christians have experimented with "yes" answers to each of these questions but never resolved them. With variations, the prevailing view of salvation for all of them hinges on Christ embodied in us as God was incarnate in Christ. Combined with an instrumentalist view of the Christian Church and its members, this notion of salvation contains real possibilities for distortion and abuse. That is where we are today.

The Protestant Reformers faced these questions in the person of *Andreas Osiander* (†1552), an early Lutheran who led the reform movement at Nüremberg. When Luther died in 1546, Osiander tried to step in and restate the pivotal doctrine of justification by grace through faith alone. The aim of justification, he said, is to make us morally good with the essential, divine righteousness of Christ residing in us through faith. For the leading Reformers of the day,[16] however, this view turned Luther upside down and came at the worst possible time. They denounced Osiander's views emphatically, and he died shortly after starting the squabble. One hundred years later, Osiander's writings resurfaced and his ideas blossomed into the very avenue Pietism took in the 17th Century.

The Pietist agenda provides a foundation for the Enlightenment world view of the 18th Century and later.[17] That includes the perfectibility of the human (both goodness and expertise), accents on human experience (religion) and empirical truth (science), and a high valuation of the instru-

---

[16] These included Phillip Melanchthon, John Calvin, and Wolfgang Musculus. Calvin assesses the threat at length in the *Institutes*, 1.15.3-5, 2.12.5-7, 3.11.5-12. The modern fascination with Osiander led to the publication of his collected writings in 10 volumes (Gutersloh Verlag, 1975-2005).

[17] See Merwyn S. Johnson, "The Three-Legged Stool: Pietism and Post-Modern Theology," in *Theology Between East and West: A Radical Heritage (Essays in Honor of Jan Milic Lochman)*, ed Macchia and Chung (Wipf and Stock, 2002), 317-339.

mental means (technology) through which we humans can harness nature for our purposes. Different from the Reformation, the modern paradigm brings Pietism and Modernism together. This paradigm is less about the Church reacting to modernity than Christianity—conservatives as well as liberals—helping to create and shape the era. The "acids of modernity"[18] are alive and well among us in both Church and culture.

The figure of *Dietrich Bonhoeffer* (†1945) stands out in this discussion. He has become a prism for the paradigm shift now taking place. A young, promising, German Lutheran theologian, Bonhoeffer was reared in the strongly Pietistic church of his day. His Reformation studies and pilgrimage, however, led him to a singular focus upon Christ alive and acting as his own person: the larger framework for *Christ in us*, he found, is *our life in Christ*.[19] The intense pressures of Nazism from 1933 to 1945, showed how *Christ in us*—the one-sided, Pietistic focus on Christ embodied in the inner self—provided fertile ground for the idea of a superior race destined to rule others. When Hitler tried to make the Protestant churches an arm of the German State, Bonhoeffer became part of the Confessing Church movement, the only group in Germany to publicly oppose the wholesale Nazi takeover of Germany. In October 1940, he joined the active German resistance, was discovered after a time and imprisoned.

From his wartime prison cell, in a hostile situation, cut off from everyone and everything, Bonhoeffer came face-to-face with the separation of Church and World he

---

[18] The phrase was coined by the skeptic Walter Lippmann in *A Preface to Morals* (George Allen & Unwin, 1929).

[19] The breakthrough insights are stunningly visible in Bonhoeffers' primer for an underground seminary, *Life Together* (1938), the first chapter on "Community." See *Dietrich Bonhoeffer Works*, Volume 5, 27-47.

had inherited as part of his Pietism. His circumstances drove him to ask: Is Christ at the center of the World as much as Christ is at the center of the Church? His reflections on this question are recorded in a series of letters and papers from prison. They have become the breakthrough discussion of where the gospel is at risk in our time and where reality lies beyond the Modernist-Pietist paradigm.[20] Bonhoeffer was eventually tried and hung for his resistance activities, but his single-minded focus on Jesus Christ was sharp and clear to the end, noted by those who watched him die.[21]

Bonhoeffer's struggle foreshadows the post-World War II, cultural dis-establishment of Christianity in America and the Church's growing alienation from its own message and efforts—at the extremes of Modernism-Pietism. The watershed moment was probably 1966-68, when membership peaked and the Church began to lose its youth.

Like Dietrich Bonhoeffer, many Christians in America today live in motion, at sea, unmoored from the cultural supports of our recent past. We, too, sense that the Gospel is at risk among us, and the questions we are raising sound remarkably similar to those of the Reformation era, especially in the early 16th Century. We, too, are seeking solid ground on which to stand. Like Bonhoeffer and the Protestant reformers Luther and Calvin before him, our way forward will surely find its bedrock *in Christ*.[22]

---

[20] See Dietrich Bonhoeffer Works, Volume 8.
[21] See the camp doctor's comments, in Eberhardt Bethge, *Dietrich Bonheffer: A Biography,* Rev Edition (Minneapolis: Fortress, 2000), 927-8.
[22] See Merwyn S. Johnson, "What Is the Nature of the Reality We Seek?" in *Case Studies in the Life and Theology of Dietrich Bonhoeffer,* Fourth Edition (Charlotte, 2016), 57-66.

ESSAY 18, AFTERWORD:

BEDROCK FOR A CHURCH ON THE MOVE.

The essays in this book arose out of the spiritual struggle of modern American Christianity to regain its footing. For some time now America has been battered by a rapidly changing, advanced, technological culture that is moving away from the religious elements that gave it birth. The old language, worship styles, and church programs no longer touch large numbers of American Christians the way they once did. Stop-gap measures to be "relevant" in the new environment—new strategies, tactics, programs, fund-raising schemes, structures, rules and policies—do not work, either.

The immediate backdrop to these changes is the massive devastation of Europe and Asia from two world wars and numerous international police actions. As Paul Tillich observed in 1948, the social, economic, and technological changes stirred by World War II threaten "the end of the Protestant era."[8] The effects have only intensified since then, and now have caught up with American Christianity. We are facing a major, historical watershed—a paradigm shift (see sidebars P.1 and 17.1)—in religious and cultural outlook.

With these concerns front and center, this essay provides the context for this book of essays, at four points:
(1) The Paradigm Shift Now Underway from Within.
(2) The Paradigm Shift Now Underway from Without.
(3) The Church Dispute over Gays and Lesbians as a Prism.
(4) Bedrock for a Church on the Move.

---

[8] See Paul Tillich, *The Protestant Era* (Chicago: University of Chicago Press, 1948, abridged edition 1957), 222ff. Tillich served as a military chaplain in World War I as well.

1. The Paradigm Shift Now Underway From Within.

a. A Focus on Where God is Not.

The forces of change at work in the American Church are coming from within the Christian Church itself, not mainly from outside. Modern American Christianity joins the inner self (the "heart") with the human individual's freedom and responsibility to act for oneself alone, a space that does not require God. Many people are sunk so deeply within themselves and overloaded with choices in life, that their primary experience is isolation and alienation from their surroundings, even when crowded with other people. When the realities of life press in upon us, especially when things do not go well, the obvious question is, "Where is God?"[9] With this question in mind, for many American Christians during the 1960s "the death of God" became a viable faith option.[10]

Compounding the situation is the global awareness and increasing presence of world religions in the United States over the last 70 years. The pluralism of religions adds another layer of complexity to the already crowded field of Judeo-Christian denominations. How Christians get along with one another now entails living beside and engaging people from other religions. The situation encourages us to find a common denominator for all religions, like human ethical behavior where neither God nor religion is essential. In fact, sensibilities in the 2010s are moving toward no religion at all (the "nones").[11]

---

[9] See Robert N. Bellah, *et al*, *Habits of the Heart: Individualism and Commitment in American Life* (Berkeley: U. California Press, 1985).

[10] See *Time Magazine* articles: "Theology: The God Is Dead Movement" (October 22, 1965) and "Is God Dead?" (April 8, 1966).

[11] As of 2014, 23% of Americans declared no religious affiliation at all, inaccording to the U.S. Religious Landscape Study, conducted by

The Gospel message we have inherited does not help American Christians deal with this religious moment. Indeed, the shape of the Modernist-Pietist paradigm (1650-2000) invites the shift in process from within. We now face real crises of relevance, authenticity, and community.

b. A Crisis of Relevance.

Within the prevailing paradigm (1650-2000), American Christians draw a sharp distinction between the Church and the World. The Church is the place where God saves, blesses, and makes people good. The World is the place where people are not saved, not blessed, and not good, and where God by definition does not reside. Having persuaded ourselves of this distinction, we now face a crisis of relevance:
- of religion to life,
- of Christianity to Modernity,
- of church to community,
- of self to a pluralism of truth (science, other religions, other contexts).

The distinction affects the culture as well as the Church. With increasingly bold secularism, the World today embraces how the Church sees it, as a place where God is not and where modern humans learn to take care of themselves without any need for God or religion. Living in a secular World, Christians have urgent questions about where the Church fits in to their lives, both publicly and privately.

c. A Crisis of Authenticity.

Overlaying the concern for relevance is concern for the authenticity of the Church. Within the prevailing paradigm the Gospel presents itself as an inner truth, experienc-

---

the Pew Research center on Religion and Public Life. See the report online at www.pewforum.org/religious-landscape-study/.

ing God and loving others from within, individually. From that narrow vantage point, formal or "organized" religion seems for many people:

- more concerned for defending partisan claims than seeking God's truth,
- more concerned for pursuing cultural influence than serving others,
- more concerned for surviving institutionally than helping those in need.

These concerns challenge the Church's authenticity at the core of its operations. Wary members in mainline denominations, mainly their youth, began to leave their churches in the decades after 1970. Even the community- or mega-church movement stalled after 2010. Many pundits label the new era "post-denominational," "post-Constantinian," or even "post-Christian."[12] With the authenticity of the Christian community diminished, the Gospel itself is at risk.

d. A Crisis of Community.

From within the prevailing paradigm, at the peak of its numerical success in post-World War II America, a profoundly polarized Christianity struggled to hold itself together and handle issues as they arose. The current fault lines of liberal and conservative emerged in the Ecumenical Movement after World War II (see Sidebar 18.1).[13] The two

---

[12] The idea of a post-Constantinian era was first raised by Loren Mead, *The Once and Future Church* (Alban Institute, 1991), with follow-ups in the Gospel and Our Culture Series published by Eerdmans, 2000ff, and the Post-Christendom Series published by Paternoster, 2004ff. John Burke speaks of a post-Christian era in *No Perfect People Allowed* (Zondervan, 2005), and Diana Bulter Bass declares the same in *Christianity After Religion* (Harper One, 2012).

[13] See Robert Wuthnow, *The Restructuring of American Religion: Society and Faith Since World War II* (Princeton U. Press, 1988). The same im-

> *Sidebar 18.1. Post-WW II Liberals and Conservatives.*
>
> The more liberal side pressed for the formation of:
> - The World Council of Churches (1948ff), emerging out of the international missionary movement,
> - The National Council of Churches (1950ff),
> - The Consultation on Church Union (1962ff), and
> - Some high-profile denominational mergers:
>   United Church of Christ (1957ff),
>   Presbyterian Church (U.S.A.) (1958, 1983),
>   United Methodist Church (1968), and
>   Evangelical Lutheran Church in America (1988).
>
> The more conservative side rallied around:
> - The National Association of Evangelicals (1943ff), helped by an influx of Pentecostal churches during the 1950s.
> - The formation of Fuller Seminary in Pasadema, CA (1947), which anchored a nationwide network of seminaries fostering a fundamentalist, non-denominational, message.
> - The publication of *Christianity Today* in 1956, to give media coverage and credibility to the emerging movement called "evangelical Christianity."

sides produced competing Bible translations at this time:
- The Revised Standard Version (1952) and New Revised Standard Version (1990) among liberals;
- The New International Version (1978, 1984, 2011) among conservatives.

The initial push of the Ecumenical Movement was to bring different streams together. However, with the increas-

---

pulses were running through the Roman Catholic Church.

ing impact of an epochal paradigm shift, the challenge has become holding the streams together. Things once binding Christians together no longer work as before, whether:
- mission as a common cause;
- worship and worship styles;
- organization and polity;
- agreement within a belief system;
- mutual cooperation across partisan lines;
- shared experiences; or
- denominational identity, history, and loyalty.[14]

Every one of these previous points of unity and community is contested today. So, when a simple dispute arises, the impact can be devastating for all parties. The dispute over the role of gays and lesbians has had that effect on many churches over the last 50 years. Within the prevailing paradigm, American Christians now face a crisis of community.

2. The Paradigm Shift Now Underway from Without.

The previous section, indeed this entire book, discusses how the paradigm of Modernism-Pietism has led the Christian Church to a crisis point where the Gospel itself is at risk. On its own that would ordinarily be a sufficient concern for Christians. The paradigm shift now underway for American Christianity, however, is compounded by a similar shift happening in American culture. Because American Church and culture are so closely intertwined, a paradigm shift in either one of these affects the other directly as well.

---

[14] In 1958 and 1983, out of a merger of three Presbyterian bodies—PCUSA (northern), PCUS (southern), UPONA (north-south), major branches dating back to the Civil War (1861)—Presbyterians produced four churches: PCA (1973), EPC (1981), PC(USA) (1983), and ECO (2011). The story is similar for American Lutherans, Episcopalians, United Church of Christ, Southern Baptists, and United Methodists.

a. Meeting Human Needs.

American Church and culture converge at the point of meeting human needs. *On the religious side of Modernism-Pietism*, the ultimate need for sinners is salvation, to make oneself a good human being and to guarantee life beyond death. The ultimate means for meeting this need is the sacrifice and example of Jesus Christ, combined with the faith that enables Jesus to dwell within us. The means for meeting the needs are indispensable to the outcome.

On the cultural side of Modernism-Pietism, meeting human needs today includes:
- Providing opportunities to work, prosper, and be happy, for oneself and one's family—by means of an open market economy and advancing technology.
- Fostering emotional and relational health—by means of psychology and counseling.
- Ensuring personal inclusiveness and status—by means of democracy, education, equal rights, and authentic community.
- Providing for eternal salvation—by means of spirituality, religion, and church.

Notice: meeting human needs on the culture side includes spirituality, religion, and church. Notice also: each item in the list of meeting human needs is accompanied by the instrumental means of doing so. Though uneven in practice, American culture still promises to meet human needs at a high level.

Arguably, "meeting human needs" has always been part of humans finding ways to survive and thrive. "Meeting human needs," however, is a relatively new way to talk about human existence. It does not show up in the ancient world or in the parallel developments of the East. In Biblical times, notably the Old Testament, the language was *bless-*

ing, considered to be life as it came from God's hands, or *salvation* centered on God rescuing people from oppression, enemies, a life-threatening situation, or sin. The "poor and the needy" are people we are to help in this life, out of our own abundance. *If any one has the world's goods and sees his brother in need, yet closes his heart against him, how does God's love abide in him?* (I John 3:17, RSV). Such considerations lie behind Paul speaking from his prison cell in gratitude for help the Philippian Christians gave him: *And my God will supply every need of yours according to his riches in glory in Christ Jesus* (Phil 4:19, RSV).[15]

But also, "meeting human needs" is not the primary concern of the other theological paradigms outlined in Essay 17. The Early Church paradigm is concerned about human life and death, and the long-term destination of eternal life in Christ. The Medieval paradigm is concerned about purity of heart, coupled with human guilt and condemnation, and a vision of God stretching into the supernatural realms of heaven and hell. The Reformation paradigm focuses on issues of sin, grace, and life in Christ.

With the Modernist-Pietist paradigm, however, the focus turns to the condition of the believer, the experience of the inner self, and what it takes to fulfill the individual's needs for meaning and well-being. Crucial here are the instrumental means of salvation: Jesus Christ as the means of salvation for humanity; faith in Christ as the means of salvation for individuals; the Church as the means of reaching sinners with the message of salvation; transforming the individual by salvation as the means for transforming society. These instrumental means are embraced by Christians of every stripe in the Modernist-Pietist era. American culture mirrors these underlying concerns to a remarkable extent.

---

[15] "Need" and related words are not prominent in Bible concordances and do not show up in any major Bible dictionaries or encyclopedia.

French sociologist Jacques Ellul makes a similar point about the modern, notably Western fascination with technology to meet human needs. In some respects technology has always been about meeting human needs, he says.

> Technology responds to human needs, to permanent desires. . . . Technology makes his oldest needs and his youngest strivings come true. It gives body to his dreams. It responds to his desires.[16]

In the last three and a half centuries, however, modern society has taken technology—the instrumental means of meeting human needs—to another level. We now live in an "advanced technological society" (Ellul's term), which takes technology for granted—like the air we breathe or the water we drink. Those of us who have grown up with the advantages of modern technology now rely on it as a fixture of the world we live in. We work, we play, and we worship with the tools and instruments of modern technology. We cannot imagine living in a world without airplanes, trains, and automobiles—plus audio-visual aids, computers, internet, and smart phones.

Ellul shows how technology as *technique* (his term) insinuates itself into every nook and cranny of modern human culture—political, economic, religious, educational, entertaining, organizational, *etc*. By making usefulness the measure of all things, *technique* takes on a life of its own. It not only drives culture to ever higher levels of meeting needs but also creates new needs to be met.[17]

---

[16] Jacques Ellul, *The Technological System* (New York: Continuum, 1980), 316. See also his magesterial study of Western technological society, *The Technological Society* (New York: Alfred A. Knopf, 1964), 431. Ellul taught law and history at the University of Bordeaux as a sociologist. He was also a highly regarded Reformed theologian.

[17] *Ibid.*, 317-318. *Technique* is a technical term for Ellul, and it functions for him the same way the Law functions in the letters and theology of Paul. See *Technological Society*, xxv.

Individually and collectively, Americans spend themselves meeting these needs. We look for the best instrumental means of doing so, including the most advanced technology science can produce, while at the same time promoting individual self-reliance and self-management. On the face of it, the Modernist-Pietist Gospel seems to blend naturally with an advanced technology for meeting human needs.

b. The Gospel and Technology.

Living as a Christian in an advanced technological society, however, poses internal challenges to the Gospel. The challenges differ from the origins of Christianity, differ also from places where the needs are much simpler. Americans who visit mission outposts in Third World countries often come away amazed at the joy of Christians whose lives are simple and uncomplicated by American standards. Yet these Christians live with a clear grasp of the Gospel in all its power and truth for life, while Americans, surrounded by high tech devices, struggle to "get it."

On its face, technology is a tool to make human life better, like the simple wrench used to turn nuts and bolts. As a tool, the wrench is an impersonal thing and morally neutral. When we view our humanity in terms of impersonal, useful, morally neutral things, however, something happens to our self-image and to what the Bible describes as the image of God (Genesis 1:26). Are we just things that are morally neutral and pawns in the hands of some greater power?

Similarly, when we turn Jesus Christ into a wrench, an instrumental means to salvation, the Gospel tends to be a commodity[18] to be mastered, used, and delivered with tech-

---

[18] Besides Ellul, *see* also the perceptive assessment by evangelical theologian, David F. Wells, *God in the Wasteland: The Reality of Truth in a World of Fading Dreams* (Wm. B. Eerdmans, 1994), 58 and *passim*.

nological proficiency for technological consumption. Who, after all, is actually using the wrench? Is it I as an individual? Is it we as a community, as Church, or as society? Is it Jesus himself, or God? Is it the power of nature or some kind of fate? These are not idle questions.

In such a mixture of Gospel and technology the Gospel tends to lose the basis and clarity of its truth. As a useful means to meet our spiritual needs, the Gospel is no longer the defining center of our lives. Being useful is not the same as being precious. To say it plainly: life with God and one another is more than the impersonal, morally neutral existence of a wrench in the hands of a cosmic mechanic. Being useful does not justify us before God any more than good works. Jesus Christ—God with us!—is more than a useful means to a better life or life after death. Loving God and one another is more than making ourselves useful.

Likewise, the Church is more than a useful fixture in a culture of useful fixtures. God as the human Jesus shapes the Church with justice.

A bruised reed he will not break, and a dimly burning wick he will not quench; he will faithfully bring forth justice. (Isa 42:3 RSV)

God's justice does not calculate a person's use-value. God lifts up the least among us, those who may not be useful at all, who have no deserving, even those we call sinners, including ourselves. Such undeserving people bear the image of God, too; Christ died to restore that image to them; and *he will bring forth justice to the nations* (Isa 42:1).

Simply put, life with God is an end in itself: it serves no useful purpose other than itself. This refusal to calculate everything based on its use-value throws everything useful into bold relief. Grounded in God—*i.e.*, in Christ—we no longer have to work or be useful to justify our existence. As

Jesus says, *The one doing the truth comes to the light, so that it may be manifest that his/her works are being wrought in God* (John 3:21^{AT}). Life with God is a calling not a demand, a gift not an accomplishment, a privilege not a right. Grounded in God, our lives engage in the joy of contributing to those around us in all the ways that arise every moment of every day.

Worshipping God epitomizes this profound uselessness-but-joy-in-meaning. In worship Christ crucified and risen takes us endlessly:
- to human life at its best—love, joy, beauty, meaning, excellence, accomplishment, and hope; but also
- to human suffering at its worst without flinching—hunger, disease, death, enduring poverty, injustice, and international conflicts; and in all things
- to the reality of God's love for the world God has made, the reality of the world Christ died for.

In the covenant space of Christ, technology has a place, but not as a way of calculating human value based on usefulness. According to the Gospel, life with God is finally incalculable, invaluable, and ultimately rooted in the playfulness of enjoying God and one another, celebrating the glory, majesty, and grace of God in the process. Both the joy and the fullness of human life consist in walking daily with Jesus Christ, who is God with us in the power of the Spirit.[19]

c. The Paradigm Shift in Church and Culture.

Before World War II, American culture—the World—would have included the religious foundations that helped create it. Where the American Constitution of 1789 separates Church and State, American culture and society have always mixed them ... until recently. Since World War II

---

[19] See Josef Pieper, *Leisure, the Basis of Culture* (Pantheon Books, 1952); and Marva Dawn, *A Royal Waste of Time* (Wm. B. Eerdmans, 1999).

Americans have seen their culture and society increasingly pull away from their religion—a cultural as well as a constitutional disestablishment of religion. Christians of all stripes are struggling to rediscover the place of the Church in this new reality.

Technology still changes the way we view the world. We no longer look at nature in terms of green trees, blue skies, and the magnificent vistas of mountain formations or waves in the expanse of the seas. Wherever we are, we see our surroundings through the lens of what we have manufactured—steel, concrete, glass, video screens, audio recordings, opportunities for entertainment and travel around the globe and beyond. And, to live today—in God's providence—we have to master the intricacies of hi-tech devices.

Technology still governs our expectations. When technology has helped, fixed, moved, built, grown, comforted, healed, supported, extended, and advanced our humanity to the max, the question still presses upon us: "Is that all there is? Is there nothing more?" With that, our expectations move on to the next technological improvements. Technology thus puts us on a treadmill of making constant changes, with an impact on humanity that is not always clear or positive. The impact is mildest at the points where we have to adapt ourselves to its operational interface. The impact is greatest when we have to counter sinful people using technology against their fellow humans, in wars or criminal activity.

Technology and modern American culture are also going through massive changes—a paradigm shift—in our time. Television, global and space travel, the computer, the cell phone, social media, the internet are a shortlist of where changes are taking place. These devices extend human capacities with seemingly unlimited possibilities. But now the pace of change has quickened dramatically faster than humans can run or absorb.[20] Apart from the Church, the World is coming into its own, not only meeting its own needs but also creating its own, open-ended, "virtual" reality.

So, increasingly, the urgent question for humanity is, What is reality? Identifying reality in an advanced technological society may be the biggest challenge of all for American Christians today. God has providentially placed us in the midst of an increasingly worldwide stir. In this life situation the reality of *God with us* takes on a wholly new meaning. God expects us to live with full vigor precisely here and now. God also provides us a reality *in Jesus Christ* who is bedrock for Christians, for the Christian Church, and for life in our time.

3. The Church Dispute over Gays and Lesbians as a Prism.

a. The Dispute.

The recent church disputes over ordaining gays and lesbians to church office may help focus the changes we are now experiencing in both Church and culture. Our concern here is mainly for the church shift, but we cannot overlook the implications for the culture. Here, too, the Presbyterian Church (USA) offers a case study. The initial dispute arose in the 1970s.

From the Modernist perspective of usefulness, who may or may not be allowed to serve in an ordained capacity is a rim issue. As to who is called to office, able to perform its duties, and properly prepared for service, presumably any member can serve, including gays and lesbians.

From the Pietist perspective of the Christian Church, the issue goes to the core of her being. Individual churches carefully sift and groom the leaders who preach, administer the sacraments, and lead worship. For heirs of the Reforma-

---

[20] Thomas L. Friedman identifies 2007 as the watershed year in *Thank You for Being Late* (New York, 2016).

tion, including Presbyterians and others, the true Church exists in worshipping God, from which come all other forms of service:

> [The Church] is the assembly of all believers among whom the Gospel is preached in its purity and the holy sacraments are administered according to the Gospel.[21]

For liberals the ordination of gays and lesbians, whether practicing or not, became a litmus test for inclusiveness and social justice, with the mission of the Church on the line for them. For conservatives such ordination became a test case for the moral and doctrinal purity essential to salvation, with the mission of the Church on the line for them. Since 1978 Presbyterian liberals and conservatives have played a bruising, winner-take-all game, and whichever side won was bent on imposing its own standards on the whole church.

Two things are noteworthy for where this issue has come from and where it is going. For both liberal and conservative parties, the Pietistic questions,

Who is saved? and *Who is not saved?*

have been transposed into the cultural questions,

Who is included? and *Who is excluded?*

For both parties as well, the Pietistic question,

By what means do you become one or the other?

has been transposed into the cultural question,

How do you become useful to the society either way?

Within the Modernist-Pietist paradigm, both liberals and conservatives ask the same questions and make the same transpositions. Both sides frame the issue of ordaining gays and lesbians in the same way, and both sides join Church to culture in the process. When the dust cleared in 2011, American Presbyterians had fallen back into their habitual cycle of

---

[21] *The Augsburg Confession* of 1530, Art. VII, quoted from John H. Leith, editor, *Creeds of the Churches*, 3rd edition (John Knox Press, 1982), 70.

split and reunion, dating back to 1741.[22]

b. The Actions of the Church's Middle.

The under-reported story of this dispute involves the actions of the PC(USA) middle. I have put together a timeline (see Sidebar 18.3, end of Afterword) that traces the slow, measured handling of the dispute from 1978 until it broke open in 2010. As the conflict emerged in 1996, the *Book of Order* provision (G-6.0106b) limited but did not exclude gays and lesbians from an active role in the church. When liberals tried to overturn the limits, the Church middle blocked them. When conservatives tried to tighten the limits further, the Church middle blocked them, too. The middle refused to be moved either to the right or to the left on this issue.

Affirming the centrality of Jesus Christ to its life and work, the 2002 PC(USA) General Assembly (GA) passed the short, powerful statement, "Hope in the Lord Jesus Christ," based on the Church's confessions. The vote was nearly unanimous, but the unrest continued.

In 2006 the General Assembly received a report from a Task Force on the Peace, Unity, and Purity of the Church (PUP), along with constructive recommendations on how to deal with the church's unrest.[23] Well-chosen, diverse, and representing all segments of the church, the Task Force modeled a unity of spirit, focus, and collaboration. The Task Force

---

[22] Formed entirely within the Modernist-Pietist era, 1706 to the present, American Presbyterians have gone through repeated cycles of splits and reunions—splits when the intense demand for uniformity gets too high, reunions when all parties realize how much they truly have in common, most notably their unity in Christ.

[23] The Task Force was authorized in 2001 by the PC(USA) General Assembly, "to lead the PC(USA) in spiritual discernment of our Christian identity in and for the 21st Century." The strategy followed the course of action taken earlier by the northern PCUSA for a similar situation, different issue, in 1925.

did not try to resolve the dispute in favor of one side or the other. It recommended instead a short-term moratorium on amendments to church polity, creating time and space for the Spirit to work and for the church to develop a consensus from within. *Over the objections of both right and left, the PC(U-SA) middle passed the PUP Report with 57% of the total vote.* [24]

The liberal side, however, was unwilling to grant any more time. At the next two General Assemblies (2008, 2010) they forced modifications to the *Book of Order* in their favor. The first effort did not garner enough votes in the regional presbyteries. The second one succeeded in the vote, but what passed came from the middle. Sidebar 18.2 (below) summarizes the relevant change passed by the General Assembly in 2010 and by the regional presbyteries in 2011.

The 2010 revision picks up where the 2006 PUP Report leaves off. Tiring of the conflict, the middle resolved to end it by creating "wiggle room" for both sides to operate: allow but neither mandate nor endorse. The revision allows for every ordination exam to be contested, for local-congregations to make their own decisions, and for the fight to continue one-on-one at the most individual levels of the church. Later steps to redefine marriage in 2012 follow the same lines.[25]

In the upshot, both sides came up short. The liberal perspective did not win an unqualified endorsement. Not prevailing, conservatives mistakenly perceived they had lost

---

[24] The final vote was divided, 289 for and 221 against. The negative vote reflects a further divide, identifiable by how the parties proposed and voted on amendments:
    92 out of 221, on the left (18% of total) and
    129 out of 221, on the right (25% of total).

[25] Passed by GA in 2012, by regional presbyteries in 2013-14. The 2014 U.S. Supreme Court ruling on gay and lesbian marriage does not affect the Church's handling of such matters in its own domain.

> **Sidebar 18.2. 2010 Revision to the PC(USA) Book of Order.**
>
> - The revised paragraph (now BO G-2.0104b) begins with Jesus Christ:
>   > Standards for ordained service reflect the church's desire to submit joyfully to the Lordship of Jesus Christ in all aspects of life.
> - The paragraph makes no reference to marriage or sexual conduct but stresses the qualifications for useful service.
> - It ends with the indefinite sentence:
>   > Councils shall be guided by Scripture and the confessions in applying standards to individual candidates.
> - The paragraph requires a thorough examination of any serious candidate for ordination. Yet it neither requires nor disallows the ordination of gays and lesbians.
> - The paragraph stipulates that Scripture and the confessions are to guide the examination. Yet it does not say how these foundational authorities are to guide or connect us to "the Lordship of Jesus Christ in all aspects of life" (at the beginning of the paragraph).

in a win-lose battle, and, after forming a new denomination (ECO), many walked away.

What happened to the middle?[26] I am persuaded that the middle between the poles is as big or bigger than the two end-poles put together, likely distributed 25-50-25, or even 20-60-20. Under normal circumstances, the end-poles compete for support from the middle. The left and right poles typically raise the issues and make the most noise, while the middle seems deceptively quiet, unseen, and non-committal.

---

[26] See Beau Weston, *Leading from the Center: Strengthening the Pillars of the Church* (Geneva Press, 2003), and other writings.

The whole body does not move, however, until the middle moves, after a period of careful discernment.

Prior to 1950, self-designated liberals and conservatives in the PC(USA) established their differences in terms of the mission of the Church. For conservatives, the Church's mission is to save souls, or evangelism, by which we know who is saved and who is not saved. For liberals, the Church's mission is loving service to the community, or social justice, by which we know who is socially included and who is excluded. Notice once again that both are concerned for who is in, who is out, and by what means. For both, mission is the principal mark of the true church.[27]

The Church middle, however, does not want to separate these two facets of mission. Foreign mission workers have long understood that the two belong together. The integrity of the Gospel message entails a loving, holistic concern for the people to whom the message of salvation is directed. The same is true of local congregations. Still, at the polar ends conservatives and liberals continue to duel, debate, divide, and sap the constructive energy of the Church.

At different times the PC(USA) debate over this issue has touched on Scripture, morality, Christology, salvation, the mission of the Church, the role of creedal statements, and what constitutes unity in the Church. The discussion, however, never punched through the overlay of Modernist-Pietist ways of framing the issues.[28]

The dispute over the status of gays and lesbians left all parties exhausted, vulnerable, unsure of their core message,

---

[27] "God's reconciling work in Jesus Christ and the mission of reconciliation to which he has called his church are the heart of the gospel in any age." *The Confession of 1967, PC(USA) Book of Confessions,* 9.06.
[28] See the *2006 Report of the Presbyterian Task Force on the Peace, Unity, and Purity of the Church,* and support papers, online at www.pcusa.org/resource/theologicaltaskforceonpeaceunityandpurity.

and grasping for straws. Angry and bitter at one another, all too often the two polar opponents have given up trying to reach each other. Christians in the middle have grown weary at the constant bickering and unnecessary divisions. Christian youth have lost interest in disputes over a Gospel stuck in dry sand, regardless of the poles. Meanwhile, across the board Presbyterian churches have continued to lose members and struggle to breathe air.

I cannot stress enough how both the dilemma created and the dispute running its course fall within the dynamics of the *prevailing, Modernist-Pietist paradigm* of theology. So, for many, the way forward is stuck in:

- holding the line against secularism in the Church (conservative),
- making the Church's fellowship inclusive in a world of diversity (liberal),
- making a timeless Gospel "relevant" to a changing World (both), and/or
- finding new strategies and methods that work in the World today (both).

These various stances are not in touch with the paradigm shift at hand and have no traction. Once again on a treadmill of activity and effort, Christians today are running hard but the scenery is not changing.

5. *Bedrock for a Church on the Move.*

With authentic spiritual hunger, mainstream Christians today seek a simple, compelling message of God's grace and love for real people. They know it when they hear it and when they do not. They can tell the difference between the authentic Gospel and merely repackaging rigid positions for relevance, popularity, or leverage.

I believe the Gospel itself is at risk in our time. In the throes of a paradigm shift, we stand before God now with the question: *In this providential moment, as Christians in an advanced technological society, facing a sea change of religion, culture, and history, what is the Gospel message for us and for our time?* At this providential moment we stand before God above all, and God sends us back to bedrock, that is, to Jesus Christ.

Simply put, "Christianity" without "Christ" leaves only "-ianity," or jibberish. The Christian religion begins and ends with the figure of Jesus Christ. What Christians say about Jesus comes from Scripture. He is

◊ *God with us* (*Emmanuel*, Matt 1:23, Luke 1:32-33),
◊ *the Christ* (Mark 8:29, Luke 24:46, John 20:31),
◊ *the Word made flesh* (John 1:14),
◊ *Lord* (Philippians 2:11),
◊ *Son of God* (John 1:18, Acts 9:20, Hebrews 1:5),
◊ *the Savior of the world* (John 4:42),
◊ *God* as a human being (John 20:28).

The Church receives this witness from Scripture, both Old and New Testaments. That witness reflects the covenant which God made with humanity at creation, continued among the Hebrew people over time, and centered in Jesus Christ for all time. Coming from different times and places, the writers of the Bible offer distance and perspective on the situations and disputes closest to us. Likewise, the creeds and confessions of the Church provide insights from times when the Gospel was at risk, notably in the confessions of the Early Church and the Protestant Reformation.

Jesus Christ at the center manifests the forgiving love of God completely and decisively. Like a mirror held up before us, God's forgiving love illumines all things as they really are, including us. The truth of this love stands at the height of all truth, stronger than any alienation or suffering we can experience. As Paul says, *nothing can separate us from the love of God in Christ Jesus our Lord* (Romans 8:39). So, today, in this world, we strain to discern the reality of life in the light and truth of God's forgiving love. Jesus Christ is bedrock for that truth, as the Gospel makes plain and the Spirit makes powerful.

Sidebar 18.3. Overview of the Presbyterian Dispute Over the Role of Gays and Lesbians in the Church, 1978-2011.

1978: The General Assembly of Northern Presbyterians (UPCUSA), concentrating on the issue, declared homosexual practices to be sinful and disallowed *practicing* gays and lesbians to serve in any ordained church offices (including minister, elder, deacon).

1983: Northern (UPCUSA) and Southern (PCUS) Presbyterians merged to form the Presbyterian Church (U.S.A.), healing a division that dates to the American Civil War (1861ff).

1996: After several years of dispute, the PC(USA) General Assembly (GA) amended its Book of Order to require of church officers "fidelity within the covenant of marriage between a man and a woman, or chastity in singleness" (G-6.0106b). Votes by the GA and regional presbyteries were strongly affirmative.

1997ff: Almost every year liberals tried to repeal G-6.0106b and/or conservatives to strengthen it.

2001: The GA appointed a Task Force on the Peace, Unity, and Purity of the Church, to study the causes of unrest in the Church and to make recommendations for the Church going forward. The Task Force consisted of 20 people from all segments of the PCUSA (right, left, and middle). They worked through their differences and issued a unanimous report (in 2006).

2006: The GA passed the Task Force Report, almost unchanged, opposed by both right and left.

The Report called for a moratorium on the subject to allow the Church to heal and come to a consensus on the matter. The vote was divided, 289 for and 221 against. The negative vote reflects a further divide, identifiable by how the parties proposed and voted on amendments:

    92 out of 221, on the left (18% of total) and

    129 out of 221, on the right (25% of total).

2008: The next GA swept aside the moratorium and sought again to replace G-6.0106b. This effort failed at the presbytery level. The votes were:

> GA Committee, 41 yes, 11 no;
>
> GA Plenary, 380 yes, 325 no, 3 abstain;
>
> Presbyteries, 78 yes, 94 no, 2 no vote.

2010: The GA passed a revision to replace G-6.0106b, and the revision passed the regional presbyteries in 2011 (now BO G-2.0104b).

See Sidebar 18.2 for a summary of the changes.

A group called The Evangelical Covenant Order of Presbyterians (ECO) took formal steps to become a separate denomination in 2011.

About the Author

Dr. Merwyn S. Johnson was born at Annapolis MD while his father, a career Navy chaplain, was serving at the U.S. Naval Academy. Both as a child and as an adult, Dr. Johnson has lived in many different parts of the U.S. as well as overseas.

His formal education took place at
- University of Virginia, Charlottesville VA, (BA),
- Union Presbyterian Seminary in VA, (BD *cum laude*, Th.M. in Biblical Studies), and
- University of Basel, Switzerland (D.Theol. in systematic theology, *summa cum laude*).

His work experience includes
- Ministry as a Presbyterian pastor during the 1960s at Staunton VA, Birmingham AL, and thereafter in preaching, teaching, and pastoral care at multiple locations.
- Engagement in the Church locally, ecumenically, and internationally, at every level of the Presbyterian Church (U.S.A.) and its predecessors since 1964, most recently with In Christ Supporting Ministries, Charlotte NC.
- Teaching and writing about theology for over 45 years at
  Stephens College, Columbia MO,
  Austin Presbyterian Theological Seminary, Austin TX,
  Erskine Theological Seminary, Due West SC, and
  Union Presbyterian Seminary, Charlotte NC.

He and his wife Beverly have been married for more than 50 years and enjoy their three children and seven grandchildren.

www.ingramcontent.com/pod-product-compliance
Lightning Source LLC
Chambersburg PA
CBHW071154070526
44584CB00019B/2789